TOUGH CHANGE

TOUGH CHANGE

Growing Up on Your Own in America

Bernard Lefkowitz

THE FREE PRESS
A Division of Macmillan, Inc.
NEW YORK

Collier Macmillan Publishers
LONDON

The Free Press
A Division of Macmillan, Inc.
866 Third Avenue, New York, N. Y. 10022

Collier Macmillan Canada, Inc.

Printed in the United States of America

printing number

2 3 4 5 6 7 8 9 10

Library of Congress Cataloging-in-Publication Data

Lefkowitz, Bernard.
  Tough change.

  Bibliography: p.
  Includes index.
  1. Urban youth—United States. 2. Minority youth—
United States. 3. Youth—United States—Economic
conditions. 4. Youth—Employment—United States.
I. Title.
HQ796.L355 1987   305.2'35'0973   86–14320
ISBN 0–02–918490–8

FOR BECKY AIKMAN

Contents

Preface and Acknowledgments

In 1980 Robert Schrank, then a program specialist at the Ford Foundation, asked me to prepare a report on high school dropouts and their search for work. Our ongoing discussions of poor youngsters in America have deeply influenced my thinking, and his views are reflected in this book. Schrank has been a wise and kind mentor to many writers concerned with social issues. I owe him a great debt.

It would have been impossible for me to conduct the extensive research that went into this work without the generous support provided by the Ford Foundation. I am grateful, in particular, to Gordon Berlin, a program officer at the foundation, who approved this research grant and who shared his experience, research, and analysis with me.

Recently the condition of poor children and their families has received considerable attention from politicians and journalists. But when I first proposed this book I didn't get a lot of interest from publishers. More than one publisher responded, "A laudable idea. It certainly should be done. But this is the 1980s—who's going to read it? Who cares about poor kids?" Diane Cleaver, my literary agent, didn't give up. She fought for the book with a fervor that far exceeded whatever meager return it

x   PREFACE AND ACKNOWLEDGMENTS

could bring to her. She may not get rich from this effort, but she has my gratitude.

My analysis of the educational problems faced by poor young-sters was enhanced by discussions with Harold Howe II, former U. S. Commissioner of Education, and Paul Ylvisaker, dean emeri-tus of the Harvard University Graduate School of Education.

It will be clear from the text that William Sosa was an under-standing, thoughtful, and sensitive guide to the streets of Newark. If there were more William Sosas, there would be a lot fewer forgotten children in this country. I am also indebted to his super-visor, Jeffrey Fleischer, who was then a project director for La Casa de Don Pedro, an outstanding social service organization in Newark. For several months Fleischer and Sosa, in effect, per-mitted me to take up residence in La Casa.

Throughout the country I met many committed advocates for the interests of deprived youngsters. The constraints of space permit me to acknowledge the contributions of but a few. I want to thank, particularly:

Frank Slobig, project director of the Roosevelt Centennial Youth Project in Washington, D. C.; Dr. David Rogers, president, and Frank Karel, vice president, of the Robert Wood Johnson Foundation; Dr. Josué González, associate superintendent of schools in Chicago; the Reverend Charles Kyle of Saint Francis Xavier Church in Chicago; David Richart, executive director of Kentucky Youth Advocates, and his colleagues, the policy analysts Sandra Tuley and Debra Miller in Louisville; Dr. José Cárdenas, director of the Intercultural Development Research Institute in San Antonio; Joan McCarty First, executive director of the Na-tional Coalition of Advocates for Students in Boston; and Paul DeMuro, who was then director of youth services in Essex County, New Jersey.

For their assistance and hospitality I owe a special debt to Jack Nienaber, director of the Brighton Center in Newport, Ken-tucky, and to the center's dedicated social worker, Millie Little.

Eben Keyes flawlessly and tirelessly typed many transcripts of interviews and later the manuscript. He was a perceptive listener and reader, and I benefited from his advice and encouragement.

The first person to suggest that I write this book was my wife, Rebecca Aikman. Her professional skill, enthusiasm, and devotion sustained me through what seemed to be an effort with-out end. She is also a terrific editor.

TOUGH CHANGE

ONE

Absorbing Time

Newburgh, 1961

This book was not born of a moment's inspiration. It evolved. By evolved I mean that for more than twenty years, I have been concerned about the condition of young people who have had to grow up on their own in the United States and elsewhere. But most of my writing through the 1960s and 1970s was about adults—the laid-off factory worker, the struggling sharecropper in Alabama, the policymakers in Washington and China.

As a journalist writing about social issues, it is easier to meet your deadline when you limit yourself to adults. When they understood where you were headed, they tailored their response to fit your story. They restrained their anger. Usually, they were temperate and careful in what they had to say. Adults speaking to adults. If you wanted to write empathetic stories about responsible people in trouble, you didn't talk to kids. Kids let their rage show. They could be reckless, inchoate, menacing. Kids scared people. Unless they were five years old, hungry, and sick, they didn't evoke much sympathy.

In 1980 I began to write specifically about kids in trouble. They were in trouble in school, at home, and on the street. The

1

word I kept using to describe their circumstances was "running." They were "running" from their teachers, from their families, from their friends, from the cops, and from their employers. They were youngsters fleeing their childhoods. But why were they running? Where were they running to? And what would happen to them if they stopped running?

The more time I spent with those youngsters, the more I realized that I had asked these questions before. The image of running, of flight, had been imprinted on my consciousness many years ago. If I had to pick a moment when I first began to think about American youths on the run, it was probably on May 1, 1961, in a police station in Newburgh, New York.

Newburgh is a small river city of some 30,000 people in the Hudson Valley, about 75 miles from New York City. In 1961, Newburgh seemed a city in irreversible decline. Its shaky economy was bolstered by dozens of small, sweatshop factories, by the labor of migrants who harvested onions and apples in the surrounding countryside, by a flourishing illegal gambling industry— tolerated for years by the police and the city government—and by some highly profitable whorehouses that serviced the enlisted men from a nearby Air Force base.

The voice of this center of commerce and culture was its newly appointed city manager, Joseph M. Mitchell. And his voice was commanding. His prescription for curing Newburgh's economic ills was to reduce the welfare population, which amounted to less than 3 percent of its residents. To do that, he proposed a new welfare code that would deny assistance to all unwed mothers who continued to have illegitimate children; would limit relief to no more than three months for all but the blind, aged, and disabled; and would require all new welfare applicants to show that they had an offer of employment when they arrived in Newburgh.

Mitchell's crusade against welfare "cheats" and "chiselers" soon achieved national resonance. *The Wall Street Journal* thought he was a courageous public servant. The American Legion lauded him as a champion of the individual who stood against the encroachments of the welfare state. Senator Barry Goldwater thought he was a "terrific guy" and was said to be considering him as a possible running mate.

Whatever his administrative shortcomings, Mitchell did have a certain flair for political theatrics. This he demonstrated on

May 1, when he staged the first act of his welfare drama in the dingy squad room of a Newburgh police station. He had ordered all of the city's welfare recipients to appear there for an "audit." They would be interrogated, their records would be examined, and all those who did not meet his criteria would be instantly severed from the dole.

By 9 A.M. some 300 indigents had filled the squad room. Most of them were women, who brought their children along as proof of their eligibility for assistance. Some of the mothers leaned against the dirty gray wall where the police, on other days, held their lineups. Infants crawled on the hardwood floor, crying, sucking on their pacifiers and the nipples of their baby bottles. Social workers truculently checked names against a master list. Cops wandered among them, clasping clipboards, twirling nightsticks, and trying, without much success, to bring a little military order to the nursery.

After a while, television camera crews arrived to film the scene. Their strobes were turned on, bathing the room in a brilliant white light. My eyes were caught by one youth. As soon as the lights were turned on, he began to edge along the wall, away from his mother. He should have been in school, but I guess she had brought him along as living proof that she had a dependent child. He was a gangly kid, all arms and legs, and his blond hair bristled in a crewcut. A couple of years, I imagined, and he'd be enlisting in the Marines. Suddenly he bolted for the door. He had made it halfway across the room when a burly cop stuck out his arm. The kid slammed into it, doubling up, more with surprise than in pain, I thought. "Go stand by your mommy," the cop told him. "You can't go until we say you can go."

At the end of the day, as I drove back to my newspaper, I tried to frame the story in my mind. Mitchell had proclaimed the audit a success. He had discovered a mother of five who had earned in the past month three dollars more than was permitted by his welfare code. The yield wasn't great, but that, after all, wasn't the point of the exercise. "The point," said Mitchell, "was to scare the hell out of these people." But my mind wasn't on Mitchell or his welfare crusade. It was on that one kid who had tried to run.

I was twenty-three then, the product of a working-class family in Brooklyn, not so far removed from the kid that I couldn't imagine what he was thinking when he tried to run. If it had been I, when I was fifteen, what would I have told the kids in school when they asked me why I had to spend the day in a police station? How could I explain that my mother was being interrogated because she was suspected of being poor? Whatever she was doing must have been bad, otherwise why would she be in a police station? I would have felt guilt by association, because whatever she was doing fed me, clothed me, sheltered me. If she was a criminal, so was I.

I decided that I would have cut out, too. I would have run so far and so fast that the camera crews and the cops and the social workers would never catch me. If I were that kid, I'd be thinking: The way it is now, I'm guilty by reason of birth. If I screw up on my own, at least I can say it's my own screw-up. No more answering for mommy's sins.

Isaiah's Decision

Events diverted me from the metaphysics of adolescent flight. Events: New York State ruled that Joe Mitchell's welfare code was illegal; Joe Mitchell was indicted on a charge of accepting a $20,000 bribe; Joe Mitchell lost his job. I suppose I should have been pleased at the spectacle of the scourge of welfare cheats standing trial for bribery. But it was like walking away from a four-course meal with an empty stomach. The debate over his welfare campaign was never resolved on its merits. No public judgment was delivered on the morality of reducing the sixty-nine-cent-a-day food allotment for welfare recipients. The thought lingers that a more discreet and skillful bureaucrat could have succeeded where a Mitchell failed with, for example, a program euphemistically entitled Casework Consolidation and Cost Reduction Initiative. Mitchell's undoing was that he had no talent for artifice; but he did tap a deep-running current of hostility against the welfare class, a current that would run ever more swiftly in the next twenty years.

Through the 1960s I worked as a newspaper reporter in New York, then as an evaluator of overseas programs for the Peace Corps. While my memory of Joe Mitchell's brief celebrity faded, the vision of the kid with the crew cut haunted the decade. It was an experience that would not let go.

In 1964 I wrote a series of newspaper articles on poverty

in New York City. At that time, the city reported that 25,000 youngsters were dropping out of school each year. I met one of them at a group home for adolescents in the Bronx. Isaiah Fulton was seventeen years old and black. He had left high school in his junior year, and a few months later he left home.

Isaiah was running, too, but not exactly for the same reason as the kid in Newburgh. Isaiah thought leaving home would ease the economic burden on his family. It was not the shame of poverty that separated him from his mother and sisters and brothers; it was his concern for their survival.

"I didn't want to go, and I miss Momma," he said. "She was makin' it best she could. But there was six of us at home, and the other kids was younger than me. Every time I sat down at the table I was takin' food off their plate. My mother was havin' it hard enough. I didn't want to make it harder for her."

If you looked at it from his family's difficult position, his decision to strike out on his own made some sense. There would be one less mouth to feed. At an earlier time, it might also have made sense for Isaiah. If he were able to find a job and achieve some independence, he could return later and help those he had left behind. He might have been able to do that if the times were different. He might have been able to do that if he had left home in 1955, instead of 1964.

In 1955, George Smith, a friend of mine, dropped out of junior high school in the Williamsburg section of Brooklyn. He was fifteen years old. George went straight from the classroom to a job running coffee and sandwiches for the work crews in the lumber yards. George had an advantage—his uncle was a foreman in the yards. George's Irish relatives and friends had found him the job.

Truth was, most of the kids in the neighborhood envied George. While we were slaving away in high school, George was living the life of a grownup. By the time he was eighteen he had his own apartment, his own jalopy, and his own girl friend. He was also able to contribute thirty dollars a month, not an insignificant sum in those days, to the support of his parents and his eleven brothers and sisters. For George Smith in the 1950s—poor but white and wired into the work world—leaving school and finding a job was a reasonable alternative, a rational option.

It wasn't so rational for Isaiah Fulton. He didn't have a network of kin and friends to hook him into a job. In the eight months since he had left home he had worked all of two weeks, washing dishes in a luncheonette. When the Italian cook's nephew came around to the restaurant looking for work, Isaiah was out on the street. Although the American economy was booming in 1964, it wasn't booming for kids like him. In New York City then, some 72,000 young men and women between the ages of sixteen and twenty-four were out of school and out of work; half of them did not have high school diplomas. More than 150,000 single people in New York earned less than $1,200 a year; each month 1,000 more people went on welfare.

In the 1960s, a journalist or policy analyst had no difficulty obtaining data on poverty. Michael Harrington's book *The Other America* helped to make poverty a priority concern on the nation's social agenda. Various public agencies were quantifying the increase in welfare dependency in New York, hunger in Appalachia, school dropouts in Los Angeles, and infant mortality in the South. But there was no statistical category for youngsters like Isaiah, who left home and school in their youth, who had been cut off from many of the vital sources of support—family, school, and community—that guide and shape adolescence. Officially, they were invisible.

Other American adolescents were highly visible as the decade wore on. Middle-class white youths roamed the country searching for psychedelic revelations and sometimes ended up dead in a cellar in the East Village or shivering in an Army greatcoat in a doorway on Haight Street in San Francisco. They were the subjects of many cautionary books, television documentaries, and magazine stories. Those accounts inevitably began with an evocation of the stable, seemingly conventional families they had left, with a portrait of their distraught parents, and with the pained response of teachers and counselors who remembered how bright they were in high school. We feared they were squandering their privilege and advantage. In their tragedies, we read catastrophe for our own children, if they slipped away.

Remember the trigger words of that disordered decade: alienation, anomie, unconnectedness, atomization. White words for white kids. Remember how Joan Didion began her celebrated essay on the "hippies" who gathered in San Francisco in the spring of 1967:

> The center was not holding. It was a country of bankruptcy notices and public auctions annoucements and commonplace reports of

casual killings and misplaced children and abandoned homes. . . .
Adolescents drifted from city to torn city, sloughing off both the
past and the future, as snakes shed their skins, children who were
never taught and would never now learn the games that had held
their society together. People were missing. Children were missing.
Parents were missing . . .[1]

Then, we mourned the missing children of the center. Now, twenty
years later, nothing has changed. We still mourn our lost children.
They are children whose promise was bright, whose future seemed
limitless. Their pictures appear on milk cartons and on subway
posters. Pictures of smiling children, family snapshots that reveal
a gap where they've lost their front teeth. Usually, they're white
children. Whether they're white or black or Hispanic or Asian,
their parents are working and their brothers and sisters are in
school.

We are not sure how or why they disappeared. They may
have wandered off or they may have been abducted. What we
do know is that everybody is sick with worry about them. And
there is good reason for alarm. The morning television shows
tell us that our worst fears for them may be realized. They may
be drug addicts. They may be prostitutes. They may have been
impressed into child slavery. Their families, neighbors, friends,
the police, and social agencies are all desperately trying to find
them and bring them home. Those of us who don't know those
missing children personally can feel their parents' desperation.
For if it's the neighbor's child today, it may be our child tomorrow.

There is another legion of missing children, but we don't
refer to them as lost. We call them losers. They do not claim
our attention as the children of the center do. They are not our
neighbor's children. They are mostly poor adolescents—black,
white, Hispanic. They represent a disproportionate number of
the youngsters who drop out of school each year. Official reports
estimate that there are about 800,000 dropouts annually, although, as a later discussion will make clear, I believe the actual
count is much higher. They are part of a larger force—some 5.5
million young men and women—looking for work without success.

The federal government estimates that every year there are
730,000 to 1.2 million runaway and homeless children.[2] The statistics are projections based on the number of youngsters living in
short-term foster care, in group homes, or otherwise served by
public agencies. But some analysts say that count is short, that

many more youngsters have had little if any contact with social programs and, if they have stayed at all in public facilities, it's been only for a few days and weeks. In the last decade millions of these adolescents have disappeared into the streets of America, living and dying in the shadows. They are the unmourned and forgotten children. No one knows the precise number of poor adolescents who have left home and school: There is no central registry for these young people; they are not visited by census takers; their pictures don't appear on milk cartons. But you can find them riding the subways of New York or sitting on park benches in the Boston Common; at night they huddle in the cellars and hallways of Woodward Avenue in Detroit, in the abandoned buildings of the Hough section of Cleveland, in the twenty-four-hour arcades of the Loop in Chicago, and in crumbling shotgun houses in the desolate Fifth Ward of Houston.

The Parking Lotters

The data on those youngsters are soft. Their absence goes largely unreported, and unless they ask for help or are arrested, they are barely noticed, except when they force the outside world to pay attention. It is not too wild an exaggeration to say that their departure is regarded as inevitable, virtually a rite of growing up. "Charley's days here are numbered," the high school counselor says in the same matter-of-fact tone he'd use to note another student's impending graduation or acceptance into college. "Soon, Roberto will be leaving the house," the mother of the fifteen-year-old says. She could be talking about his birthday or confirmation. It is just one more milestone in his passage to adulthood.

They have been part of America's social landscape for more than twenty-five years now, one generation of wanderers bleeding into another. In 1965 Douglas Glasgow, a sociologist, noticed a group of eighty to more than a hundred young men who hung out in a parking lot on 103d Street in the Watts section of Los Angeles. In the community they were known as the Parking Lotters. Glasgow found them the most tragic of all the youth in Watts. They were "always around, idly walking 103d Street, in the Parking Lot, or on the corner, without hope, beaten into submission. They no longer give a damn. . . ."[3]

In April 1982 I spent a day in Fort Lauderdale, Florida, re-
searching a study of youth unemployment for a group of foundations. Fort Lauderdale that week was swarming with college kids
on their spring break. The beach was a carpet of thousands of
young bodies, soaking up the beer and the sun, kids giggling
and flirting, keeping time with the beat from their tape decks.
That afternoon I was driving through the black part of town on
the way to the airport. As I waited for a light to change, I saw,
on the opposite corner, a whitewashed shanty with a hand-lettered
sign that said "Spirits." Behind the liquor store was a hard-packed
dirt parking lot, filled with perhaps fifty or sixty young men and
women, most of them I would guess in their early teens. All of
them were black. It was a school day, but they weren't dressed
to go to school. Most wore T-shirts and undershirts, cutoffs and
sneakers. What I noticed first was the almost total absence of
animation. They seemed to be just standing there, frozen in place
under the withering Florida sun. I heard no laughter or giggling.
They stirred only when someone passed a bottle of wine or a
joint. They looked like a bunch of kids waiting for something,
anything, to happen. Kids standing in a parking lot, absorbing
time.

The cliché is hard to resist. Here, separated by a ten-minute
drive, were two Americas. On the beach was one group of kids,
which had been given official license to act a little wild, to go a
little crazy, to trumpet their youthful vitality. They had society's
permission, because in a few weeks they would return to the legitimate business of securing their futures.

The other kids in the parking lot had no future. What I found
so sad was that they had resigned themselves to their fate. This
was the last stop, the end to flight. This is where the kid in Newburgh and where Isaiah Fulton would come to rest—in the insen-
sate hush of a wine stupor. A dedicated social scientist might
have dissected the scene behind the liquor store: Where did the
youngsters come from? What had happened in the time between
the innocence of childhood and their numbed resignation in the
parking lot? What if anything could they or we do to bring them
back to life? These questions deserved more careful reflection
than is permitted by the changing of a traffic light. They deserved
a book. All I could think of at that moment was that if these
kids suddenly awoke they might create a little more mischief than
the kids on the beach. We all might pray for the safe return of

the kids whose photographs appeared on milk cartons. But we'd pray that the kids behind the Spirits shop would just stay where they were—in the parking lot.

If, indeed, all poor youngsters had been as passive as that congregation in the parking lot, then the waste might have gone unnoticed by policymakers. It was only when adolescents turned dangerous that a policy had to be devised to contain the menace. The Summer Youth Employment Program, the most extensive and costly employment program for poor adolescents, was intended to cool down the "long hot summers" of the 1960s. It was and is a form of social insurance against the recurrence of the urban riots that devastated dozens of inner cities in that decade. Better to provide some time-killing jobs and pocket change than to have to mount a machine gun on the steps of the Capitol, as was done when Washington burned in 1968.

Rioting subsided in the 1970s and the 1980s, but the image of the potentially lethal adolescent persists.

When I first began to inquire into the condition of this abandoned generation, I spoke to Aaron Sadove, an executive at Consolidated Edison in New York. Sadove, a retired Army officer, was committed to educational and vocational opportunities for poor youngsters. He had organized a small but effective training program at the utility and he was trying to generate support for a much larger citywide effort. He impressed me as somebody who really cared about what happened to them.

Without much calculation, rather spontaneously, I asked him during a pause in the interview: What comes to mind, what do you feel, when you see one of these kids, not the kids in your program, but a kid in the street? He leaned back in his chair, closed his eyes, as if to call up a long-suppressed image, and said: "I see a kid sitting across from me in the subway car. He's smoking a cigarette. He has a radio the size of a grand piano, and he keeps turning up the volume. His legs are stretched out so nobody can pass. He is staring at me with a look I can describe only as hate." And how does that kid make Sadove feel? "I can only think of one thing. I want to get up, walk over to him, put my hands around his neck and. . . ."

Sadove, a civilized man who had worked hard to find jobs for minority youth, suppressed his violent impulses, as most of us do. With the exception of the rare vigilante who acts out our fantasies, we check our rage by constructing an invisible wall that runs along the middle of the subway car; we stare at our shoes, hide behind our newspapers and books. When we reach our subway stop we sigh with relief.

This is our urban survival kit. We think the walls we build will shut these young people out of our lives. That is, we hope they will. We pray they will. But what we cannot shut out is the fear and loathing we feel toward them. The price these youngsters have exacted for our indifference is fear. We walk the streets of our cities fearing that the child-killer is waiting in ambush.

Twenty years ago there was concern that the young men in the Watts parking lot would burn down our cities; now we fear that they will kill us. And we cannot dismiss this feeling as urban paranoia. Even those analysts most sensitive to the condition of poor young men and women confirm that our anxiety is at least partially justified. Claude Brown, who described his own childhood in Harlem during the 1940s and 1950s in *Manchild in the Promised Land,* writes, "The present-day manchild is a human paradox. Compared to Turk, Dunny and Sonny [youths Brown knew when he was growing up], he is a considerably more sophisticated adolescent. He is more knowledgeable, more sensitive, more amicable—and more likely to commit murder." Brown goes on to say:

"Today's manchild is an enigma to his predecessor of 30 years ago. He obtains the biggest gun he can find—usually a sawed-off shotgun or a .45—sticks it in the face of some poor working person and takes all of $5 or $10 *and* his life—a maniacal act."[4]

Brown and other correspondents from the front lines are quick to add the qualification that not all kids raised in poverty end up as marauders. The kids raking leaves in the park or sweeping subway platforms are reminders that not all children of poverty have given up on honest labor. But the impact of these reminders is blunted by the too-frequent front-page photograph: the black or Hispanic kid, head bowed, hands cuffed behind his back, flanked by two burly detectives. That picture sticks.

The details that accompany the photograph almost seem interchangeable from story to story. The kid has dropped out of school. He's left home. He's out on his own. He's been picked up before, maybe ten or twenty times, for stealing cars, muggings, breaking and entering. Now they've got him for the big one, for shooting down a grocer or busting the head of an old lady. An implicit theme runs through all of these stories. So many of these kids seem to grow up in a divided world. A paper-thin membrane separates the two provinces of their youth. On one side of the membrane is civilized order maintained by family, community, and schools. On the other side is the street—the jungle. The message of these stories is that the membrane is stretched so tight that the slightest, tiniest pinprick can destroy it. Once that protective shield is pierced, the child is lost to the streets and cannot be reclaimed, or so the popular literature would have it. To grow up alone on the street is to run wild, is to be stripped of conscience, morality, and humanity. The street youth is transformed into a deadly night creature, a cold-blooded savage. That is the message embodied in the stories of violent crime and in the stationhouse photographs.

The message, however inaccurate and exaggerated, has been accepted as fact by millions of Americans. Brutal, senseless, random crime has become all but synonymous with "youth crime," a term that, when decoded, is taken to mean crimes committed by black and Hispanic youth. It doesn't matter much that this interpretation is not consistently supported by official statistics of violent crime issued by local police departments and the FBI. The crime statistics run in the back of the paper, the crime stories up front. The occasional attempt to portray the street kid as a victim rather than as a criminal is dismissed, in this season of national indifference, as yet another example of grotesque liberal sentimentality.

In crime stories where the suspect is a youth, the favored pronoun is "drifter." As in, "A nineteen-year-old drifter was charged yesterday with. . . ." It is an evocative word. It conjures up an individual floating free of all restraints, prowling silently through dark alleys. In crime stories, some of which I wrote, the characterization of someone as a drifter almost amounted to *prima facie* proof of guilt.

In a society of laws, conviction is followed by punishment. Since we had already convicted them, it rationally followed that our response to these youngsters, the policy we devised, would have as its primary objectives their control, containment, and punishment. It is a policy, as we shall see, that has been implemented with a passion.

Then and Now

On the surface, the Parking Lotters in Watts and Isaiah Fulton at the youth shelter in New York seemed like the natural progenitors of the kids I was to meet twenty years later—the kids behind the liquor store in Fort Lauderdale. They were poor. Many were black and Hispanic. If they had any strategy it was to wait, to stand in place, until something happened. In the 1960s and in the 1980s, they absorbed time.

But the similarities were deceptive. In reality, great changes had taken place in the actual conditions of their childhood and adolescence and in their prospects for securing a stable and productive adulthood. By the mid-1980s, the odds against them had lengthened significantly. Getting over youth and growing up was a very tough change.

For one thing, there were many more poor kids now than before. For another thing, poor kids were getting poorer. Congressional studies found that the poverty rate for children had risen by 54 percent in just ten years, from 1973 to 1983. In fifteen years, the number of poor children had increased by 3 million. They represented 40 percent of the total population living in poverty and were the largest single group among the poor. In 1985, the U. S. Census Bureau reported that there were 8.1 million white children living in poverty, 4.3 million blacks, and 2.3 million Hispanics. Forty-seven percent of black children and 38 percent of Hispanic children were poor, as against 15 percent of white youths.[5]

Poverty for white youngsters is often a short-term setback: Parents split up, a wage-earner loses his or her job. Not so for minority children. They are born into it, and it remains with them for much of their childhood. "The average black child can expect to spend more than five years of his childhood in poverty; the average white child less than ten months," the Congressional study said. And poverty in the 1980s, the study noted, is a lot worse than poverty in the 1960s. In 1968 the poorest fifth of all families had, on the average, 91 percent of the income they needed to pay for their basic living expenses. Fifteen years later they had only 60 percent. Much of childhood and adolescence is devoted to scrambling for the tough change that will allow them and their families to get by for another day, another month.

A common shortcoming of such studies is that they fail to

say what happens when this period of *official* poverty, as measured by federal standards, ends. Is a family that has risen out of welfare dependency now able to move out of the anarchy of low-income public housing into a better neighborhood, or does rising above the poverty level mean just enough money to pay for a pair of super Pumas or a case of beer every month? The improvement in economic status has significance only when a child is able to see progress in the material condition of his family; when, for example, his parents can afford to rent a graduate's gown at his high school commencement.

Many reasons account for the spread and deepening of poverty in this generation of youngsters, and they will be examined at length in the following sections of the book. But that discussion is enhanced by a brief review of three elements central to how poor kids grow up in America today. They are parents, education, and jobs.

PARENTS

For all kids, family life just isn't what it used to be, in our realities or our fantasies. Perhaps the Christmas card picture of Mom and Dad and the grandparents unwrapping junior's gifts around the fireplace never held true for *some* less-than-picture-perfect families. But it was even more foreign and strange to children born between the late 1950s and the early 1980s: In those years the proportion of all children living in female-headed households more than doubled—from 9 to almost 20 percent. For black kids, especially, the space in the picture where the father was supposed to be standing was blank.

In 1980, 48 percent of all black births were to unmarried women; by comparison, 11 percent of white babies were born to single white women. Between 1976 and 1984, the number of black female-headed families increased by 700,000—a rise of 30 percent. Forget, for the moment, the social and psychological effect—for most of the youngsters I met it was the most devastating of all their deprivations—and concentrate on the economic consequences. Three out of every four children, whether they're white or black, who are born to single mothers are poor.

You fall behind when there's no male provider around, but you really end up in the dust when your mother is a poor teenager. In 1980 more than half a million babies in the United States were born to teenagers. (This is a distinctly American phenomenon. Teenage pregnancy here is 96 per 1,000; in Canada, by comparison, the rate is 44 per 1,000, according to the Alan Guttmacher Institute.) More and more, these teenage mothers are likely to raise their children without a father present. In 1982 more than half of the teenagers who gave birth were unwed. Twelve years before, less than one-third were. Take one unexceptional year: In 1982, approximately 261,000 female-headed families were formed by teenagers. "A family is formed when a child is born," says Senator Daniel Patrick Moynihan of New York. "When an unwed teen-ager gives birth, a broken family is formed."[6]

Not only are adolescents having more babies, they are having them when they are younger. Senator Moynihan cites studies that show that the age of sexual maturity for young American women is now under thirteen years. In 1982 girls fourteen or younger gave birth to 10,000 babies. "For the first time, American preteens can have babies," Moynihan points out.

There is no mystery about how these children will grow up. Most of them will grow up poor. Adolescent mothers account for more than half of all women who receive welfare payments. If your mother is black, single, under thirty, and a high school dropout, your chances of being poor are more than 90 percent.[7]*

EDUCATION

We know that if you're a child whose mother is a teenager who dropped out of school, who can hardly read enough to make out her electric bill or add up her grocery purchases, your prospects of winning a scholarship to Yale or just making it past the eighth grade are not much better than winning the lottery. In 1985, almost 41 percent of Hispanics between the ages of twenty and twenty-four had dropped out of high school, as had 23 percent of blacks, compared to 14 percent of whites. In many American cities the dropout rate is much higher than the national rate. Approximately 80 percent of Hispanic students drop out in New York, 70 percent in Chicago, and 50 percent in Los Angeles.

* By comparison, the poverty rate was 12.5 percent for children of black married couples where the father was over thirty and had completed high school.

The black dropout rate in these cities runs about 50 percent or higher.[8]

Dropout rates are but one indicator of present and future problems. But there are more foreboding predictors. Perhaps the most telling is literacy. Occasionally, a kid who drops out of school may through luck, charm, or connections land a white-collar job, but how will he hold the job if he can't read or write? One comprehensive study finds that 13 percent of all seventeen-year-olds, 44 percent of black youths and 56 percent of Hispanic youths are functionally illiterate.[9]

Jobs

It has never been easy for poor youths, especially poor minority youths, to find jobs. In the 1980s it seemed almost impossible.

What is especially disheartening for so many poor youngsters coming up in the 1980s is the unlikelihood of any improvement in their prospects for employment. The economy, recovering from the recession of the early 1980s, created almost 7.5 million new jobs in less than two years; but teenagers claimed only 3 percent of the new jobs. Unemployment rates for young blacks in 1985 were more than two and a half times those of white youngsters. The jobless rate averaged about 42 percent for young black women and men. Only eight out of every 100 black teenagers in 1985 held full-time jobs; one-third of Hispanic adolescents held jobs.[10]

Those statistics do not really capture the desperation felt by youngsters trying to achieve economic self-sufficiency. The official unemployment rates do not count youngsters who have given up looking for jobs. Out of work, out of school, often out of their homes, an estimated 1.4 million young men and women, most in their late teens and early twenties, drift. When they do manage to latch onto a job, it's often temporary, rarely pays more than the minimum wage, and infrequently offers a full week's work. The argument is often advanced that if minority youngsters can be persuaded to return to school and earn their diplomas, they will have a much better shot at getting a job with some promise. The kids know better. All they have to do is look at their friends who did stick it out, who did graduate. The unemployment rate of 1983 black high school *graduates* was 37.5 percent, as against a 23.5 percent unemployment rate for white high school *dropouts.* [11] With such bleak prospects, it is not a stunning surprise to find that one-third of young inner-city black males in a national survey say they have a better chance of supporting themselves through crime than in the legitimate job market.

No matter how bad things are now, they're likely to get much worse. Studies in 1985 project an "aggregate poverty rate of just over 10 percent by 1990, with the rates for blacks and Hispanics rising to 40 percent and 33 percent respectively."[12] By the year 2000, 20 percent of all American families will be headed by single women. Female-headed families will grow at more than five times the rate of husband–wife families, the Federal Bureau of the Census projects. We can assume that in the absence of any dramatic innovation in social policy, as single-parent families proliferate so too will poverty among American children.

The Rehabilitative Ethic

The data tell us that this generation is poorer; parents are younger and more fragile; and their prospects are dimmer. Numbers and percentages are but one means of gauging the differences between generations. There are other, less quantifiable, measures. They are concerned with emotions. They have to do with how today's youngsters feel about themselves and the world they know.

No one would claim that the youths who burned down their communities in the 1960s were bursting with optimism about their futures. But there was a sense of movement and ferment. A thirty-five-year-old man recalling the riots that gutted his Newark neighborhood says, almost wistfully, "Man, there was action then. Whatcha got now?"

Attention yielded policy. And policy was translated into programs that brought a presence that could be seen, if not always felt, on the streets: Head Start, CETA,* community-based organizations, Job Corps, Vista, public health centers, free lunches and breakfasts, public housing, urban and rural cooperatives, literacy programs, and alternative schools. Outsiders turned up in the poor precincts of the country—community organizers, youth workers, doctors and nurses, job-trainers—and they talked of re-

---

* Comprehensive Employment and Training Act

form: reform of the welfare system, reform of the schools, reform of the juvenile justice system.

The rehabilitative ethic colored the rhetoric of the outsiders. The message they carried to the dark interior was that systems, institutions, *and* individuals could be rehabilitated. Stasis was rejected as defeatism. No social problem was permanent, given enough public funds and personal commitment. The life of the Newburgh youngster could be redirected by humane social workers, engaged teachers, and sympathetic employers. The guys in Watts could escape the parking lot by learning a trade and applying that trade to the restoration of their devastated community.

It's an open question whether the public initiatives of the 1960s ever constituted a cohesive youth or family strategy or were mainly a series of disjointed, reflexive spasms. The debate continues over whether the programs directed toward youth were intelligently conceived or whether, as Senator Moynihan contends, too much emphasis was placed on services and too little on improving the material condition of poor families. And the jury is still out on whether the architects of these efforts ever really intended or expected to raise substantial numbers of youngsters out of poverty or if their true purpose was to stage a political magic show to create the illusion of concern in the midst of social rebellion.

What is indisputable is that by 1980, when I began to spend time with a new generation of kids on the street, the rehabilitative ethic had withered. Despite popular mythology, public funding for poor children and school-age youths was never great in the 1970s. In that decade benefits for kids in the AFDC* program declined by one-third. Although the number of black children in female-headed families increased by nearly 20 percent in the 1970s, the number of black youngsters receiving AFDC benefits decreased by 5 percent. "The fiction of any great explosion in anti-poverty spending in the 1970s is simply wrong," says Senator Moynihan. By comparison, older people in America achieved large gains. The cost-of-living increases in their Social Security payments had significantly reduced poverty among the elderly. After taking into consideration in-kind payments such as Medicaid, the incidence of poverty in the aged population had been reduced

---

* Aid to Families with Dependent Children

to 3.3 percent; the poverty rate for preschool children was 18.2 percent. In the 1980s American children were six times as likely to be poor as were the aged.[13]

Still, whatever poor youngsters were getting was deemed to be too much. In the first term of the Reagan administration the operative word was "cut": cut food stamps, cut child nutrition programs, cut the welfare rolls, cut employment and training, cut support for community-based organizations, cut legal services. The administration was not talking about marginal reductions; it wanted to eviscerate. Federal funding for inner-city schools was slashed by 21 percent, for employment and training by 35 percent. Funding for programs conducted by organizations in poor communities was reduced by 58 percent. Even in 1981, before the impact of the reductions hit home, a bunker mentality took hold. In a pamphlet directed at black parents, a community organization in Miami advised, "Stock up on beans, dried milk and potatoes. You are going to have to make your supplies go a long way."

The sociologist Philip Slater has written that the characteristic American approach to social problems is "chronic denial interspersed with occasional brief flurries of murderous punitiveness."[15] But this was something else indeed; this was vengeance defended and justified by an elaborate ideological construction. The administration's leading ideologue on matters of domestic social policy was Charles Murray, whose book *Losing Ground: American Social Policy 1950–1980* advances the striking thesis that the net effect of assistance to the poor has been to create a class of indolents. Social intervention, he argues, has enticed poor blacks and Hispanics and whites into a life of sloth. His rhetorical question is: Why work when you can live better on the dole than on a paycheck? Murray's solution: "Scrapping the entire welfare and income-support structure for working-aged persons, including AFDC, Medicaid, Food Stamps and Unemployment Insurance and the rest. It would leave the working-aged person with no recourse whatsoever except the job market, family members and public or private locally funded services. It is the Alexandrian solution; cut the knot, for there is no way to untie it."[16]

Murray's solution was somewhat more extreme than earlier proposals along similar lines, but hardly novel. It was the rational extension of a logic that had been building for two decades, among liberals and conservatives alike. It is a logic rooted in the conviction that the young people, who are the subject of this book, form a dominant part of a convenient typology: the underclass. Murray locates these youths in an undifferentiated mass occupying a substratum of society that is simply unreachable. By conventional diagnosis, they are afflicted with irreversible, terminal social pathology—nothing will help them. The term "underclass" is an awfully useful invention; it allows society to abandon its lepers without a twinge of guilt.

In the 1980s the underclass hypothesis and social practice began to converge. In the schools, "difficult" students were treated as if they had an infectious disease. They were isolated from healthy youngsters—quarantined. If they were unable to cure themselves, they were invited to leave the school. The most sensitive and dedicated educators were saying, without apology, that increasingly scarce resources should be expended on behalf of the most promising students. "Maybe the truth is we can help the kid who's one step from the bottom, but we can't do anything for the kid at the bottom," a Hispanic educator in Chicago told me. He didn't explain how you tell the difference between the near-bottom and the bottom.

In a temporary shelter for kids who have left home, the director enthusiastically describes his plans to leave the child welfare system and go into the restaurant franchise business. "When I started working in this shelter, I believed all these kids needed was some help straightening out their lives, a push in the right direction, some professional family counseling. That was ten years ago. Now, I know I can help some kids, but it's infinitely more difficult. The kids I see now come out of a world that says, 'Whatever my life is, I have to accept it.' There is such a deep, profound fatalism, it's almost like a catatonic state."

Even inside the home, some parents have also given up, surrendering to social Darwinism. I met a thirty-three-year-old mother of six in Newark. Her oldest child, a boy of fifteen, had left home and disappeared three weeks before. It was the fourth time in three months that he had run away. He had been picked up on minor charges by the police six times in the last year. She had decided not to report his absence. "Let him go," she said, trying to hold back her tears. "Let him grow up away from here. I have to think of the other five. He's going to ruin them. I have to give them a chance to live."

Triage is the fancy word that arises in the policy discussions in Washington. Other words with the same meaning are heard in the tenements of Newark. Those thirteen-, fourteen-, and fif-teen-year-olds who can survive by their own wit and agility will; those who can't won't. That is the big difference between the kids I met in the last five years and the kids growing up in the 1960s: the sense of total abandonment.

When you feel abandoned, as does this generation, there are two instinctive reactions. You sink into a somnambulistic pas-sivity: The seventeen-year-old mother sits in the dark room in mid-afternoon in Harlem, absently spooning baby food into her three-month-old's mouth. The other reaction is to take care of business. Ricardo, an eighteen-year-old who has served two years and four months for an attempted bank robbery, is asked what he expects to happen to him now that he's back on the streets of the South Bronx. "I be dead in two years," he says, "or I be driving the white Cadillac." There were not too many kids I met who said that abandonment by society had encouraged them to become model citizens.

Unpunished Crimes

Between 1980 and 1985 I researched and wrote four national studies on issues concerning poor youth.* Two of them concerned the problems confronting disadvantaged youngsters searching for jobs. A third examined the quality of health care in low-income communities, with emphasis on family planning programs for ado-lescents. The fourth was a report on poor students in public schools, particularly high schools. During those four studies, I spent time with approximately 200 adolescents, almost all of them poor and most of them members of minority groups. When I say I "spent time" with them, I mean that I did not conduct a conventional social science survey. It would be more accurate to say I shadowed them. That is, I spent days and sometimes weeks with them in their schools, on the street, in community

* "High School Dropouts and Work," a report to the Ford Foundation in New York, July 1980; "Jobs for Youth: What We Have Learned," a report to the Edna McConnell Clark Foundation in New York, 1982; "The Funding Partners Community Care Program," a report to the Robert Wood Johnson Foundation, Princeton, New Jersey, April 1984; and "Renegotiating Society's Contract with the Public Schools," which appeared in the Fall 1984/Winter 1985 issue of the *Carnegie Quarterly,* a publication of the Carnegie Corpo-ration in New York.

health centers, and in their workplaces. Altogether I visited twenty-nine cities and localities, from Stebbins, a tiny Eskimo settlement in Alaska a couple of hundred miles from Siberia, to Modesto, an agricultural center in north-central California.

I learned a lot about the lives of those youngsters and the changes they were going through, but when the studies were completed I was dissatisfied on three counts.

To begin with, I was limited by my assignments. In a study of how minority students were performing in school, I was pretty much confined to what happened to them in the classroom. But I suspected, for example, that the decision to drop out of school had as much to do with a youngster's friendships outside of school, the family's economic condition, and early childhood experiences as it did with a student's ability to achieve passing grades in six classes between 8:30 in the morning and 2:45 in the afternoon. I realized, finally, that any discussion of some of the critical transitions in an adolescent's life—the decision to leave school, to have a baby, to separate from the family—would be incomplete unless I understood how each significant element fed into the others. I needed to learn about the whole life, not a single piece of it.

Another source of discontent was the dominant voice in these reports. As was true of many foundation reports concerned with youth issues, adults—policy analysts, elected officials, employers, teachers, counselors—were the principal sources. The youths themselves were peripheral; they provided a stroke of color, a touch of authenticity, but they were hardly central to the discussion. That wasn't unusual. One of the obvious reasons legislation providing assistance to low-income youngsters has such a hard time winning approval in Congress and state governments is that kids don't have clout. Their problems may be real, but what they have to say about their own lives is usually treated as immature, inarticulate babbling; adults know what's best for them. A similar attitude permeates research studies on youth.

The adults I interviewed for these studies led me to youngsters who, while poor and in some difficulty, were considered basically trustworthy. They were having problems, but they were still hanging on in school or were enrolled in training programs or were responding to assistance provided by social agencies. The tough cases were missing. They had slipped out of orbit and were gone. Parents and teachers would say, "If you want to meet a rough kid you should go talk to Thomas or Carla." But I didn't have the time to find them; besides, they were incidental to my basic assignment—a luxury I couldn't afford.

But after I completed those assignments, the thought of the Thomases and Carlas nagged at me. They were the ones in most trouble. They were the ones the experts said couldn't be saved. They had the least hope and the most rage; their fate, people told me, was to kill or be killed. What I didn't know until I began to seek them out was that there were so many of them. Rather than aberrations, they were typical of what happens and what can happen to all impoverished adolescents in this generation.

So this book began to take shape out of the omissions and deficiencies of my earlier research. I wanted to concentrate on kids at the bottom, kids struggling to survive on their own. I wanted their voices to come through clear and strong. Although adults would be present as sources to discuss and amplify the issues raised by young people, to consider the policy implications of issues, they would not drown out the views of the youths who were at the heart of my inquiry. Also, I didn't want to focus on a single dimension of their lives. I would try to understand what happened to them before they left home and school, what they encountered on the streets, how their experiences affected them, and what they thought needed to be done to reclaim their lives.

My ultimate purpose in writing *Tough Change* was to discover what they have lost and what they are looking for. In the stories of their lives, I hoped to find unifying themes and connections that, while not diminishing the youngsters' individuality, could serve as the framework for a national mission to salvage their futures.

My research for this book took almost a year and a half. I traveled to fifteen cities and localities,* where I spent time with 280 youths. As my inquiry proceeded, I came to an important realization: I should not entirely limit my investigation to minority youths. The problems of poor white youngsters were not as grave as those confronting minority teenagers, but they were serious indeed. In 1984, the Bureau of Labor Statistics reported that 1.3 million white 16- to 19-year-olds were out of school and didn't have a diploma. The number of white high school dropouts between 20 and 24 years old was 2.5 million. Changes in the labor

---

* New York, Newark, Cleveland, Washington, Boston, Flint (Michigan), Detroit, Pittsburgh, Louisville, Houston, Fort Worth, San Antonio, Chicago, Kansas City (Missouri), Newport (Kentucky), and small rural communities in Appalachian Kentucky.

market made it tougher than ever before for blue-collar white kids to find jobs. Growing numbers of white kids were being rejected by their families. Schools often treat poor white kids with the same indifference they show minority students. The drug and street cultures have almost as tight a hold on troubled white youths as they do on Hispanic and black youngsters. Radical changes in sexual values thrust the responsibilities of adulthood on the kids, black or white, who are least prepared to assume them. And most displaced kids, regardless of race, encounter cynicism on the part of the social service system that is supposed to help them.

Of the 280 youngsters I met, 110 were black, 120 were Hispanic,* and 50 were white. A total of 160 were men and 120 were women. Seventy-five percent of the youngsters were between the ages of twelve and nineteen. Because I was interested in patterns that developed in preadolescence, I included 42 youngsters in the 10–12 age group. I also wanted the perspective of young adults older than high school age, so I sought out 28 men and women who were between the ages of nineteen and twenty-four.

I also wanted to investigate how the perception of class and actual economic status influenced the youngsters and shaped the response of different institutions to them. There would be value, I felt, in comparing the experiences of impoverished young people with those who came from working-class and middle-class backgrounds. Of the youngsters I included, 210 had families who earned less than $11,000 a year; 43 had family incomes between $12,000 and $20,000 a year, and 27 had family incomes above $20,000.

Where it was relevant, I also drew upon my earlier research, which involved some 200 youths in nineteen cities.† Although most of those encounters were focused on a single issue, their inclusion enriched the ethnic, social, and cultural understanding I brought to the present work. Not all of the kids I met in those previous efforts were living apart from their families, but all of them were hurting. This book, then, is the product of my experi-

---

* The Hispanic population included the following subgroups: sixty-seven from Puerto Rican families, thirty-eight from a Mexican-American background, and fifteen whose families came from Central America and Latin America.

† New York, Cleveland, Albuquerque, Miami, Fort Lauderdale, Boston, Baltimore, Philadelphia, Chicago, Minneapolis, St. Paul, San Francisco, Oakland, Phoenix, Scottsdale (Arizona), Modesto (California), Denver, Seattle, and New Orleans.

ences with almost 500 young men and women in nearly every region of the country.

Some of the young people I met saddened me. Some made me laugh. Some I disliked intensely. Some scared the hell out of me. And some I loved. A very few of the youngsters asked me to help them, and I tried to respond with my limited resources and influence. Most didn't ask for my help. The adults they had encountered in their childhood and adolescence hadn't done a great deal for them, and they didn't expect much from me.

If my response was different to different kids, my point of view in writing this book has been constant. I wanted to find out what had happened to them before I came on the scene. And I wanted to learn, from them, what could be done to save them and the kids who would come after them.

This was the focus of my inquiry. It was the focus because I believe in the possibility of change. I don't believe in fate, and I don't believe in a permanent underclass that has lost the capacity to hope and dream. I think the strangling cords of race and class can be cut when individuals and institutions make the effort.

The following pages describe at some length what I learned in this investigation. But my most important discovery can be stated in a few words: What's happened to most of the kids I met is a terrible crime. I don't use the word casually. By crime I mean the waste and destruction of lives. That destruction is the consequence of conscious acts of commission and omission. I refer to the acts committed by the youngsters themselves and by the adults and institutions responsible for plotting the course of their lives. In this book, I will hold them all accountable.

TWO

To the Brink

Days of Decision

Adolescence is a time of instability, running to chaos. Order is anathema to many teenagers; risk, experimentation, drama, confrontation, challenge, and rebellion are the stuff of growing up—as much for kids in Harlem and Appalachia as for the Kennedy clan coming of age in the compound at Hyannisport. As the psychoanalyst Anna Freud, among many others, has observed, the inherent turbulence of the teenage years is so disordering that it becomes very difficult to distinguish between commonplace "adolescent upsets and true pathology."[1]

Life for most adolescents is a blur: You're always on the move, always running. Why sit when you can stand up? Why walk when you can run? The theme of motion, of flight, recurs in the literature of adolescence. The analyst Sandor Lorand has written that adolescents are "not ready to adapt to the overwhelming pressures and demands of reality adjustment . . . they become impatient and impulsive; they attempt to regress and run away."[2]

The psychologist Erik Erikson found among discontented youth—and how many youngsters can be considered "contented"?—a "craving for locomotion . . . 'being on the go,' tearing after something, or 'running around.' "[3]

What makes growing up in poverty different is that the occasional periods of freneticism of middle-class youth becomes a constant frenzy among deeply impoverished youngsters. And it isn't confined to restless, hyperkinetic youth; adults, young children, the elderly, parents, older brothers and sisters, neighbors, business people, street hustlers, cops, social workers—everyone seems to be caught up in the churning. It is hard to find the quiet center here. The message the kids get from the adults around them is that the turmoil they see in their childhood is not something you grow out of.

One late afternoon in August 1984 I was shown around the low-income Seventh Avenue housing project in the Lower Broadway section of Newark by a man in his early thirties who lived there. We stood in the common area of the project. One hundred or more tenants were clustered around an overflowing garbage dumpster. Their children, some no more than two or three years old, crawled through the spillage of glass fragments and rotting food. Their mothers gulped down booze and argued about who was going to buy the next bottle. A man, red-eyed and shirtless, fell to his knees and stretched out on a concrete ledge. He began to snore. That afternoon, as on every summer afternoon, the main attraction was the dealing. Grass, coke, and heroin passed from palm to palm without any pretense at concealment; there wasn't a housing authority cop or city policeman in sight. The little kids stood at the edge of the crowd, watching, picking up the moves.

The man who was showing me about waved at all the people around us and said, "They're just crabs in a pot. They're in boilin' water, they're turnin' red, a few minutes they'll be dead, and they're still kickin' and screamin' and clawin' at each other. It never changes—every day they all jump into the pot."

Well, not everybody. During the month I spent in and around that housing project, I met a number of relatively stable families. The parents, whether on welfare or working, tried hard to provide the essentials of life for their families, maintained order in their households, and worried constantly about what would happen to their children in the streets. But they were largely invisible. They lived their lives behind the doors of their apartments. What was visible, what the kids saw on the roofs of the project buildings, in the hallways, on the landings between floors, in the basements, and out in the courtyard was squalor without end.

As a developmental psychologist, Erik Erikson interprets

youth as an early chapter in a life history. One of the hardest lessons learned during childhood and adolescence is that the process of growing up is irreversible, that this passage contains an element of historical fatality. School, puberty, work, occupation, parenthood—these are some steps that individuals take toward finding themselves. With each step, we fix and narrow the choices and decisions that await us in the future. This unfolding of a life history presents a painful conflict for many kids, especially for the youngsters growing up in the Seventh Avenue project. They want to know how the story will turn out, they want to find themselves as individuals and adults. At the same time they are afraid they will drown in the squalor around them. They want their lives to turn out differently; they seek the power to separate themselves from their environment, to be their own person. In Erikson's phrase, they seek an "open future." He writes that "in no other stage of the life cycle are the promise of finding oneself and the threat of losing oneself so closely allied" as in adolescence.[4]

Nowhere is that threat more palpable and pervasive and frightening than in the communities of poverty. It is a mistake to think that the impulse to escape is felt only by a few youngsters under extreme stress. Anthony J. Alvarado, former chancellor of the New York public schools, who once served as superintendant of an East Harlem school district, proposes a redefinition of who is at the greatest risk of dropping out of school. What he has to say about kids leaving school applies with equal force to kids who also decided to leave home. "High risk is not the five percent of the kids who already are not showing up in junior high school," he says. "High risk has to be redefined for almost the entire population. At any given moment, any one of these kids could drop out, because something hits them and they have nothing. They don't have any resources to deal with it. Whether it's substance abuse, whether it's sexuality, whether it's family, whether it's life, whether it's not being able to cope academically, whatever it is."[5]

Some would interpret the act of leaving home as an aberrant expression of underclass pathology: crazy people acting crazy. But for many kids, leaving is not a pathological response but an attempt at reconstruction. The words "underclass pathology" are too glibly used in America today. Robert Schrank, a sociologist,*

---

* Schrank's analysis is not purely theoretical. In the early 1960s, he supervised the job-training program of Mobilization for Youth, one of the earliest community-based antipoverty efforts of the decade.

says, "The guy sleeping on a street grate cradling a bottle of wine, now that's a case of underclass pathology. This guy's given up. The kid, who's trying to do something about his life, he's different. He hasn't surrendered yet."[6]

Most of the youngsters I met saw that first break with their families and school as a chance to rewrite their own life histories. If they stayed, they would end up as one of the crowd around the garbage bin. They were competent at one thing: They knew how to run. That first day when they ran, they thought they had embarked on a redemptive flight. That comes through clearly as they describe their feelings and thoughts during their first hours on their own.

THE FIRST BREAK

Ruby Howard, * *February 16, 1983, Newark.*   That snowy Wednesday morning Ruby got up early and put on her best dress, the pink one with the white collar and eyelets. She made her own breakfast, and she was walking out the door when her mother called after her, "How come you all dressed up today?" Ruby was prepared. She knew her mother would be curious, because most school days she wore jeans and a sweater. "I'm in the assembly program this week. I told you, you never remember," she said. But Ruby wasn't going to school. She was all dressed up because she was going out to look for her father.

Ruby's father, James, had left the family when she was six. Now fourteen years old, Ruby had seen him only twice in the past eight years. The week before, her cousin Sheila had told her that she had heard James was working for the telephone company downtown. "I have to go find him," Ruby had told Sheila.

The reason she wanted to see him was the fighting. These days, it seemed Ruby was always fighting—fighting with her mother, with her three brothers and two sisters, with the kids at school.

> I been fighting as long as I can remember. I can't take but so much. I can ignore somebody for a certain amount of time

* The names and a few identifying details of the lives of the adolescents who appear in this book have been changed, except when noted, to preserve their privacy and to allow for a time in the future when they may want to put this period of tough change behind them.

and then that time is up. That's when I want to fight. Lots
of girls, who think they're tough, they get you, they make murder. They make you want to punch them in the face. When
I got an attitude, or my mother makes me mad, I go outside
and fight. It's not right, but I do it 'cause I need action real
bad. Fightin' gets all my anger out.

Up to junior high, Ruby did pretty well. Her reading and
math scores were at grade level, and because she had a pretty
voice she sang in the school chorus and in the church choir. She
hoped that someday she would become a professional singer—a
new Diana Ross. In the seventh grade her life slid downhill. She
was fighting almost every day, and she seemed to spend more
time waiting outside the assistant principal's office than she did
in class. Frequently the school sent notes home to her mother.
"I'd get to feelin' the school'd be as happy if I left as if I stayed."

Ruby cut a lot in the seventh grade, as much as three or
four days a week. She had discovered boys, and she spent a lot
of time where they hung out—in arcades, at the big train station
downtown, and on 42nd Street in Manhattan. "I never fight with
the boys," she says, "and the boys don't fight with me." All of
this led to nastier and uglier confrontations with her mother.
Mrs. Howard had a night job as a cleaning woman at a hospital;
she had six kids to worry about. She was losing patience with
Ruby.

> She was always hollerin', tellin' me this, tellin' me that, when
> I knew I wasn't really doin' nothin' wrong. It was just that
> she didn't approve of it, 'cause she thought it was goin' to
> get me in some trouble. And I never—I only had one charge
> against me, that's assault and battery. I never been to the youth
> house [the detention facility for youths in Newark]. I never
> been to jail. I couldn't take it no more. I felt dead. One day
> I might just disrespect my mother. I might curse her out all
> day, hit her. So I just say I better leave.

The answer to her problems, Ruby thought, was to persuade
her father to come back to the family or, failing that, to move
in with him. At fourteen, she looked back at the few years she
had spent with her father as a shining period in her childhood.
"When my father was home, he just talk to us. He bought us
what we need and what we want. He never hit us, he just talked
to us. If there's somethin' wrong, he let us know. My mother

when we was actin' bad, she'd holler and then she'd say, 'Do you hear me?' Everybody hear her; *of course* I hear her. But my father even when I'm bad, he did see the good in me."

Now it's a few minutes after noon, and Ruby Howard, shivering in her blue parka and pink dress and black rubber boots, is standing on Broad Street, outside the phone company, waiting for her father to come and rescue her. Ruby spots him walking out of the building, carrying a lunch pail, shooting the breeze with a couple of other linemen. She stops him and says, "Daddy, I gotta talk to you." He looks at the chubby little girl with those unblinking eyes staring at him behind her thick glasses.

"Go home to your momma," he says and keeps walking.

"But—," she starts, trying to keep up with him.

"I got no time for you," he says, aware that his friends from the phone company are staring at him. "Can't you see I'm busy? Go to your momma."

What is Ruby going to do now? She doesn't want to go home. Her father won't talk to her. There's always New York, Ruby thinks. The train station is only a block away and from there it's a half-hour to Manhattan, and Times Square. That's where she spends the rest of the afternoon, huddling under the marquees of theaters showing porn movies, eying the pimps and prostitutes, the dealers and the addicts. "I see people with big old hands takin' drugs. Or red eyes. I see a lot of prostitutes, dirty lookin', sittin' in the street." Finally she is approached by a young man who looks a few years older than she. He says, "You better watch out for the pimps." She says, "I know they make me feel like— dirty." He suggests they go over to the Port Authority bus station where it is warm.

Inside the station, they buy coffee and crullers. Ruby tells her new friend about her father and her mother. The more she talks the angrier she gets. Then she sees a white woman in a fur coat, loaded down with packages, rushing to catch a bus. "I decided to do something wild," Ruby says. She steps into the woman's path. Ruby glares at her for a second—and then spits into her face. The woman drops her packages and screams for a cop.

It is a little after midnight, and Ruby Howard is sitting in the squad room of the Port Authority police station. Her first day away from home is almost over. But Ruby isn't contrite or frightened. She is still boiling inside.

Her mother walks in, sees her daughter snapping her gum,

reading a comic book. To claim her, she has had to miss a night's work. "You had enough?" her mother asks. "You ready to come home?"

To both questions, Ruby answers, "Not yet."

Ralph Ortiz, March 22, 1982, Chicago.   Another Monday. Ralph fidgets in his seat. The history teacher drones on. Ralph takes down the homework assignment in his notebook. He is very good about doing his homework, never misses a day. Ralph is a good, if not spectacular, student at Roberto Clemente High School on the Northwest Side of Chicago. This is no small accomplishment at Clemente, where an estimated 70 percent of the 3,500 students leave the school before graduating and where in 1983–84 only 58 of the 434 seniors were reading at grade level.[7]

If you wanted to pick out a single student who would beat the odds, who would graduate and perhaps go on to college, you could do worse than bet on Ralph. He is polite to his teachers, usually attentive to what they are trying to teach him, and popular among his circle of friends. He is slender and good-looking, with a smooth cocoa complexion, and he moves with an easy, flowing motion, with nothing of the gawky awkwardness of the typical teenager. Ralph is a neat, unostentatious dresser. In the spring, his usual outfit consists of chino trousers, sneakers, and a pullover shirt. His blue and white sweat socks are invariably rolled two inches above his sneakers. A blue bandana handkerchief sticks out of his back pocket.

Most kids moving over from junior high school to high school are rattled by the feverish pitch: the rushing from one fifty-minute class six or seven times a day to another; the different teachers, each imposing his or her own standards and demands on their students; the sheer size and complexity of the institution—all these 4,000 different students, the huge lunchroom with its wall of deafening noise, the rigid pecking order of race and class and academic status. But Ralph seemed unperturbed by the fragmentation of high school. He exudes a rare self-assurance, a quiet confidence that marks him as a leader even though he's only a freshman. This is life number one for Ralph Ortiz.

At home, Ralph is just as much in command. His father is gone, and his mother, Lydia, works off and on. In Chicago, unlike Newark, there are still some factory jobs, although here, too, they are dwindling. Lydia has worked at a glass plant, a paper factory, and now at a woodworking shop that manufactures advertising displays. The work is hard, but Mrs. Ortiz considers herself lucky, because there just aren't that many jobs around for a thirty-year-old Mexican-American mother of four who never went beyond the sixth grade, and who can't speak English very well. When she can arrange it, her employer pays her in cash, without declaring her income to the IRS. This allows her to receive welfare payments while drawing a salary. Still, the income for this family of four is never more than $12,000 a year.

In her absence Ralph plays father. He makes meals for his three younger brothers, orders them to do their homework, watches out for them on the street, washes their clothes, and bathes them before his mother arrives home. Not only that: Ralph fills the role of the provider. Once a month, for the past two years, he has given his mother $100 or more. "The first two times I brought money home, she didn't know where I got it from," Ralph remembers, "because I wouldn't tell and she started beating me up. But then, after a while, she took it without questions. My brothers didn't mind 'cause they needed money, and my father wasn't giving us anything, or nothing like that."

Whatever doubts Lydia Ortiz has about her oldest son and the money he brings home are partially deflected by his obvious popularity. At fourteen, Ralph seems to be the most popular kid on the street. Not a night goes by when the doorbell to their sixth-floor apartment doesn't ring every ten minutes.

"Mrs. Ortiz, could you tell Ralph, Maria would like him to call?"

"Mrs. Ortiz, Guillermo says he has to see Ralph. Very important."

"Mrs. Ortiz, ask Ralph to come over to Julio Martinez's house right away."

There is pride in Mrs. Ortiz's voice when she says, "The bell doesn't stop ringing. You can see, everybody wants Ralph. He is the big star."

Lydia Ortiz is proud of her son, appreciative of what he does at home, pleased at his progress at school. Ralph is protective of his mother; he knows that her life is hard, her burdens many. But there is something missing between them: They rarely express emotion. Their relationship is almost businesslike. "I felt like I was going along with the program. My mother tells you to do something, you do it, that's it. And if it's done right, or if it's done wrong, she'll tell you about it. I personally could never hug my mother. I don't know why, that's the way she projects her feelings towards me."

At times Ralph can't help but feel resentful toward his mother and his brothers for all the responsibilities he has to shoulder.

> My mother was having kids and I was fucking changing diapers. At home, I'd use my authority as a father, and I could win some small battles. I could tell my brothers do this, do that, and they'd have to listen. But when my mother came home and she said, Why don't you do this? I was just a kid again, a baby.
>
> At times I really hated the program. I thought a lot about leaving. I'd try harder and harder, but I couldn't get no response. But I felt it was important to stay. I didn't have so much love *from* them, but I had so much love *for* them. And I wanted them to know that, as much as possible, because I really felt committed towards them.

Dutiful son, surrogate father—that is life number two for Ralph Ortiz.

Life number three is on the streets. For the last three years, since he was eleven, Ralph has been the leader of the Avenue Boys, one of dozens of street gangs on the northwest side of Chicago. In his neighborhood, the gangs are made up of Mexican-American kids. Outside of his neighborhood there are other gangs—black gangs, Puerto Rican gangs, white gangs. Almost every block has its own gang. Ralph grows up believing that every street, every piece of turf has its own colors, its own flag to which you pledge allegience, to which you owe absolute fidelity. "It's like the whole nation is wearing a color. We've got the blue and white flag; over there there's the red and yellow, and the rich people are wearing their color, they're wearing green. That's what people die for—their color."

The colors of Ralph's gang are blue and white. That's why he's always careful to let his bandana hang out of his pocket and to wear his blue and white socks rolled over his sneakers. The colors tell the kids at school or on the street: Don't mess with me, I've got plenty of bodies and firepower behind me. Ralph's crew has been selling dope since he was nine or ten, starting with grass, moving up to angel dust, pills, coke, and heroin. They sell in adjoining neighborhoods, in arcades, in the suburbs, sometimes at a drive-in movie where kids hang out. Ralph keeps half of the money he makes from dealing; the other half goes to his family.*

Money and protection drew Ralph into the gang world, but what kept him in and sealed his loyalty was something else that, at that age, he couldn't find at home or in school. It was power. And it was shared intimacy. "Being recognized as a leader, that gave me a type of power and I took advantage of it. If I wanted somebody to listen to me, I'd ask the guys to go get him. And if I wanted somebody hurt, I'd just tell them to do it. And if I had to prove myself, for me being the ruler, I'd go do it. There wouldn't be no problem, 'cause I knew I had the power." With the gang, as long as he asserts leadership, he retains authority. With his mother, he assumes many responsibilities, but in the end he has no authority.

With the gang members, Ralph never felt he had to hold back. He could open up to them.

> It was like if you felt like crying, go ahead man, cry. You'd cry and let it out, feel better. That's how we started growing more together, being stronger. The gang was my emotion. If I felt something, everybody felt something. If I didn't, nobody did. That's how we were communicating. Not just by being cool or bad, but how we felt. Our feeling was that if something was hurting one of us, we'd do something about it. If it has to be done, it will be done.

In the bloody, vicious world of Chicago youth gangs, there was no lack of opportunity for gang members to prove their loyalty to each other. The guys in Ralph's gang got their chance one summer night when he was twelve. They were standing on the street, three blocks from Ralph's house. They were flying their colors in no-man's-land, on the border of territory claimed by a hostile gang. Ralph's uncle, a Vietnam veteran, passed by, and Ralph warned him, "Why don't you go home. You know how dangerous it can get over here."

His uncle ignored him and—"We walked down the block, and it just happened, we were all singing and a guy came out with a shotgun and blew him off in the head. Like that, and he was dead."

---

* Eventually Ralph gives back a quarter of the earnings from drugs to the gang.

That night Ralph's gang struck back. "The guy's family had a candy store. We went down there and blew it up. We went to the guy's apartment and blew it up—blew off his leg. Then we blew up his car. That's the way it was going—we were blowing up everything."

The gang, says Ralph, didn't worry about retaliation, didn't worry about the police. They didn't worry about anything because his uncle's killer had violated the one inviolable rule: "You don't get back at anybody through the family. That's the one thing you don't do. And if you do, you're up for grabs. That night the gang was family, and we acted like family."

The next morning Ralph goes back to his three separate lives: high school student, son and surrogate parent, and gang member. He can never be sure whether his mother or other relatives know about his life on the street. He can't be sure whether the teachers, who see his colors hanging out of his pants pockets, know. But nobody tells him to stop. Nobody says, "Stop dealing and stealing and destroying." "I still thought I could keep my worlds separate," Ralph says. "I could split up my school world, my family world, my street world. Shit, I was only twelve. I never thought I'd have to choose."

On March 22, 1982, Ralph chose. He did what he always did—left school at 2:45, stayed home taking care of his brothers until 4:30, and went out to hook up with the gang. They kidded around with some girls for a half-hour, and one of the guys said, "Let's go for a ride." They got into the guy's red convertible. The top was down. Ralph was sitting in the front, next to the driver, a third gang member in the back. Out of the corner of his eye, Ralph saw the purple Camaro cruising west on East Main, saw the sun glinting off the doublebarreled shotgun. Crack, crack, crack. Three shots splintered the windshield, showering glass on Ralph and the driver. Ralph ducked under the dashboard, grabbing the wheel with one hand, coming down hard on the brake. The car skidded toward the sidewalk, plowed into a parked car, and stopped dead. The driver was holding his face in his hands. Blood ran through his fingers. "First, we fix your face," Ralph said. "Then tonight we settle up."

The Avenue Boys met that night. After a couple of hours, Ralph said, "What's the use talking?" He reached into his bookbag and took out his gun, the pistol he always carried with him when he was on the street. "We know what we gotta do. Let's do it."

One gang member said he didn't want to go with them. "Fine, it's your decision," Ralph said. He ordered a violation* for the kid. "We banged him twenty-five times on the knees and ankles with a bat. We broke both legs, but I thought he got off cheap."

They found the guy who had shot at them a few hours later. "We hit him in the head," said Ralph. "We didn't think about it, just did it. Wasn't no other way. If we didn't do it, the gang was dead, we was all dead. At home or in school, if somebody snaps on you, you can say, I'll let it go this time, 'cause it ain't worth gettin' in trouble for. But on the street you don't show no weakness if you wanna live."

The next morning Ralph decided not to go home.

> I just couldn't live the lie any more. The killing made me realize my life was out on the street. What I was doin' in the house or in school was pretending. I was a kid, and I was feelin' old, and I couldn't play any more games. I remember when I made up my mind. It was about dawn, and I was sittin' on the floor of this basement where the gang stayed. I was smokin' a cigarette, and lookin' up through this window with grates on it. Somethin' told me it'd be a long time before I could go home again, and I could feel my stomach sink. I thought right then maybe I was losin' something important, but I didn't know what it was and I didn't know how to find it.

Bill Craig, January 24, 1982, Newport, Kentucky. It's a short stroll across a bridge from downtown Cincinnati to Newport, Kentucky. Over the years, many thousands of solid Cincinnati citizens have taken this walk in pursuit of a few kicks. In this old, tired river city of 23,000 they could find wide-open gambling, prostitution, strip shows, and an interesting variety of other vices. During the 1950s and 1960s, the city fathers, despite highly publicized federal investigations, openly promoted forbidden pleasures as the principal industry; if fun-seekers dropped a bundle at the blackjack tables at the Flamingo or the Yorkshire, everybody got an equal cut. The Mafia's cut, it was rumored, was more equal than anybody else's.

---

* In Chicago gang jargon, a violation is the penalty imposed on a youth who has broken the rules of the gang. A kid who is approached to join a gang and refuses may have to run a gantlet of gang members who beat him with a paddle or bat. A member who decides to leave may be beaten twenty or thirty times. A kid who doesn't wear the gang colors when he's inside gang territory may have his arm broken.

Good-government reformers have cut into Newport's action in the past decade. The gambling casinos have been shut down. Some of the most overt prostitution has been curtailed. The strippers are supposed to keep their G-strings on. Yet, for all the reform initiatives, no one argues today that Newport has been purged of sin, only that the focus of its corruption has shifted. Instead of offering outsiders a bawdy playground for relatively innocuous, victimless transgressions, Newport now breeds an evil virus that infects, mainly, its young and poor.

I first visited Newport after interviewing youngsters in the coal-mining country of Appalachian Kentucky. I followed the same route north as that traveled by thousands of Appalachian families after the Korean War. When the mining was mechanized, the company towns were abandoned, and thousands of miners were fired. They were lured to Newport and other towns to the north by the promise of clean, steady work. Most of the decent living space had already been occupied by the earlier German, Italian, and Irish settlers, so they crowded into the congested, already decaying West End section of town. No coal is mined near Newport, but the West End, with its squat brick buildings, broken sidewalks, and rusting cars calls up the same dark, dour mood that weighs so heavily on Welsh mining towns. Instead of slag heaps, the natural landmarks of the West End are garbage dumps and landfills.

That is what intrigued me about Newport and teased me back for a second visit. Listening and talking to the kids of the West End, watching them at home and in the streets, the first impression is that this is White Harlem. In a five-block walk, an eleven-year-old boy gets a half-dozen offers to buy or sell drugs, a school bus driver tells of confiscating three or four pints of liquor every day on the way to grade school. West End childhoods do not lack drama. Blood feuds nurtured in the hollows of Appalachia are settled on the sidewalks and back alleys of Newport. The implements of survival for many children are the shotgun and the switchblade. When a teenage girl is asked who was important to her as a child, she lists more people who died violently than are still alive.

When I was in Newport, a social worker asked a young West End man to compose a history of the "successes" in his life. He wrote:

Age 0–10

Learned how to walk, learned how to talk, learned how to
read, learned how to write. Learned how to cross the street
by myself.

Age 10–15

Learned that you have to watch out for perverts. Learned that
there are serious drugs that can hurt you bad. I shouldn't
hang out with bad company.

Age 15–20

Learned that I shouldn't get in any trouble by the police.
Learned that I shouldn't have quit school. Learned that I can't
find any good job here. Learned that love hurts.[8]

This boy grew up in a community where the "official" unemployment rate in 1983 was 14 percent and the actual rate, which
included seasonal and part-time workers and discouraged workers
who had stopped looking for jobs, was more than 20 percent.
Almost 30 percent of young adults aged twenty to twenty-four
were out of work. More than a quarter of the families lived in
poverty, and another 25 percent barely exceeded the poverty level.
Forty percent of the families were headed by a single woman,
and 80 percent of the apartments and houses they lived in were
listed as deteriorating and delapidated.[9]

Statistically measured, the conditions of life for young whites
in the West End may not be quite as hard as they are for black
youths in Newark or the Fifth Ward of Houston, or for Hispanic
youngsters in the Humboldt Park section of Chicago. But there
are some things that cannot be easily measured. One is hope.
Another is the sense of possibility, that feeling that the future is
open to all those ready and willing to explore it. I found that
among West End adolescents there is more fight, more determination to challenge fate; they don't seem as resigned as some black
and Hispanic youngsters I met. Perhaps the difference is that
they know they have, if nothing else, their whiteness going for
them, not an insignificant advantage in America.

But race is not enough to sustain their faith for long. It doesn't
take long, no longer than their eighteenth or nineteenth year,
before they feel that their futures have been foreclosed. In Newport, the plants that attracted their parents and grandparents have

been shut down. The two leading employers, a brewery and a clothes manufacturer, have reduced their workforces and are rumored to be considering relocation. But when there is nothing else, there is always the underground economy. Jack Nienaber, director of the Brighton Center, a private nonprofit service organization in Newport, estimates that one-third of the young women in the West End will earn money as prostitutes during their adolescence, and half of the teenagers in the area will buy and use hard drugs—pills, angel dust, heroin.[10] A majority of the kids, he says, start drinking heavily by their ninth or tenth birthday. Half of the young women become pregnant before they are sixteen. Only 30 percent of the kids will graduate from high school. "This town is permeated by sleaze—sleaze and violence," he says. "The sleaze isn't as obvious as it once was, but scratch the surface and you find dirt."

One of the great quests of youth, Erik Erikson has written, is for fidelity—"the search for something and somebody to be true to."[11] Surrounded by rot, Newport youths, as Newark youths do, yearn for somebody to believe in, somebody who affirms their hopes, someone who shields them in their vulnerability. This yearning is especially intense here because of the Appalachian legacy of loyalty and fidelity. Many Newport youngsters live and breathe the past, the past of grandparents who brewed moonshine in the hills of Eastern Kentucky, who struggled to survive in the shadow of coal tipples, who cannonballed their coal trucks down the twisting roads of Floyd and Harlan counties. In their early adolescence, before they began to assume their own separate identities, young West Enders see themselves as the embodiment of family myth. For them nothing is more important than proving themselves to their families, thereby winning and preserving the family's love.

When I talked to these youngsters about their family history, love came up in almost every conversation. "I felt so bad when I got in trouble 'cause I know my family loved me so much," a youngster will say. Explaining why he almost killed another teenage boy who made an uninvited pass at his sister, a West End boy tells me, "I did it because I love her. When you love your family, you'll do anything for them."

When family love is withheld or denied, the youngster loses more than his parents' affection, protection, and devotion. He is denied access to an elaborate and romantic family mythology.

He is shut out of an intimate family history that not only illumi-
nates what he believes was a heroic past but serves also as a
blueprint for his future. In a community where it's nearly impossible to find external models to guide his growth, maturity, and
vocational development, he has to invent his own future. He is
truly alone.

As the Newport boy wrote in his "success" story, love hurts,
and lost love wounds deeply. The manchild exiled in Newport
learns quickly to harden his heart against hurt. Bill Craig began
to build his fortress when he was very young. His father left the
family when Bill was born. In the next eight years his mother
remarried, got divorced, and married again. She had twelve children by her three husbands, but by the time Bill was ten only
two brothers and a sister were at home. Eight of her children
were being raised by relatives. "I had two thoughts when I was
a kid," says Bill. "Did my being born drive my real father out
of the house? And, the other thing, was, if she didn't love me
enough would she give me away like she gave away my other
brothers and sisters? I'd lay in bed late at night thinkin' about
that."

His own appearance heightened his fears. He was a skinny
kid who developed acne early. A speech impediment made him
slur his words. It took him a long time to ask for something.
His face would redden, and he would hop from foot to foot as
he tried to get the words out. His mother would sometimes say,
in exasperation, "Billy, say what you wanna say. I don't got the
whole mornin' to wait on you."

June Craig did have a lot to worry about. There were all
those kids, some home, some away; she was gaining weight; some
days she would feel her youth slipping away; the relatives—her
grandparents, cousins, uncles, brothers-in-law—were always dropping in, asking slyly, "Are you gonna be able to keep *this* man?"
Her husband, who worked in a hardware store, developed a heart
condition when Bill was eight. He gave up his job and began to
collect disability benefits. When Bill quarreled with his stepfather,
June would shout at him, "Do you want to kill my husband? Keep
this up, and you'll be buryin' him." Bill thought, "He's not my
real father, he's a stranger they want me to love. I want my mother
and that's it."

In the swirl of family life, Bill began to feel something like
a castaway. When his uncles went on a hunting trip, the runty

kid with pimples on his face and marbles in his mouth was left behind. When the family got together for a party, Bill wasn't the kind of kid you'd spend a lot of time with talking about guns and duck blinds. In his isolation, Bill began to invent his own world. He began to use and then deal grass. On Monmouth Street, the main shopping thoroughfare of the West End, where new dance lounges and pornographic book stores each year replaced failed convenience stores and clothing shops, Bill scored grass with money he stole from his mother. He was nine years old. "All I had to do was walk down the street and say, 'You got any reefer?' Hey, they didn't give a shit how old you were."

Bill didn't walk the street alone. He had a partner. Bill had known Johnny Bayley since they both were infants. "He knew more about me than my own mother did," Billy said.

> His parents with me were sweet. My family was sweet toward him. Sometimes with him I could act like a kid. When I was over his house, we'd get on his bed and jump up and down.
>
> I missed my parents' love, but me and Johnny, we used to give each other love. Johnny once looked at me and said, "Don't think I'm queer or nothin', but I have to tell you somethin'—I love you." We'd start holdin' each other and tellin' each other we loved each other. We used to have dreams that when we grew up we'd get a big place together. I guess it was the two of us against the world.

On the night of January 24, 1982, Bill had one last, bitter argument with his stepfather. His parents had discovered a cache of marijuana in his bedroom dresser, and his father told him, "This is a drug house." His mother said nothing. The argument continued late into the night. The next morning Bill threw a few clothes into a sack and left home. He knew where he was going: He was going to hook up with Johnny Bayley, and together the two ten-year-olds would live out their childhood.

All that day and night Johnny hid Bill in his parents' basement. He took food from the refrigerator and brought it down to their hiding place. But there are limits to the guile of ten-year-olds. The next morning Johnny's parents found the plates in the basement and called Bill's mother. Before she arrived, Bill left. Johnny decided to go with him.

> Johnny and me, we were so much the same. He felt, his stepfather's kid, his stepsister, was getting all the attention. He'd

been smoking reefers since he was eight. When we skipped
school, we skipped together. It wasn't one leading the other.
We did things like we were part of the same body. The only
difference was our mothers. After he left his house with me
and his mother found out, she told him to get the fuck out.
My mother was always trying to get me back.

They spent their first day on the outside, trying to sell grass,
planning how they would manage on their own. By nightfall, their
long-range plans had not evolved, and they had to confront the
more immediate problem of where to stay. They settled on an
all-night White Castle restaurant. "We sat at a table in the back.
I'd fall asleep and he'd wake up. Then he'd fall asleep and I'd
wake up," Bill remembers. "We kept ordering coffee all night.
One time an old guy came into our booth and started making
passes. Johnny told him, Get lost. But what I remember most,
what Johnny and me wondered about later, was nobody asked
what two little kids were doing in that place all night. They acted
like it was just normal."

The next morning Johnny slipped back into his house and
brought Bill extra clothes—a couple of pairs of pants, three or
four T-shirts, a light windbreaker, and a sweater. These would
be all the clothes they had for the next two years. That night
they took their meager belongings to an embankment alongside
the railroad track. They tried to sleep there, but it began to rain
and it was cold, so they returned to the White Castle. The following night they slept in an abandoned building, but someone spotted them and called the police.

"We were draggin'," Bill says. "We couldn't keep doin' this.
We had to find a place to stay for a while, at least till the spring.
Then we thought we could sleep outside."

Johnny knew a twenty-two-year-old drug dealer who had an
extra room in his apartment. He offered to let the two boys stay
there if they would sell drugs for him and pay him half the profits.

We were scared where this all was taking us. We were scared
all the time. We were goin' down this long road, and we didn't
know where it would end. But we didn't have too many choices.

I told Johnny maybe we should go back home for a while.
But he said no. He said we'd be all right as long as we had
each other and we didn't get involved with other people. He
said, You could live anywhere and be happy if there was love.
It was just the way I felt.

Those first nights away were the beginning of a long journey that lasted more than three years. It was a journey filled with danger, violence, and tragedy. And when it was over only Bill would be around to tell all that happened to two ten-year-old boys who lost their childhoods in Newport, Kentucky.

The Lost Dream

Three young people leave home. Ruby Howard spits in the face of a white woman. Ralph Ortiz binds himself to his street gang. Bill Craig forms an alliance with his best friend. By conventional standards that measure happiness at home and success in schools, their lives did not seem especially unhappy. It is true that Ruby was rebuffed by her father, that Ralph was forced to assume the role of a father when he was still a child, that Bill felt his mother didn't understand him and didn't give him as much love as he wanted. But these hardly seem adequate explanations for rejecting the two central institutions of their childhood, their schools and their families.

Paul Osterman, an economist at Boston College, has constructed an index to determine how ready high school dropouts were to take jobs. Only 20 percent of these young men and women, he found, are so seriously disturbed that they require long-term employment training and psychological therapy. This bottom tier consisted of youngsters, Osterman said, who not only "can't read, write and do arithmetic" but have had "such devastating life experiences that they were just blown away."[12]

Osterman's ranking system is concerned specifically with what is required to prepare poor youngsters for employment. But it also provides a rough guide to the different levels of the youth population I studied. That is, I found that perhaps 20 percent of the youngsters I met would require long-term psychological counseling and an extended course of basic remedial education to equip them to enter the mainstream of American adolescents. Ruby, Ralph, and Bill, while they had difficult and troubled childhoods, had not been, in my view, devastated by their experiences; their economic status, their performance in school, and their families' relative stability would place them in the top 40 percent of the youngsters I met.

Ruby was two grades behind in her reading, but she was talented in art and music and involved in extracurricular activities.

For a youngster brought up in a family that spoke only Spanish, Ralph had done quite well; his reading and arithmetic scores were average for his age and grade. Bill had failed arithmetic once, but otherwise his overall grade level was average and in reading and social studies above average.

At home, all three had problems. But none of them had been sexually abused, severely beaten, or thrown out of their homes. Their parents were not heavy drinkers or drug users. It was just the opposite: Their parents demonstrated genuine concern about their progress in school and the perils of the street. These three were poor, but they were not severely deprived. At different times, the parents of all three had received some form of public assistance, but they had enough to eat. The families even had a few relative luxuries. Bill's parents had a car, and he had a stereo. Ralph's mother managed to buy a secondhand washing machine when she had one of her occasional jobs. Ruby's mother had a color TV.

I met black children in Houston who had to sleep on the floor, whose railroad apartments didn't have any heat in the winter, who huddled under the same coverlet with their brothers and sisters. I met young women in Floyd County, Kentucky, who wore the same pair of jeans for three years. I met kids in Newark who lived in tiny basement hovels where there are huge, gaping holes in the walls, where steam pipes snake across the ceiling, dripping scalding water, and where toddlers sleep in their own excrement. That is extreme deprivation. By comparison, Ruby, Ralph, and Bill were not severely deprived.

If by conventional standards they were not desperately poor, they had not been abused, and they had not failed in school, why did they break away? I have a direct answer for that. Even some children who grow up in relative, rather than absolute, poverty do not have what we usually consider a normal childhood and cannot be judged by conventional standards. They do not grow up with a vision of an open future. The adults who surround them do not provide models of success and achievement that would inspire them in school and afterward. Children like Ralph, Ruby, and Bill don't perceive themselves as part of the mainstream. They identify, in School Superintendant Alvarado's resonant phrase, with the imperiled 95 percent who live on the verge of chaos and anarchy. When they review their life histories, they reveal an accretion of hurts and traumas that are largely invisible to outsiders.

Their experiences are like scar tissue covering a wound that has never really healed. An unforeseen accident or misadventure can reinfect them. It doesn't have to be a big thing, only the latest thing. A spark can touch off a firestorm in their lives. When children must exercise constant vigilance to survive, they don't have much opportunity to exercise the Dream, to cultivate a vision of what they can someday make of themselves. The Dream is the adolescent's lodestar as he or she navigates toward adulthood. In his comprehensive study *The Seasons of a Man's Life,* the social psychologist Daniel J. Levinson writes, "In early adulthood a man has to form a Dream, create an initial structure in which the Dream can be lived out, and attain goals through which it is in some measure fulfilled."[13]

But that may not be possible for these children. Every day they devote themselves to getting over until the next morning. In their world, there is no room for the Dream. The central question Levinson poses is: "If he lives in a disorganized, fragmented, polluted, crime-ridden world, how can he keep the worst features of collective life from becoming part of his individual environment?"[14] Every young man and woman I met was forced to confront, from their earliest days, this question: How do I keep myself from being overwhelmed by the environment that surrounds me?

They clearly understood that cutting themselves off from their families, their education, and their community life would not end their distress. They had few illusions that leaving would assure them control over their surroundings. From a thousand frightening stories passed along the grapevine by adults, older brothers and sisters, and veterans of the streets, they knew that alone, at the mercy of strangers, they would be exposed to a collective life at least as threatening as the one they were running from.

Still, they ran. They did not slip quietly into the night of the city. They were mobilized by rage. It was a rage that had been building for a long time, for months and years. Ruby expressed that rage when she spat into the woman's face. Ralph felt that rage when he and his gang hunted down their enemy on the streets of Chicago. Bill and Johnny were enraged when they felt they had been denied their parents' love.

Ruby did not leave only because she was rebuffed by her father. Ralph did not leave only because of his commitment to the gang. Bill did not leave only because he had a fight with his parents over drugs. Those were but the latest in a long series of episodes that left them with a sense that they were powerless to control their environment. They felt as though they were instruments of a larger design that they did not understand and that they could not hope to master. They were denied the Dream. And that is what enraged them.

How did it happen? What went wrong? When did they lose the Dream? The answers to these questions can be found only by retracing the journey undertaken by a generation of young Americans. For it is in the half-buried, seemingly banal details of their childhood and early adolescence that the larger mosaic of their lives is foreshadowed.

A good place to begin is at the beginning.

THREE

Childhood

Willie's Story

All the way through my research I was nagged by a sense of incompleteness. It was as if I were catching hundreds of kids in a freeze frame; it was roughly equivalent to projecting an entire life from a snapshot in a high school yearbook. I never knew how the picture would change in six months, a year, five years.

Lacking a time machine to transport me into the past and the mystical power to read fortunes, I found a guide who led me back through his childhood, brought me into his adolescence, and carried me forward into his young adulthood. When I met William Sosa during the summer of 1984 he was 30 years old and working for a community organization in Newark called La Casa de Don Pedro.

He reminded me of a fullback. He was not a breakaway runner, an artful dodger. He was the bull you brought into the game if you needed two yards on third down. He was built close to the ground, with a massive chest and arms bulging like barrel staves. His face looked as if it had been gouged and stomped in a thousand pileups. But his dark brown eyes were intelligent and inquisitive; they seemed to say, I've seen a lot, but I'm ready to learn something new. His smile could light up a stadium.

In social work terminology, Willie was an "outside" man, a street worker. His forte was putting out fires on the street. In the summer I spent with him in the desperately poor black and Hispanic neighborhoods of Newark, he fought what seemed like a thousand fires.

A fifteen-year-old girl shows up in school with her body a mass of bruises inflicted by her father, who doesn't like the people she's been hanging out with. Her older sister calls La Casa and says, "We need Willie." A sixteen-year-old boy is fired from his first straight job for smoking grass and, too ashamed or frightened to come home, has been riding the trains for two nights. His mother, surrounded by her eight other children, pleads with the La Casa receptionist, "We need Willie."

That summer I often thought only Willie stood between the wild, half-crazed kids in this Newark neighborhood and the lockup or the morgue. His accomplishments derived from his awesome talent as a chill-out artist. By listening, talking, sympathizing, arguing, pleading, and sometimes even judiciously going a little crazy himself, he bought time. With a little time, he believed, he could introduce reason into the most volatile conflicts; with a little time, he could activate the clanking social welfare machinery; with a little time, he could save a life or maybe just delay disaster. If he could get these kids to chill out even for a few days, then maybe somebody somewhere could figure out an answer. Willie Sosa's job, for which he was paid $15,000 a year, was not to find the big answers. It was to win a temporary truce in the small, deadly wars that were fought every day and every night in the rubble of Newark. And in that job he was remarkably effective.

He was effective because he was part of the community. He'd spent much of his life here on these streets, and now, when ambition or money might have lured others out to a safer sanctuary, he chose to stay. He lived right around the corner from La Casa, in the eye of the storm. He also knew everybody. He knew their parents and grandparents, knew the towns and villages they had come from in Puerto Rico, knew who had stabilized their lives and who was drinking every afternoon in the lot behind the projects. Willie, prowling the streets in his rumpled jeans and the sweatshirt with the faded U.S. Marines logo, was somebody you could always talk to about the rumors of layoffs at the plant, about the new principal at the high school, about the cutbacks in food stamps, about the old lady with diabetes who refused to go to the *Americano* hospital for treatment until her leg turned black and had to be amputated. In a community where silence was the only defense against a thousand silky-voiced snoops, everybody talked to Willie.

Willie Sosa was the keeper of the secrets. A child's history is composed of two parts. One consists of the written record of growth and development: a birth certificate, a doctor's examination, the first report card, the elementary school diploma. The second part is hidden from public view. It's composed of thoughts and feelings, of concealed fears and protected visions of the future. Willie was privy to the undocumented secret history of childhood. He knew how different, how special it is to grow up poor in America.

That's not something visiting "professionals"—the teachers and social workers—can learn as they hurry about their rounds of classrooms and tenements. To those unengaged observers, the sudden, surprising turns of adolescence can appear incongruent with the carefully composed faces children put on every morning for the outside world. Johnny seemed like such a serious, dedicated student. Why is he dropping out? Linda seemed so happy with her family, so enthusiastic about college and a career. Why is she having a baby at fifteen and leaving the house? Willie knew why, because he had explored the hidden interior behind the façade. The startling disjunctures of adolescence didn't startle him at all. It was what he expected to happen to a kid who grows up in these circumstances.

The secrets confided to him by the poor children of Newark had revealed more than perhaps anyone should know. He had learned that these children are never secure in the protection of their families and communities. He had learned that from birth they are in fear of abandonment. Every day Willie refereed the endless tug-of-war between a child's desire to explore the unknown and a fearful parent's attempt to control and regulate a kid's curiosity. If the kid broke the rules set by parents and the schools, he wouldn't get sympathy and understanding. He could expect only certain and swift punishment. Willie knew from his own life and from the lives of his constituents that a kid's first mistake can be his last, that you don't get too many second chances on the streets of Newark.

Willie had lived the life. I don't mean by that that his experiences exactly paralleled those of the youngsters he was trying to save. What he had gone through was, as such travails can be measured, worse than what many of these teenagers were going through. Most of the kids in the Newark barrio knew that. Their parents knew that. And they also knew that Willie had come through all of it and had managed to turn his life around.

William Sosa is the inner voice of this book. I will not devote a great amount of space to his memories of his own life and to his experiences with the young people of Newark. But what I learned from him has greatly influenced and informed this writing. He was, in a sense, my mentor, and the effect of his tutelage can be found in how this work is organized, how issues are defined, and how I propose to ameliorate some of the problems that burden youth.

This is not to say that I consider his epic struggles representative or typical of what all poor youngsters experience. I don't think any one individual or community embodies the diverse problems of an entire generation, any more than I believe in a single, monolithic culture of poverty. I agree with Bernard Rosenberg and Harry Silverstein, who in their brilliant study of juvenile delinquency argue that there is "more difference than sameness" among poor youth.[1] Rosenberg and Silverstein write:

> That people of poverty are alike in sharing common economic circumstances is obvious and indisputable. That they similarly interpret and respond to their common condition is much less certain . . . failure to recognize the validity of this proposition results in treating all low-income people as if they were a single social unit, which in turn produces frustration and despair.[2]

Amidst poverty, differences abound. First-generation Mexican-American families still exult in their arrival in the Land of Promise and cling to their optimism and hope. Second-generation Puerto Rican families are more inclined to a weary surrender; they have been around too long and seen too much to be buoyant with hope. Black teenagers in an isolated neighborhood in Houston appear more fearful of engaging white authority figures than do their counterparts in Harlem or Roxbury. The New York boy looks directly at me in a conversation; the Houston boy stares at his shoes. The pregnant black Fort Worth girl rejects the option of abortion. In her community, it would be considered an unforgivable sin. The pregnant black Bedford-Stuyvesant girl does not inject sin into a discussion of her pregnancy. She may or may not decide to have her child, but religious belief is not the deciding factor for her.

The interplay between youngsters and the resources and economic opportunities present in the neighborhood—what one analyst calls "community ecology"—influences how different youths view their future. In Chicago, black youngsters believe that they have a shot at the few remaining well-paying factory or manufacturing jobs where credentials are less important than the ability to acquire skills at work. Black youths in Newark despair of cracking the white-collar world of Manhattan without high school diplomas and advanced training. The poor white high school dropout, living alone in Louisville, thinks that if the going gets really rough, somebody in his large extended family will find him a pickup job. The poor white dropout in Newport, where there are few jobs for anybody, doesn't know of many mentors in the legitimate economy.

With that caveat, I have to say that in one respect all impoverished children are alike: They all pass the early seasons of their lives *in extremis*. Willie Sosa's experiences in his childhood, adolescence, and early adulthood embody not the particulars but the essence of the universal struggle. How he reacted to the tough changes of growing up—with confusion, fear, anger, rage, cunning, and rebellion—is how, with some distinctive, individual shadings, most of the youngsters I met reacted.

For those who are committed to the repair of devastated lives, the universal elements of Sosa's experience are of central significance. Most of the poor kids I met did grow up with great voids and gaps in their emotional and social development. When adults try to help them, they must begin with an understanding of the universal injuries these adolescents have suffered—and an appreciation of the strength it takes for them to overcome their deprivations.

That is why William Sosa's life had transcendent importance for me. If we recognize that his story is not the exceptional case but an all-too-common tragedy, we will understand what we have not yet comprehended in the United States: That intercession can succeed, but it will require an empathy and commitment far beyond what we have demonstrated up to now.

William Sosa was born in Puerto Rico. When he was less than a year old, his father, who had been a field worker on the island, found a factory job in Perth Amboy, New Jersey, a tough, blue-collar town. Soon after, in 1953, he sent for his wife, William, and William's two sisters. The Sosas rented a three-bedroom house in a tract development. By 1960, when William was seven, the Sosas had seven children, with an eighth on the way. *Willie's story:*

My father was makin' pretty good money, a hundred and somethin' dollars in the early 'fifties. We had beautiful food, a nice house. I can't remember when we didn't have a TV. But then my father started gettin' in with this crowd, and he started drinkin'. I think I was about four when I seriously seen him drinkin', 'cause he used to take me to the bar. Show off his son, and stuff like that. I used to drink my soda while I watched him drink boilermakers, the shots of Seagrams Seven.

I don't think my father ever told me a story. He never set me down and said, I love you. When he was drunk, he wouldn't like us gettin' on his lap, or anything close like that. When you're five, six, seven—the maturing years—is when you need to know your father, and those were the years that my father was an alcoholic, so I really didn't know him.

When my father was drinking, a lotta times he'd come home and beat up on all of us. My father was about six-three, a big, huge guy. He was so giant, he used to paint the ceilings without a ladder. He was really brutal. We used to fight him when we was kids, my brother and sister and me, we used to hang on to his pants and try to bite him.

He'd beat up my mother real bad. The first time I saw him do it, I thought if my mother didn't get away from him, he'd probably kill her. I kind of freaked out. I said, "Hey, what are you doin'? You're beatin' up my mother. You're goin' to have to pay for this. When I grow up you're gonna have to pay for it."

Sometimes he beat her so bad, she landed in the hospital, but not for long periods. There was a time when my mother, to protect herself, hit him with a bat and knocked him out. I loved him and everything, but I felt hurt about what he was doin' to my mother. I could see the alcohol was destroyin' his life, but I didn't understand why he had to drink and why he had to be violent. It was just like he started really goin' downhill.

What went wrong with my father? My father wanted to come over here, he wanted to live better, he wanted to have the things he didn't have in P.R. He wanted everything to

be better *right then.* The money *was* better, but the money
wasn't everything. He began to see that a lot of Americans
didn't want to deal with us. Didn't want to deal with how we
looked, what we were, how we spoke, how some of us couldn't
read or write, how some of us weren't used to workin' inside,
how some of us weren't used to all the competition to keep
what you had and get what you wanted. Here you couldn't
relax, and for my parents who came from the island relaxin'
was a big part of life. So my father became hard, you know,
because they say that the Puerto Rican people are a loving
kind of people, but he became hard—*we* became very hard.

In the family everybody was lookin' out for themselves.
My father's dream wasn't passed on to the kids. Now, my
mother and father would say, I want you to grow up, go to
school, be a good boy. But they weren't planting the seed.
They were concentrating on right now. And then my father
began to realize, maybe, that the dream he had wasn't really
truth. That what he was looking for, he could have found right
on his own island. Maybe if he tried, he coulda made the dream
come true for us, the next generation, but he wanted the dream
so much that he didn't work to plant the seed.

What broke it for us was one day I was seven and walkin'
down the stairs in the house and my mother was sittin' on
the couch, and she was all beat up. Her eyes was swollen and
blood was spattered all over the wall. The thing was my mother
was six months pregnant, then, with my sister Esther.

That was the downfall of the marriage. He beat her up
so bad she had to go to the hospital. First of all for the injuries
she had, plus they wanted to supervise the pregnancy. At that
point, they put my father in jail for six months for beating
her up. So they had to put us in a foster home. They split
the kids up. I stayed with my brother Stevie and my sister
Priscilla. The smaller children stayed with another family, but
I never met them.

The family were nice people, they treated us good. The
only thing was it hurt me a lot 'cause I didn't understand
why my mother wasn't around. I was seven years old, I was
sayin' to myself, Wow, here I am, nobody's home, my mother
she's not comin' back. What did my father do to her? I just
couldn't understand what was goin' down. I was tryin' to be
the man, to analyze the whole situation, but I couldn't.

When my mother came home, I felt relieved. I thought
everything would be all right. I didn't know my mother wasn't
going to allow my father back. She sat the kids down and
said, "We have to make it together. We have to be strong

to survive." We had to survive on whatever welfare gave us.

Welfare affected me tremendously, tremendously. Because I'd never known what hunger was until I'd gone onto it. I never knew what not having a decent pair of pants was like. I never knew what it was like not having a pair of shoes, except for a $1.98 sneaker to last for the whole year. I didn't even like to go to my friend's house, 'cause I'd see five or ten pairs of pants in his closet and I only had one or two. I had a teacher who used to call me Patches. My clothes always had patches. But she said it with love, she never said it bad. At Thanksgiving she brang us a whole meal with a turkey—a whole grocery. She was the only one that ever did anything. My father hasn't given us a penny since I can't remember.

My mother didn't have no money left over. The welfare check always had a funny thing of running out—by the twentieth or the twenty-third of the month, it's already gone. I never had breakfast. Mostly our big meal was rice with milk. If I ate rice and beans with a little piece of meat, I was satisfied, because I knew that was what I was goin' to get for the day. I was thin as a bone. Real skinny little belly. Sometimes I would catch myself wanting to eat over at my friend's house rather than eat a meal at home.

One night somebody gave us bread and my mother made a bread soup. We just had juice, soup, with the bread in it. The bread couldn't fill my stomach up. And I said, No, man, I ain't gonna take this any more. I ain't gonna take this lyin' down. The next morning she'd be sittin' down, she'd be cryin' on the milk box. And watchin' my mother sittin' there and cryin', I started to realize that things weren't goin' to get better.

A few days later me and my buddy was in somebody's house playing with matches and we started a fire, and almost burned it down. I should have stopped him, but I didn't. I really didn't give a damn any more. I found other kids who felt the same way, who were rebelling; we'd tear down the clotheslines, break windows, paintin' car windows with soap. I was startin' to do my little mischief.

Understand—before my father left I was a home boy, I was always in the house. Today, you see these kids, they start hangin' at three or four, right on their own street. But I really didn't go out. My father would let me out for one hour, watchin' me right there in the front. Even after the foster house I didn't hang much. But then we couldn't afford the house and we moved out to the public projects. That's when I began to learn to hustle.

In our old house, everything was more quiet, and it was more settled. But the projects were loud. And a lot of people were on welfare—everybody was lower class, everybody was in the same mess. I had the feeling—that's where I belong. And it was different at home. My father had run my mother down physically, mentally. He'd really hurt her. She wasn't the same any more. She was depressed, and I hated to see her like that. I didn't want to always come home to the same thing—one meal and that's all—boom. I'd look forward to Halloween when I could go get some money or candy. Yeah, Halloween was like training to be a hustler.

I started hustling, shining shoes in the bars in Perth Amboy, when I was nine, ten. My brother and me'd go out four times a week, Mondays, Wednesdays, Fridays, and Saturdays. Fridays and Saturdays were the best nights, we'd stay out till two or three. At first, we'd come home with ten, fifteen bucks. All you'd get was fifteen cents, a quarter a shine. Sometimes they tip you and sometimes they don't, depending. If we did a trick, like singin' or dancin', instead of givin' us twenty-five cents, he'd slap dollars on us. But that wasn't what we was about. We was out for big bucks.

It happened by accident. We didn't intend to do it. I was shinin' shoes, and my buddy said, "Hey, there's five dollars on the bar, the guy's drunk." I'm thinking, Should I? Should I not? Should I? Then I say, Yeah, let's go for it. Once we did it there was no turning back. 'Cause it was an easier way for me to hustle.

Fridays, Saturdays was big payrolls. Besides, there was no school the next mornin'. You got to get a good crowd at the bar. You watch for the guy who's very stoned, you gotta pick your mark. You don't do it on anybody; you do it on a guy that you know you can get over. The guy's a drunk, bent over, and, whoosh, you rip the money off the bar. A lot of nights my brother and me, we'd be comin' home with a hundred, two hundred bucks.

My brother was smaller and slicker. Really fast. I always told him we gotta bring the money home. He was always wantin' to spend it, and I was thinkin' about bringin' it to my mother. My mother could be a strict disciplinarian. She'd bang us up when she had to. I had to know how to say things to her in order for me to get over. I couldn't come up with the wrong thing or she's liable to hit me with a bat or somethin'.

When I'd come home with big money, my mother would ask me about it. What we'd do to get over—we'd spill the polish out of the can and make believe it was almost empty. I'd say to her, "Look into the box, see how much work I did!" My hands would be all dirty from shinin' shoes, you know. She made me promise that I didn't steal it. *But I did steal it.* In my mind, she must have known.

I was doin' business. I was busy. My thing was hustlin', okay? I had a purpose: I had to bring in money somehow. I was the little man and I thought by doin' this, I could help out my family. We didn't talk about the right or wrong of it. *You are out there to make money.* That is the only thing you talk about. Well, damn, if hustlin' is wrong, then why is this cat at the bar drinkin' all his money away? He must not be doin' no justice to his family. So at least we'll do justice to *our* family—that's the way I thought. It may have been rippin' off the drunk was gettin' back at my father, the drunk. Yeah, it might have been. But I didn't think about it. My head then was just to go out and get as much money as I can.

From nine to twelve were the days of my hustling as a kid. So that was the pattern. Once I began to hustle, my life was already set. I was goin' to be a hustler in any way that I can. I was already set then, when I was a kid.

Some things have changed since William Sosa was growing up in the late 1950s and early 1960s: Hungry kids can get a free lunch in school; food stamps supplement the welfare check, and the underground economy, with its income from legitimate and criminal work, has proliferated through all levels of society. Does this mean that poor children grow up today more secure than Willie Sosa did twenty years ago? Do they feel more protected against misfortune and adversity?

It may sound strange, but most of the adolescents I met grew up with a more palpable and immediate fear of abandonment than Sosa did. I'm not suggesting that their parents care less for them than Sosa's parents did; it's only that the constant message they receive from the outside is that their survival and well-being count for little. From infancy, they learn that life is cheap.

It's not that they have a vague sense of unease engendered by patched-up jeans and not enough money to get into a Prince concert. I am talking about the solemn awareness, based on solid evidence, that the institutions of society, and some of the people closest to them, don't give a damn about whether they live or die.

Starting Life in the Fifth Ward

Houston, October 1981. Althea Walker, a fifteen-year-old black girl who was two months pregnant, waited on Lyons Avenue in the Fifth Ward for a bus that would take her to Jeff Davis Hospital—where, she had heard, she could legally and safely get an abortion.

To local residents Lyons Avenue was known, with some affection, as Pearl Harbor. Across the street from the bus stop were the burned-out remains of the Classic movie theater. From where she stood, she could see down the block the blank marquee of Club Matinee, also burned out. On this street, part of the main shopping thoroughfare of the predominately black community, the only functioning businesses were a funeral home, a liquor store, and a hock shop. Through the early morning haze the glass and chrome skyline of white Houston was visible, a shimmering city constructed on the wealth realized in oil and gas, insurance, and real estate. In all her life, Althea Walker had never entered one of those business buildings. They might just as well have been on Mars. What she knew too well, what was completely normal for her, was Lyons Avenue—Pearl Harbor.

It took twenty minutes for the bus to come, and then another forty-five to get to the hospital. That gave her a lot of time to think, and Althea, an intelligent and exceedingly gentle youngster, had a lot to think about. She thought about her discovery that she was pregnant. "The first thing that came to my mind was, 'Oh, God! How am I going to take care of it?'

"I was in the room talking to my sister. I said, 'I don't want it.' My sister said, 'Don't cry. It's here. You can't do nothing about it.' I said, 'I can have an abortion.'

"My mom, she was listening. 'You want to?' she said.

" 'Yes,' I screamed out."

Althea's vivid memories of her own childhood was one reason for her decision not to have the baby. She hadn't forgotten that when she was ten her family had been thrown out of their apartment. "We got put out. I guess Mama missed the rent, and we had to leave. They took our furniture. We had our own phone, our own TV, our own bed—and they took it all. We just didn't know how to appreciate it. So He took it—God took it, taught us how to appreciate what we got. I guess I was raised hard. And I guess I was wondering, Was my baby going to be raised the same way?"

Althea didn't have to guess about what her life would be like as a teenage mother. All she had to do was recall her own mother's life.

Mama was 14 when she got pregnant with my brother. My grandmother put her out, gave her fifty dollars and told her to get a job. My grandmother took the baby. I thought that could happen to me, 'cause my mother's got all my brothers and sisters to take care of and she's always got to hustle up money. When I told my grandmother I was pregnant, she said, "*I'm* going to have me a little baby." My mom said that could be a problem.

My grandmother—she just likes for you to beg from her. Sometimes it just makes me sick. Like maternity clothes: She thinks just because we poor, I ought to run and grab anything she gives me. She got some clothes look just like they come from the 1940s—some dresses come way up to here. I'm not trying to be ungrateful but—hand-me-downs!

She also had to consider her feelings about the father. Her feelings were very firm.

I didn't want to tell him at first. I was hinting on it for a f-e-e-w weeks and then I said, "I'm pregnant."

He like to fainted. He got a big old smile on his face. When I told him I wanted to have an abortion, he got mad. He asked me, "What you going to do that for?"

I said, "You going to help me take care of it?"

He asked to marry me, and it scared me. When you're pregnant and you're young, the boy thinks he owns you. He tell you, you're going to stay here, and you're going to do this, and you're going to do that. When you don't get married, you still have yourself for what you can do. Having a baby and getting married—it's like two mistakes in one. So I told him, "No, no way."

Like a lawyer delivering a summation to the jury, Althea marshaled her arguments for an abortion: Her mother's hard life raising Althea and her brothers and sisters; her grandmother's interference; Althea's opposition to marriage as a teenager; the fact that this had been the first time she had sexual relations; how motherhood would interfere with her education and her social life. Her mother did not try to dissuade her; she managed to raise $200 to pay for the abortion. In Texas, Medicaid does not cover the cost of an abortion. (Althea did not consider the alternative of putting the baby up for adoption; neither did any of the other young black and Hispanic women I spoke to in Houston.) Althea went ahead and made the appointment at Jeff Davis for an abortion.

But now, as the bus carried her to the hospital, her resolve wavered. Everyone except her mother seemed to be saying that she should have the child. "My sister, my grandmothers, my friends—everybody wanted me to have it. I just screamed, 'Why you all trying to tell me what to do? It's me that's going to have to live with it, not you all.'" Yet she couldn't help but remember what they had told her: An abortion could kill you; you had terrible pain; you were commiting an awful sin.

And she remembered, too, that all of her girlfriends were trying so hard to *have* a baby, and here she was, *the lucky one,* killing it. Louise, her best friend, had been taking castor oil for months to bring on pregnancy. "Louise she's all of fourteen. She's done tried months, days, years, she's just not gettin' pregnant. She figures that her mama don't love her, and she thinks she can have something that she really loves and wants to hold onto. She can fall back on her baby and have somebody to love. Like if your baby's growing up, you can talk to it, and he won't go back and tell nobody. That's wonderful."

Could all her friends be wrong? Could her grandmother be wrong? Could her sister be wrong? The more she thought about it, the more an abortion amounted to a repudiation of her mother.

> My mama tried with me, she tried with all of us—and it weren't easy. Once when I was real little, I asked her, "Mama, what's the best age to have a baby?" And she said, "When God says you should have one." If God would want you to have a baby, could it be bad? My mama knows when she wants something, I'll get up even though I could be sick. My baby could be the same way with me.
>
> I began to think: If Mama could go through with it, I can, too. I'm thinking: Maybe I can take care of it. If God didn't want me to have it, He wouldn't have gave it to me—'cause I tried in every way not to. I'm thinking real hard now: If I have the baby in the summer, I can spend all the time in the world with it.

Just then, as the bus was pulling into the hospital stop, Althea changed her mind. "I wasn't scared or nothing. I wasn't thinking about the pain. I was just thinking, *I want it. I think I can do it. No, I don't want no abortion. I'm going to have it."*

Certain considerations did not enter into Althea's decision, because she simply was not aware of them. Althea had done some thinking about how her life would change *after* her child was born; but she hadn't thought much about her pregnancy. When she walked into the Winifred Wallace Maternity Center at the hospital, the room was crowded with women. They sat on the floor, on window sills, in each other's laps. Some of the women had already given birth, others were plainly pregnant. Althea saw many girls who looked younger than her.

It took four and a half hours before a doctor saw her. After he examined her, he told her, "Your blood pressure's up. I'm not sure, but you may have hypertension. I think you'd better come to the prenatal clinic twice a week."

Althea did some rapid calculations. Traveling back and forth to the hospital took two hours. The clinic took two hours. There would be waiting time. Every day she came to the clinic would mean that she would miss another school day.

"But I go to school," she said.

"You know a lot of babies are born dead," the doctor said. "And the main reason is that the mothers don't have prenatal care. The decision is up to you. You tell your mother that."

Althea knew that there were clinics in Houston that provided care after school hours. But the clinic at Jeff Davis was the only one that did not charge pregnant mothers under the age of sixteen. "I guess I'll come," she said.

As she was leaving the maternity center, Althea heard an announcement on the hospital's public address system. "Mr. Esperanza, please come right now to the third floor desk. Your baby is dead." A lot of babies were born dead at Jeff Davis. Some 14,000 babies.

Forty percent of all babies born in Houston are delivered at Jeff Davis. The infant mortality rate at Jeff Davis was 15.2 deaths between the time of delivery and one year of age per 1,000 births, as against a rate of 3.8 in private hospitals in Harris County, which includes Houston. For babies born at Jeff Davis, the "perinatal" mortality rate—babies who die between the twentieth week of pregnancy and twenty-eight days after delivery—was 27.7 per 1,000; it was 9.3 at private hospitals in the county.[3]

More than 60 percent of the hospital's maternity patients are classified as "high-risk" patients. Low-birth-weight babies account for 60 percent of all infant deaths. Teenage mothers give birth to 25 percent of all low-birth-weight babies. Althea herself was 20 pounds underweight.

Two years before Althea Walker came to Jeff Davis, an administrator at the hospital had testified before a Congressional subcommittee investigating, among other concerns, the fact that Houston had the highest infant mortality rate in the country. The administrator said that good prenatal care could detect more than 80 percent of life-threatening complications. "We could do that if we had enough people and could spend enough time with each patient," he testified. "But the truth is we're bursting at the seams."[4]

Althea gave birth to a baby boy on April 19, 1982. The birth was three weeks premature, and the infant was 2 pounds underweight. Three weeks after delivery, Althea took the baby home. She named him Joseph. Later she nicknamed him "Sunny." "That's 'cause every time I smile at him he smile at me," she said.

She decided to drop out of school for a while, although a number of teachers had urged her to stay in. "I want to spend all my time with Joseph," she said, " 'cause I want him to be loved. My mama says she didn't spend that much time with me but she still love me. She says she wished she could have, but she had to get back out and keep going. I want to give Joseph my time."

Two years later, when Althea was seventeen and Joseph was two, she left her mother's apartment and moved in with a twenty-two-year-old man who drove a delivery truck. "I left 'cause my grandma was nastier and nastier. She tried to make Joseph her baby. She always sayin' she a better mother than me." A visiting public health nurse who came to Althea's and her boyfriend's apartment—a two-room unheated apartment for which they paid $300 a month—found the baby was 11 pounds underweight and suffered from an intestinal disorder. She reported that Althea appeared listless and was vague when questioned about Joseph's health. Althea said that she often stayed in bed with the baby until the late afternoon. The nurse prescribed vitamins for Althea and the baby and suggested some changes in the baby's diet. On the form, in a space marked "General Comments," the nurse wrote: "Mother says she is bored staying home alone with the child during the day." In another section of her report, headed "Indicated Treatment," the nurse wrote: "May have to consider removing child from parents for a period if health deteriorates."

Althea had been living apart from her mother for six months when her closest friend, also an adolescent mother, told her she was going back to school. Her friend explained that an infant-care center had been established in the school. Her baby was being taken care of while she was in class. If she wanted to see the baby during the school day, all she had to do was drop down to the center between classes or during her lunch hour.

Althea visited the center. In one section, there were twenty-two children between the ages of two and four. The center opened at 7 A.M. and closed at 5. There were many signs on the walls: GOT A PERSONAL PROBLEM?—SEE THE CLINIC. TAKE CONTROL OF YOUR LIFE. Under a picture of a pregnant teen-ager was the caption: Expect the Unexpected. What she liked most about the center was that she could look through the window while she walked down the school corridor. She could check on Joseph all day long. She decided to enroll Joseph in the center and return to school.

When I last saw Althea she had been back in school a year. Joseph's weight was almost normal, and his intestinal disorder had disappeared. She was attending child development classes twice a week in an adolescent health center, also situated in the school. She no longer seemed listless; she was doing well in school and was optimistic about her future. One big change was that she was now taking birth control pills. "I got plenty of time to wait for a new baby," she told me.

Althea also appeared much more receptive to advice from adults. She understood that it was hard to grow up all alone. With Althea I attended one of the child development classes where birth control and family planning were being discussed. One of the young mothers was adamant in her opposition to postponing having more children while she was still in school. She reminded me of Althea two years earlier, when she told the family planning counselor: "If God's willing to give me a baby, I'm willing."

After the class, Althea said, "When that lady asked that girl do she want help, she was all Miss High Class. She didn't want no help. But I told them, Yes, I think I can use help. I know I can.''

Accepting Sadness

Some children need more help than others. Althea seized the opportunity when it presented itself and took the first step in a steep climb. I don't know if her youthful resilience will carry her and her child through a hard life. But at least she's made a start. Many others I met in the Fifth Ward were less prepared for that sudden, shocking lurch from childhood dependency to adult responsibility. It wasn't only that their psychological stability was undermined. The total environment of their childhood ate away at their health and physical well-being.

Dr. Susan Pokorney was one of two physicians who practiced at the adolescent health center that Althea attended. Dr. Pokorney recalls one of her first patients.[5] "Dee was a fifteen-year-old who already had a baby and was now twenty, twenty-four weeks pregnant. I had trouble getting a history from her, because she wouldn't take her thumb out of her mouth. She'd come to the center in her housegown, with slippers. Clearly, she was *very* indigent. She just answered 'yes' or 'no' to my questions. She didn't know when her last period was. She really had gotten no care, had no comprehension of what she should be doing to help herself.

"Her attitude about having a baby was an acceptance of sadness. Her feeling was: 'That's the way life is.' Probably the most therapeutic thing we did was to hug her in the waiting room when she walked in."

Dee had her baby. Soon after that, the center discovered that her first child, now thirty months old, had developed recurrent vaginitis. "We really worried about sexual abuse. Dee was living alone and she'd leave her child with friends off and on. She'd be gone for periods and she could never really explain what she was doing during those periods."

The center brought Dee's case to the attention of county welfare officials. Eventually her children were taken from her and placed in foster care. She still comes to the center for her health care. Partly, says Dr. Pokorney, that's because the staff arranges for her to visit her children. But she also comes "because at the center she can find some company," the doctor says. "Besides, it's a warm place to go."

And so life begins in the Fifth Ward.

If the prospects for a healthy childhood are chancy at best at birth, they don't improve significantly as children grow older. I don't mean to single out only the Fifth Ward, where 40 percent of the 65,000 residents have incomes below the poverty line; in almost every community where children grow up poor their health is endangered.[6] In north central Flint, Michigan, a predominately black community of 81,000 people, the infant mortality rate is close to three times the national average. In the Fort Worth neighborhoods called Polytechnic and Stop Six, where the population is composed of poor blacks and whites, infant mortalities are two and a half times the national rate.

As you travel about in a country that has made enormous technological advances in treating and preventing childhood illnesses, there is no escaping the fact that it is *still* dangerous to your health to be young and poor. Partly, it's a matter of being able to pay for good health care. Robert J. Blendon, vice president of the Robert Wood Johnson Foundation, which specializes in health care issues, estimates that perhaps 55 percent of the poor in the United States have "reasonably decent health insurance,"[7] including Medicaid. "A few others have a little hospital insurance and the rest have nothing," he says. The Medicaid eligibility requirements and reimbursement schedules vary widely from state to state. In Texas, for example, only one-quarter of Texans whose income is below the federal poverty guidelines are eligible. In 1982, a national survey conducted by the polling firm of Louis Harris and Associates found that more than 12 percent of Americans—21 million adults and 7 million children—have great difficulty in paying for basic health care.[8]

During the past twenty years a variety of programs were introduced to reduce inequities in medical care. One of the most important was the establishment of health centers where parents in poor communities could bring their children. But since 1981 federal support for those centers has been reduced, with more than one-third closed down.

For poor families, health care becomes as much a problem of accessibility as cost. Dr. Will Risser, medical director of the Houston adolescent center, says, "If a poor kid needs an ENT (ear, nose and throat] evaluation, he'll have to go to the public hospital system. He'll spend all day at the general pediatric service, and then he's referred to the ENT service, and he'll get seen if a young, inexperienced pediatrician is on top of the situation enough. Then he has to go back another day and wait in the ENT clinic. Understandably, many of these kids' parents never follow through. It's humiliating and it's a drag."[9]

It is in routine health services, which more privileged children take for granted, that the gap between poor and more advantaged youngsters is the widest. Consider the matter of eyeglasses. In his practice at the Houston center, Dr. Risser has found that perhaps 15 percent of his teenage patients suffer from impaired vision. If he were serving a middle-income population, the solution would be relatively simple: Inform their parents and have them buy eyeglasses for their children. It's not that simple in the Fifth Ward of Houston. "The problem is, it means the parent has to get them to an eye clinic and cough up some dough for an impairment that isn't life-threatening. The kid just can't see that well. The parents are absorbed in survival issues. The glasses get forgotten."

When Brenda Shapiro, an educational consultant, organized a job-training program for high school dropouts in Miami, she found that more than half of the youngsters suffered from longstanding hearing and visual problems that had never been treated.[10] Colorado State University, which tested high school dropouts for a training program in 1981, reported that 67 percent of the young people had physical impairments that had not been detected previously in the school system.[11] A 1980 study of one hundred juvenile offenders in Dade County, Florida, most of them from poor families, found that half had difficulty with visual-motor skills, "indicating an organic factor contributing to school failure." Dr. Judith Amster, a remedial learning and learning specialist at the University of Miami, says, "When you walk into the classroom, you can always spot these kids. They're the ones sitting in the back of the room with their feet up on the desk and their hats pulled down over their heads."[12]

That image of kids peering at the blurred letters and numbers on the blackboard, slouching deeper into their seats, finally pulling their hats down over their faces to hide their inadequacy—that image mesmerized me.

Poor eyesight is an impairment that is relatively easy to diagnose and remedy. The origins of other illnesses are more difficult to identify, and treatment involves more than a ten-minute examination and writing out a prescription. Dr. Risser in Houston discussed one young patient at a staff conference. "Now this fourteen-year-old girl has right shoulder pain," he told the staff. "She had pneumonia, but she should be over that. You have to wonder at the meaning of the pain. Her parents are breaking up. She's a kid under stress. You only get the idea of stress on the second or third visit. Then she'll tell you about the problems she's having. You have to ask what's going on when she gets the pain. Does having pain get the attention from her mother that she wouldn't otherwise get? When she displays pain, she's kept home from school. She stays in bed. She's fed, she's taken care of. Pain brings her a reward; pain brings her attention."

Children treated at the Houston adolescent clinic are fortunate. There an integrated staff composed of physicians, social workers, psychologists, nutritionists, and infant care specialists consider how the child's total social and economic environment affects his or her well-being. That kind of comprehensive treatment is not available to most poor kids. The doctors they will meet won't often stop to consider how environmental stress affects their development, what part it plays in their recurrent illnesses, and how it distorts their most intimate relationships. Unless the illness is grave, a band-aid and an aspirin will tide them over until the next time.*

Exercising Control

It's a rare child whose life is free of all stress. At a stage in American culture where the expectation of perfection in our children has never been higher, where they are expected to be perfect students, perfect athletes, perfect entertainments, perfect family therapists,

---

* Most private doctors and public health physicians and nurses do not provide comprehensive treatment of childhood illness. They treat the physical symptoms of illness but rarely probe for the environmental sources of sickness. If they did, they would find many more instances of stress-related illness. In Kansas City, a comprehensive adolescent treatment program was established at a high school where most of the students were poor and black. Between October 1982 and March 1983, the adolescent health center at the school reported 370 cases involving psychological and emotional stress.[13]

and perfect friends and companions, it's no wonder that sometimes they break down simply to relieve the pressure. Illness,
physiological or psychological, offers them a moment's surcease;
it's their way of shrieking, Enough, enough! But the pressure
bearing down on poor youngsters, particularly poor minority
youngsters, is of a different order. It is unceasing and unrelenting.
Everywhere I went its source was always the same: the crackling
tension between the self-control and discipline expected of them
at home and at school, and the seductive freedom and excitement
that tempted them in the street.

The parents of poor children do not demand that they be
perfect. They demand that they control themselves. From early
on, the *good* family demonstrates its strength and responsibility
by controlling the child; later, the school is supposed to assume
its share of the burden of control. In dozens of conversations
with parents of children who had left home and school, the same
thought was repeated in almost identical words: *I tried to control
Charles. I wish I had been able to control Lisa. The trouble with the
school was that they were too soft on Roberto. They should have controlled
him.* Almost from birth, these parents wage a Manichean struggle
for control of the mind, body, and soul of their child. The great
fear that haunts so many poor families is that with the slightest
easing of the family restraints, their children will revert to a primi-
tive, primordial state; the good boy or girl will become the Wild
Child, a savage, barbaric, cunning creature of the jungle.

Are we hearing only the normal concern of parents anxious
about their children in a world of unkind strangers? Not according
to Rosa Garcia. She is fifteen years old and lives in Edgewood,
a poor neighborhood in San Antonio, populated mainly by Mexican-Americans. Rosa is a child teetering on the brink; neither
she nor anyone who knows her can be certain whether she will
finish high school or drop out, remain at home or run. In a school
composition, Rosa wrote:

> Right now it's only me and my little sister that go to school. I
> really want to graduate, but I dought it if I do. Graduating is my
> only hope. But I am barely making it! I am trying to, but its hard,
> and that's life! All my sister and brothers are drop-outs, I see the
> way they are right now, I wouldn't like to be like them!

Rosa is capable of learning. Anyone who spent a little time
with Rosa would be impressed by her intelligence, sensitivity, and

seriousness. She is a very warm and endearing young woman, who cares deeply for her family. Rosa is in trouble because her life is spinning out of control, and she doesn't know what to do about it. It was a mystery to me, as I listened to her describe her life out of school, why she hadn't collapsed entirely.

Rosa's recent history is littered with corpses and broken bodies. Three months before I met her, someone shot her grandmother as she was walking on the street. She is still in the hospital. Two months before, her uncle heard the sound of gunshots. When he opened the door of his house, his body was riddled with buckshot. He died a few hours later. "We all know who hit him," she says. "They live right in front of my house, but nobody will do anything about them."

Not long ago, Rosa's sixteen-year-old cousin discovered she was pregnant. But she will have to raise her baby alone; her boyfriend was shot and killed during a fight at a party. "Everybody is a little crazy right now," Rosa says, and then adds, apologetically, "I had to skip out on school a little to go to all the funerals."

In Rosa's intimate circle, those who have not been shot or stabbed are wounded in other ways. On her way home from school, she often runs into her thirteen-year-old brother and his friends, who hang out in the alley a couple of blocks from where she lives. "Two years ago he was into grass and snorting spray paint. Last year it was acid and beer. But now he says that won't do anything for him. So he's using heroin. I see him every day in the alley, passing the needle. He's always with the older men of the barrio. They don't even try to hide it from me."

Her older brother, who is nineteen, dropped out of school in the seventh grade. He doesn't work. "When he was eighteen, he made his girlfriend, she's only fourteen, pregnant. He was with her all the time when she was pregnant. Then when she had a baby, he left her. He doesn't help her for nothin'. The girl sent letters to him for child support, but he says, 'I don't care.' When the girl brought the baby to our house, my brother punched the girl in the eye. I hate my brother. When I say something to him, he hits me so hard I have to call the police."

Her seventeen-year-old sister has two children. Although she has an apartment in a public housing project in Edgewood, she frequently visits Rosa's parents. "My mother and her fight all the time. My mother sees her life going down, but when she says somethin' my sister screams at her. With all the fighting and arguments, my mother gets all nervous. When my sister leaves, she starts to shake and cry. It's a little hard to concentrate on my homework in my house."

All around her Rosa sees young lives in decline. One friend, who just turned eleven, a small, frail-looking child who could pass for eight or nine, has had three miscarriages. Her closest friend recently left school to have a baby. Out of self-preservation, Rosa has tried to distance herself from her sisters and the girls she grew up with. "I'm afraid I'll be like them," she says. But she worries, "My sisters and my friends are going to hate me because I don't hang with them. They think I'm actin' like I'm too good for them. Yesterday, just yesterday, there was a note in my school locker. Some girls said they were going to beat me up in the second lunch period."

Like Ralph Ortiz in his Chicago high school, Rosa Garcia has compartmentalized her life. In school, aside from some difficulty with English and science, she gives the appearance of having her life in order. White blouse, blue pleated skirt, hair neatly cut in bangs, book bag slung over her shoulder—she could be any one of 2,000 kids in her high school. Who could imagine what this tiny, slender young woman, who giggles behind her palm, whose voice hardly rises above a whisper, has to endure every day after she leaves school? No one could imagine, because no one has bothered to find out. No teacher, no counselor, no principal knows Rosa's life. "Sometimes I think nobody around here has problems like I do," she was saying as she gathered up her books and waited for the announcement that another school day was over. "But last week I talk to this other girl and she says, 'Yes, we're the same.' And here I thought I was the only one."

I asked Rosa if she had ever discussed the monumental struggle to control her life with any adult at the school. "I wish my teachers knew," she says. "But my teachers talk to me about my marks, and my counselor talks to me about my credits, but they never talk about my house." There is a long silence as she thinks about my question. "I need to go to talk to somebody who could help me," Rosa says. "But who? I don't think the teachers care. They're nobody special, just people like me. Teachers are not going to do anything anyway—they're just gonna listen to me."

Time to go. I have to talk to another kid, in another barrio in San Antonio. Before I leave her, I ask one question: What does Rosa think is going to happen to her?

"I want to go somewhere," she says, with a catch in her voice. "Anyplace. Anywhere away from my neighborhood." She looks up at me and whispers almost indiscernibly, "I wish I could live with somebody else."

I turn away to hide my tears. I can't think of anything to say. I'm just like one of her teachers: All I can do is listen.

The principal edict the welfare system delivers to recipients is: Understand the rules, live within them, and your subsistence will arrive in the mail the fourth week of the month. The rules: Here's food stamps, but don't let me catch you using them to buy a quart of beer. The rules: Here's your welfare check, but first you've got to prove that your niece who's staying in your apartment isn't paying any rent. The rules may be stretched and bent but never conspicuously broken. Charity is earned by self control.

In many poor families love is also earned by self-control. The kids are told: In this household you will get love, affection, kindness, and protection if you meet the basic condition: You must always exercise self-control; otherwise the deal is off.

Earned love. It is a hard concept to grasp when you're very young and you think you're entitled to love as a birthright. If you're five years old and you're just itching to find out what's going on outside the door to your project apartment—what's so bad about that? "I tell Edward a hundred times there's trouble out there, but that boy jus' don't listen," says Doris Armistead. "So I had to teach him. I had to tie him down."

Now I am getting ahead of the story. Let's back up. It is 1974, and Edward Armistead is five. He lives in a public housing project in Hough, the predominately poor, black corridor of Cleveland. Edward has a singular, consuming passion: to break out of the boring, sullen, bitching routine of his days and hit the streets at the age of five. " 'Cause when you're young you really don't care 'bout anythin' 'cept street stuff," Edward remembers. "It don't have to involve drugs or nothin' like that, you like goin' out, playin', disobeyin' your mother. Your mother tells you, 'Don't go out with that friend, he's bad.' You still go out with him anyway, 'cause you don't think he's bad. You just think you want to go out and have a good time. When my mother tells me, 'Stay inside,' I don't listen, 'cause I have to get out. That's been the problem all my life; if my mother gets on my nerves, I won't listen."

When he was a child, Edward had some opportunities to get out. His mother worked a few afternoons each week at an umbrella factory, and she left him at the Marcus Garvey Community Center,* a few blocks from their project. He was supposed to return home at six when his mother came back from work. But he was often late, slinking in some times at eight or nine. Mrs. Armistead was hearing some disquieting murmers from the street. Edward was always trying to hustle at the community center: Buy me an ice cream, buy me a soda, buy me anything, he pleaded with the adults there. When they refused, he stole a few pennies from the other kids, their lunch money or treat money. Hardly a day passed when Edward didn't get into a fight. His neighbors told Mrs. Armistead that her son was hanging out on the fringes of the Blue Maxes, a notorious project gang.

One afternoon, after coming home from work, Mrs. Armistead called to her son from the window. "I called and called but he won't come up and I said to myself, 'I can't control that boy. I gotta do somethin'."

Mrs. Armistead borrowed a ball of thick packing rope from a neighbor and went downstairs and dragged little Edward back up. She sat him down in a chair, tied his hands behind him, tied his wrists, tied his ankles to the legs of the chair. "I had to do somethin' to show him I mean business." she says. Then she left the apartment to visit a neighbor.

She was hardly out of the door when Edward was tipping the chair over. He began to roll on the floor with the chair tied to his back, until he reached the wall beneath the window. Then, bracing his feet, Edward uncoiled all that pent-up energy, jumped up, crashed through the window and fell two stories to a patch of grass below. Miraculously, he was uninjured except for a few cuts from the shattered window. "I never dreamed the boy could jump that high to the window," Mrs. Armistead recalls.

"That's how much I like to go outside," Edward says.

As Edward grew up, Mrs. Armistead was constantly frustrated by her son's ingenious schemes to elude her restraints. Beset by a host of other problems, including some disastrous relationships with men, she put her trust in the institutions of the community, particularly the school. Maybe they can control him, she thought.

---

* The name of this community center has been changed.

The school tried. It did try, but Edward resisted. "I'm a jumpy person, nervous. I always wanted to go out of school, have fun, forget about work. I never be listenin' or paid attention, never concentrated, always be talkin' and talkin' and talkin'—constantly. So they put me away."

Mrs. Armistead had tried to tie him down; his teachers now tried to put him away. "It was the coatroom, there was a lot of coats all the way around the closet. The teacher would throw me in and make me kneel down. It wasn't so dark, there was a little light, and I could see the teacher and everything through the keyhole. In a way I loved it; it was my special place. It was like a seclusion room."

The coatroom could not contain Edward's furies any more than his mother's rope could. What once could be passed off as a kid's restlessness and high spirits had turned ugly, violent. The least provocation—a sly look, a whisper—and he'd be punching away. The school tried to punish him, make him feel ashamed. "The penalty they give me was moppin' the hallway. I'd be moppin' and moppin' and when I was done I'd be pickin' on people again."

The school had begun to give up on Edward Armistead by the time he reached the sixth grade. They suspended him, first for a few days, then for a week or two, and finally for a month. The message got through to Edward. "They didn't want me, so I didn't want them.

"I played hooky all the time. Stayed over a friend's house, and sometimes I used to stay home and fake sick. Once my mother knew I was fakin' and she let me stay home anyway. She say, 'I know you don't want to go to school, I know you not sick either, you can stay home.' Then she say, '*But* you have to mop the floor up.' School or home, they always had me moppin'."

One day, in the sixth grade, as Edward was cutting up in class, he looked up and saw his mother standing in the hallway, watching. Without a word, she reached into her handbag and took out a belt. She walked over to his desk and beat him. "It made me feel funny. I never expected my mother would come. And to hit me! The kids were saying they hoped that their mother wouldn't do that to them.

"Later on when I come home, I feel like cussin' her out or just runnin' away from home and school at the same time. Just do nothin' but be lazy and no work at all. Even though I was young, I had that in mind, that I didn't like nothin'. I just wanted to go out and have a good time and just play games."

Which is what he did. He stopped pretending—going through the motions—that he was a school kid, and he was gone from the house for longer and longer periods, months at a time. Mrs. Armistead gave up: If the school couldn't contain him, how could she be expected to? Mrs. Armistead went to juvenile court and petitioned to have him adjudged an "incorrigible" youth, "a person in need of supervision." Her petition was granted, and Edward Armistead was placed in a state juvenile training institution for two years. He was fourteen years old.

Edward's life had come full circle when I met him. Just as he had ten years before, he was spending his time at the Marcus Garvey Community Center. As part of his "rehabilitation" program, the state had found him a job at the center. His experience qualified him for his new position: He mopped the floor.

At different times, when Edward had been away from home, living by himself or in the state institution, he thought about returning to his mother and making a new beginning. But he was also afraid that his mother, remembering how he had fought against her attempts to restrain and control him, would turn him away.

> Two years before, when I was real bad, my mother really didn't want me home. She was happy when I left. So when I got out of the state school, I needed an apartment, a place to stay with my mother, 'cause nobody else would take care of me like a mother.
>   But I was only home for a little before she kept tellin' me she was goin' to throw me out. And she finally threw me out. Well, I really left before she could throw me out. I said, "I'm goin' to leave so you'll be happy and I'll be happy." So I left. I guess I felt like she was abandoning me.

For her part Mrs. Armistead says, "I didn't think there were any choice. Edward brought trouble into the house. For the sake of the other children, I had to let him go."

An outsider finds it difficult to know precisely where a parent should draw the line between meeting the needs of one child, and protecting the security of the rest of the family. Some might consider Edward a "throwaway" or rejected adolescent; others may believe that Mrs. Armistead had no choice but to exorcise a destructive force from her household. But there is no question in my mind that the specter of abandonment casts a long shadow across the adolescence of many poor youths and emerges often as the critical element when they discuss their reasons for leaving home.

Freud ranked the fear of abandonment high on the scale of childhood terrors. In every childhood there is a moment of apprehension that a parent will walk away, leaving the child alone and forsaken. For most children the moment passes, and they are restored by parental love and protection. But the moment does not pass so quickly in broken, severely disturbed, and deprived families. The vast majority of the youngsters I met could recall long stretches of time in their childhoods when they went to sleep at night and woke every morning uncertain where they would spend the next day and who would take care of them.

Willie Sosa arose one morning to find his mother was in the hospital, his father in jail, and his very survival entrusted to a family of strangers. What have I done? Willie asked; Why is this happening to me? He could answer in retrospect, at least, that the breakup of the family was due to circumstances—his father's violence—that were beyond his control. Not so with many other children, who blame themselves. Abandonment (they have come to believe) is a just punishment for their crimes, the most heinous among them their refusal to resign themselves to the restraints imposed by their parents. Unsuccessfully, I tried to persuade them that abandonment is often a no-fault act forced upon poor families by harsh circumstances. They didn't see it that way. They thought they had brought it upon themselves by defying their parents.

Losing Possession

The fear of abandonment is stimulated by many sources—most, dimly perceived—that have nothing to do with disobedience. Signals warning of imminent abandonment appear like flashing yellow traffic lights all along the way from early childhood through adolescence to young adulthood. One warning sign is the childhood and adolescent experience of the parents themselves. They, like their children, have been thrust into adulthood long before their time. A growing number of them have their children while they are still teenagers and, despite their ardent pledges of total love and total commitment to their babies, remain self-absorbed and unsure of their capacity to perform as adults, let alone parents. Grimacing through their braces (when they can afford them), fretting about their complexion, anxious about their next date, their reserves of patience are easily exhausted.

An important aspect of parenting is the affirmation of what a very young child is thinking and feeling, to let the child know that the parent understands and approves. In this way, the child doesn't feel isolated and disconnected from the all-powerful authority figure in the family. But adolescent mothers, with little knowledge and understanding of the parent's role, will not say to the baby, "Oh, you feel sleepy," when the child rubs her eyes. She just puts her to bed.

The urgent need to have a baby is often interpreted as a desire to find love in a loveless word and to bring purpose and direction to the adolescent maze. There's another need that young mothers hope to satisfy through their babies: simple, no-strings-attached companionship. It comes as a shock to teenage parents when children don't respond on a grown-up level. It's not that kids don't talk; it's that they don't communicate as buddies and confidants. When adolescent mothers find that their babies can't serve as surrogates for their own mothers or other absent adults, they tend to withdraw. And their silence is met by the child's silence—or by expressions of frustration and anger. This behavior is carried over to school. Researchers agree that inarticulateness and detachment at home breed inarticulateness, detachment, and resistance in school.[14]

Nancy Curry, Professor of Child Development and Child Care at the University of Pittsburgh, who counsels many adolescent mothers, recalls a scene I have witnessed many times myself in impoverished communities. Mother and child are waiting in line in a supermarket or doctor's office. The child, growing impatient, makes noise, misbehaves, starts to cry. The mother starts to walk away, as if to leave the child, and over her shoulder, whispers, "Gooooodbye." The threat of abandonment may stop the crying, but it does nothing to assuage the fear of rejection.

In the Middle Ages, parents sometimes waited for six months to name their babies because the incidence of infant mortality was so high they were afraid they would lose them. They didn't want to give a baby an identity if it was going to die soon after birth. In white and minority slums, adolescents also fear their babies will be taken away from them. Their professions of love and commitment may be genuine while the child is in the womb, but after birth many youngsters pull away from their babies. They have learned that in these communities few possessions are permanent. Everything is fluid. What you have today—your parents' affection, a new television set, food stamps—may belong to someone else tomorrow.

Almost from the moment a child is born, the teenager knows somebody is looking over her shoulder. It may be her own mother or grandmother. It may be a child welfare agency. It may be a fatal illness. To protect themselves from the anguish of loss, adolescent mothers are understandably cautious about investing too deeply, committing themselves, to their babies. The child who is denied the warmth and affection of its parents is also denied the assurance and nurturance of teachers. Teachers, like parents, don't bubble over with warmth, don't rush to cuddle and embrace the suspicious and diffident child.

The tension between parents and children may be closer to the surface when the parents are teenagers, but it's there even when parents are older. Parents raised in poor families were expected to become self-reliant early in life; they were required to contribute to the family's welfare without receiving emotional rewards; that was their job. And it's this "job" that they now pass on to their own children. Peter Blos, a child psychologist, has described an adolescent he calls Ben, who challenges his parents' efforts to control him. Blos writes of Ben's parents:

> Both parents had had a deprived childhood, and both were forced, early in life, into emotional self-sufficiency. This very similar background made both of them seek in their marriage and parenthood the gratifications of receiving and being given, without the obligation of reciprocity. The father makes this parental position quite explicit when he says that he "expects Ben to give me first; then I will give him too." In a very real sense, the child was forced into the role of the parent.[15]

If children like Ben decline the role of parent, if they don't want to "give first," if they are not prepared to sacrifice their childhood, their parents may withdraw from them. For youngsters caught in this emotional squeeze, Dr. Blos urges an intensive course of therapy. But such expensive remedies are beyond the reach of most poor families. They also know that to invite the intervention of public agencies, whether to provide material assistance or therapeutic counseling, can be risky. The outcome of intervention is too often not the strengthening of the family but its disintegration.

In the early 1970s the sociologists Andrew Billingsley and Jeanne Giovannoni observed that the "underlying philosophy of the present child welfare system is that all families *should* be able to function adequately without the assistance of society, and that failure to perform the parental role without such assistance is indicative of individual pathology. . . . Services designed to alleviate social and environmental stresses on families are virtually nonexistent." They go on to say, "The child welfare system . . . was—and is—almost exclusively focused on placement of children away from their families; services to children in their own homes were not (and are not) extended to any significant degree."[16]

In the past fifteen years, there have been efforts to redirect the child welfare system toward keeping the child in the family. Some temporary shelters for adolescents, community organizations, advocacy groups, and public agencies try to coordinate services to children and families and, what may be most essential, to find the money to keep the family functioning. It's astounding the wonders a little extra cash can work.

In Newark, the Puerto Rican parents of a twelve-year-old girl were alarmed because she left the house early in the evening and wandered the streets until the early morning. She wasn't doing her homework, her grades began to fall, and the parents were concerned that they were losing her. The father worked during the day at a factory and the mother had a cleaning job at night in a nursing home in a suburban community. In the past the mother had driven to work in the family's old car. This had allowed her to stay at home with her daughter until her husband arrived home from work. Then the car broke down. The family didn't have the $350 it cost to repair it. Every night the mother spent two and a half hours on a bus to reach her workplace. Her daughter was alone in the apartment; in the early evenings of the summer she could hear the street beckon to her.

A counselor at La Casa de Don Pedro, the local community service organization, managed to secure a special grant to pay for the car repair. The counselor also arranged for the girl to enter an after-school remedial program and to receive counseling. "But the money was key," the counselor said. "It got the family past the emergency and started them thinking about long-term actions."

Practical, pragmatic interventions seem more the exception than the rule. When school officials or child welfare caseworkers discover that a boy has been beaten by his parents because he's spending time with the "wrong crowd," or that a teenage girl is kept locked in the house because she's been seen hanging out with boys on the street, they too often assume that the parents are acting irrationally and that the safe, responsible thing to do is to get the kid out of the house. The fear of losing a child to one or another child welfare bureaucracy silences many poor families who would otherwise seek help when adversity strikes.

What has changed in the last twenty-five years is the capacity of poor families in America to cope by themselves with the severe social and economic pressures that beset them. In the past many poor and minority families and communities were justly celebrated for their dedication and perserverence in the eye of catastrophe. When misfortune struck, families banded together and survived, sometimes all by themselves and sometimes with the unselfish support of friends and neighbors. They formed their own version of the *landsmanshaften,* the communal village societies Jewish immigrants transplanted to the United States.

"The spirit of black communalism has waxed and waned according to circumstances, but has never died," Billingsley and Giovannoni wrote fifteen years ago. "Caring for others' children . . . is a well-established feature of the black community."[17] That still happens in black and Hispanic and poor white communities, but less often. The poor family that finds itself in deep trouble today cannot count on a helping hand to pull it out.

To understand and—more importantly, I think—to feel the precariousness of poor adolescents today, you need to compare their present circumstances with what happened to other kids who suffered painful losses earlier in this century.

Lessons from the Past

In his sixties, Robert Schrank can look back on a life filled with notable accomplishments: union organizer; supervisor of Mobilization for Youth, a model antipoverty program of the 1960s; New York City Commissioner; official of the Ford Foundation; now a nationally recognized authority on workplace issues. But when he was twelve years old and a student at P.S.34 in the Bronx, he was, in the timeless argot of school administrators, a "disruptive" child. Schrank fought with the other kids, raised havoc in class, defied the teachers, and sometimes just refused to show up at all.[18]

Schrank had reason enough to be disturbed. Just as he was about to enter adolescence his mother died while having an abortion. Schrank, his father, and his two sisters moved in with relatives. Altogether there were ten people in the household. Schrank's father, a politically committed man who had immigrated from Germany, found only one way to deal with his son's anger. "Being German and being authoritarian, he couldn't understand my rebellious behavior. So I got the shit beat out of me, regularly, for rebelling. After a while I found out that the beatings didn't really matter. You get whipped, you just say, Okay, you know, this is a whipping, I'll get through it. It doesn't change your behavior, really. The trick is not to get caught. So that became another game."

His father was convinced that school was not for his son, but he also knew that the boy had a certain mechanical aptitude. Robert was called, in his family, "the boy with the golden hands."

"When I was nine, ten years old I could take anything apart and put it back together again, which I used to do regularly. So obviously, anyone who had any sense would have said, Now wait a minute, that requires a certain intelligence. I mean, an orangutan can't take a clock apart and put it together. And nobody caught that, so I was generally described as a dumb kid who was good with his hands."

His hands gave his father a way out. "My father said, 'You're not going to high school. You hate school and you're so disruptive. Go to work, go be an apprentice.' So I got an apprenticeship as a plumber, and that was the end of it."

Not quite. In his job, out of school in the depths of the Great Depression, he gained a sense of identity and place. "We were part of a network of German immigrant manual workers. It was not a disgrace to be considered a plumber or a baker. I worked with men who were mature and grown, and they made me feel mature and grown. By the time I was twenty-one, I was married and had a daughter. The guys I worked with taught me: You assumed responsibility."[19]

It is too pat to say that just the act of working straightened him out. Something was going on where he worked, some chemistry between him and other workers, that made him feel a part, a valuable part, of a larger scheme. Elsewhere Schrank has written of his early working days:

> My first boss, Fritz Hoffelmeyer . . . was a huge fat man with a bowling ball head who for the morning coffee break drank beer from a small bucket that I would keep filled by running to the corner bar. . . . All the people I knew in my youth worked with their hands and bodies. These men often referred to each other in terms of some important work achievement. My father would say, "Freddy the iron worker could take a piece of steel, and with a hammer and a good fire in no time he could make the Statue of Liberty." Willie the baker was sometimes called "Thousand Loaf Willie" because that's how many he baked every night. If you worked hard it was a badge of honor.

Work was hard. "By the end of a day of pushing a three-foot-long ratchet handle up and down, my back was so sore I was unable to bend over and tie my shoes." But you didn't have to work every day. After five days, there was the reward of the weekend. "The German metal workers were great picknickers," Schrank recalls. "They would carry barrels of beer, coolers, boxes of frankfurters and rolls on the subways. Hundreds of them would show up on a Sunday in the North Bronx at Pelham Bay Park for a picnic. The day would start out with kids' games of baseball and volleyball. . . . In the afternoon there was singing and sometimes dancing. There were inveterate pinochle players and you could be sure there was a full-fledged card-slamming game going on somewhere."

The hard work, the fellowship, the recreation could not entirely fill the void left by his mother's death. But it involved him in a process that carried him through his painful youth into young adulthood; the confusion of his childhood cleared as work gave him direction; the standards of his co-workers helped him to measure his own progress and to establish his worth in a community of men. The fun and games—what sociologists call "communalism"—gave him the opportunity to excel at something other than pushing a 3-foot ratchet handle. A beginning.

Almost twenty years later a black seventeen-year-old also found a beginning. Frank Martin,* like Schrank, lost his mother. She died when he was four years old and living in Shreveport, Louisiana. But someone else was there to care for him. "My grandmother on my mother's side, she took over from my mother. When my father went up to Detroit in 1941, my grandparents came along. In my childhood I had rheumatic fever, pains in my legs, you see. My grandparents thought that bad weather was against me, so they kind of pampered me a bit."

He may have been pampered, but he was also clearly and sternly guided through his youth. Even then in Detroit, kids were introduced to marijuana and heroin. There was plenty of heavy drinking among black youth. The street was dangerous; some of Martin's childhood friends died of stabbings and shootings.

> The funny thing about the drugs and the street gangs, people was complaining and the people in power, authorities and things, they always pushed it aside as not being very— Well, they said, it's not that bad, it's nothing to worry about. The drugs was creeping into the black areas, into the inner city. So the white folks figured out a solution. They moved out to the suburban areas, and left us black folks here in Detroit.

Whatever was going on in the street, Martin's grandparents and his father made sure he was not part of it. "We were churchgoing people," he says.

> We were from the old Southern ways, righteous people. You'd go someplace and if you did something wrong, when you got home the message was there. Your people knew about it. There were not many telephones but when you got home, whatever you did on the street, you have to have a nice, good excuse or else you get your bottom burned.
> You didn't hang around in the street, and you didn't hang around home. You'd find something to do even if you didn't do anything but wash windows or mop floors. Somebody comes to the door and say, Hey, c'mon out and play, you say, No, I got work to do. And they understand, 'cause most everybody had the same rule: You do the work in the house first, 'fore

* A pseudonym.

you do anything else. My family leave the house in charge of you, and when they came home they'd find it just like they left it. 'Cause you didn't get out of line.

School wasn't easy for him. His rheumatic fever kept him home for long stretches, and the adjustment from a two-room schoolhouse in Louisiana to the big public schools in Detroit was tough. In 1948, when he was seventeen, and in a vocational school, he dropped out. For dropouts today, the absence of form and structure that school provides is yet another loss, another sign of abandonment. Young Frank Martin didn't perceive leaving school as a loss: It simply marked the end of a transition that had begun years before. All through his youth, he had no trouble finding jobs: in gas stations, in used car lots, in drugstores, delivering newspapers. "Leaving school, it just meant I had to support myself now," he says. "I was ready."

Martin made the circuit of auto plants in Detroit. A week later he had three job offers.

> I came home on a Friday and the first thing my sister told me was, "Hey, you got a letter from the Packard Motor Car Company. It say you suppose to report for work on Monday; go in for an interview, be prepared to start work."
>
> So on Monday I had the interview, then they shows me around the plant, walking me through many different departments. Then I had a physical examination, and the good thing about it—I always like to give this example—this is the kind of application you had to fill out in those days. Just a little card, just about this long from here to here. At the top would be your name, and your age, and, if you had it, your social security number. Next would be your address and your telephone, if you had one. And then after that you'd have to give three references. Nothing about high school. Nothing about whether you could read or write. And that was all!

In their childhoods, Robert Schrank and Frank Martin suffered serious losses; they lost their mothers and they lost their place on the educational ladder. But they could overcome those losses, and their fear of abandonment, and go on, because they had access to work, supportive kin, and a community of fellowship. They were introduced to the rites of becoming an adult male in America, with all the rights, privileges, and responsibilities that entails. They had heard a whisper, a tiny murmer: The world can be rewarding. Persevere, endure, and the world will acknowledge your striving. To some degree it can be said that they made their own breaks; but it also can be said that society gave them a hand up.

Now here is Linda Ramirez, a child of the 1980s. Listening to her talk of her childhood you hear overtones of Schrank and Martin; she talks of her apartment in a housing project in San Antonio, of how the public utility turned their electricity off and for months the family lighted their apartment with candles, of how her brothers had to sleep on the floor because there weren't enough beds for them, of how she had to wear hand-me-downs, of how she had to spend weeks with her maternal grandparents to escape the constant arguments between her parents. But at a point the similarities stop, and Linda's story becomes, more than anything else, a replay of Willie Sosa's childhood.

When I met Linda she was seventeen and hanging on at school—barely. She had been missing school and for a while she had been living with a girlfriend's parents. What reminded me of Willie Sosa was not her poverty or her troubles in school or the disorder at home. It was her feeling of being alone, of having to come through the hardest times without the support and protection of adults. Schrank had an extended family and a brotherhood of workers. Frank Martin had his grandparents and an opportunity to become a self-supporting male after he dropped out in Detroit. Linda Ramirez, when she was eight years old and in big trouble, essentially had nobody but herself.

As Willie had, Linda came home one day to find her mother viciously beaten by Linda's stepfather. Her mother was taken to a hospital where she spent the next six months recovering from her injuries and from an emotional breakdown. In a similar family crisis, Willie was placed with a foster family; in a sense he was lucky, because the family was kind to him. But Linda was not that fortunate. Her natural father, who had divorced her mother when Linda was very young, did not offer to take care of the children. The courts would not allow Linda to stay with her stepfather. Her grandparents, who, Linda says, "adored me more than all the kids," could not open their home to the children. "There was some reason," she says vaguely. "They were too poor, or something like that."

Linda and a younger brother and sister were sent to what she describes as a "public orphanage" in San Antonio. It's been almost nine years now, but before she falls asleep she can close her eyes and still remember the place: the rows of bunks in the dormitory; the public showers; the small fenced-in play area, always guarded by a pot-bellied Anglo wearing a straw hat; a whitewashed dayroom with no furniture except for a few pillows scattered on the floor and a black-and-white TV with rabbit ears that had been placed on an old metal typewriter stand.

Memories of an American childhood:

The first day I knew we had to stay there, I started saying to my sister, "Boy, it's so weird in this place." It was a big old dorm and there was a lot of beds and we had to share everything together. That wasn't complicated for us because we had been sharing all our lives, sharing with each other. But it was complicated because some people didn't want to share with us. In there, it was like your things belongs to everybody. The other girls would take some of our things, like a brush or a blanket, and if we said anything the older girls would beat us up.

They wouldn't allow us to have no money for snacks, no candies whatsoever. You know how at that age you want stuff like that? We had to eat all our food, and if we didn't eat it, we were punished. The next day we didn't get to eat. I don't like spinach and stuff like that. They'd serve it and I didn't want to eat, so the next day I was hungry.

The kids in there got madder and madder—especially when they put them in those straitjackets. There was a rule everybody have to take a shower about six-thirty. The kids would fight back. There was a big old shower, and they took all of us together. Some girls wouldn't want to. A girl would start crying, "Oh, my mother, my mother . . ." They would come and tell her, "Take a shower." They would pick her up and she'd start arguing, and they'd be beating up on her. By the time you knew it, she had the jacket on, and they just carried her out. I wouldn't see her for about two or three weeks, and she would come back. It was real hard at first.

The hardest part was not knowing when they would go home.

I got lucky in that my sister and I, we slept together. We was good together, we always cried to each other in the night. We would tell each other everything: "When we gonna go home? I don't want to be here any more. Don't ever leave me." It was real hard, because every night I would cry for my mom, and we wouldn't see nobody for such a long time.

It was only like twice a month that our grandparents would come visit us, they was only allowed that much. They would explain to us what was going on. They said our mother was like in a mental hospital. The doctors wouldn't let her out 'cause she wasn't in her right mind, and they were afraid she would suicide or something like that. One time my grandparents came and told us, Your mother isn't ready for you; they would just have to keep us in longer until she was ready. I said, "When is my mother coming? Is she ever coming for us?" And they told us, "Oh, you going to come out, you're going to come out." When they left, I thought to myself, "When mom comes out, she's never going to be the same any more."

When Linda wasn't worrying about her mother, she was worrying about her little brother. Her grandparents had told her that the boy was in the "orphanage" with them, but they had never seen him. One afternoon after five months, Linda and her sister were in the play area and saw their brother.

"We were all happy, hugging him. We were sitting down and playing on the swings and talking about when we were going to go home. We were telling him how we miss you, and we would tell him how they treat us—we would compare. My brother told me he was always crying for his mom. He wanted to go home. Then he just jumped off the swings and climbed the fence. The guard with the straw hat caught him, just dragged him down, no matter how he was scratched, arms and face and everything, and they beat him and they beat him and they—" Linda stops, her words choked off.

The three Ramirez children came home after six and a half months in the institution, came home to their mother *and* their stepfather. This is how it all adds up: Linda finds her mother bloodied and beaten by her stepfather; her mother spends six months recovering from wounds, physical and psychic; Linda and her sister and brother are deposited for six unforgettable months in an institution where children are restrained with straitjackets; she comes home to her mother and stepfather, and everyone expects her to grow up smiling and contented. That's how it adds up.

It didn't add up. "See, ever since that time, I never, never got along with my stepfather. My sisters, they learned to accept him. I see him and I hate him. What I remember is he couldn't ever accept us, he wanted our mother, but he didn't want us. He once actually told her to choose and our mother chose us. She said, 'No matter what I've done in my life or what's happened to me, I'll never leave my children.' So I guess he had no choice." That the issue of choice arises, that her mother should have to explain her choice, is one of the secret disturbances of Linda's childhood.

All through the last ten years, especially after a bitter argument or a beating, Linda kept asking her mother why she continued to stay with her husband.

"I always ask her, 'Why? He's not the only man in the world. You ever see the men that look up to you, real high? And this one looks down on you instead.' And she would tell me: 'I don't know. I stay with him because he's been here for so many years. I been afraid to be alone since your dad left me. I just don't know who to lean on.' "

Who to lean on? It's a question that vexes Linda as much as it does her mother. In the year before I spoke to her, Linda's real father suddenly renewed his interest in her. Although he had been absent during most of the years when she was growing up, he now sat in his parked car outside of her high school, waiting to see her and trying to persuade her to live with him. For a month she did, and then returned home. "My father wants me, but my mother *needs* me. More than anything I want to leave my house, but I feel I should be loyal to her. I am torn from all sides." Recently, the conflict has eased somewhat because her mother booted out her stepfather after another quarrel. Linda can never be sure if and when her stepfather might return. "She's just a little shaky," says Linda of her mother. "We can be, like, together and she'll come out with something completely different from what we've been talking about. I think she's afraid she can't manage alone."

The exterior Linda presents to the world doesn't reveal all that she's gone through. She's a very lovely young woman. She comes across as more composed, self-assured, and ambitious than most of the other students. I listened one afternoon as a teacher berated her for missing a class. "Why do you do that?" the teacher asked her. "You have so much more than the other kids. You should be a model for them. You have so many advantages, why are you throwing your life away?"

Linda listened and smiled and said, "I know you're right. I *should* be better." Then, when the teacher left, Linda told me: "I just want to move, start someplace else new, where I don't know nobody and nobody knows me. Because I guess living here is like the memory's always going to be there. But I don't want to be reminded of it all the time. It's in my past, and I want it to stay there."

Because Linda was in danger of dropping out, she was chosen for a program in which she tutored troubled junior high school students. Her teachers thought the extra money she earned and the involvement with other kids might provide an incentive to remain in school. Linda described one of the students she tutors.

> This one little kid, this little boy, he tell me things, like opens up to me. I think, God, I never thought I'd be hearing that. It happened to *me.* I tell him, "When your parents argue, just don't be around, go to your sister or go somewhere and don't listen to what they're saying." When the boy says, "My father hit my mother," and all this, I tell him, "They just arguin', there's just anger. But after a while, they'll get happy again."
>
> The boy says to me, "I don't know what to do. I don't like my father no more." I tell him, "Don't feel that way. It's gonna pass by." I look at him and I say to myself, It's weird, but one time I used to be that way. But I never told anyone though, you know.

The time Linda spent in an institution stands out in stark relief—"The memory's always going to be there." There are some 200,000 adolescents in foster care in the United States, not all of them from poor backgrounds, but almost all deprived in one way or another. There are a half-million others who spend part of their childhood and adolescence in the care of some public institutions—training schools, halfway houses, shelters, crisis centers. That doesn't include the youngsters, disproportionately poor, black, and Hispanic, who are incarcerated because they have committed a status offense, such as truancy. It's not as if they have been placed in institutional care during one isolated period after which they return to the bosoms of their families. Many of those youngsters careen from one institution to another; they may know twenty, thirty, forty homes before the state judges them old enough to live on their own. I. Roy Jones, director of a temporary youth shelter in Detroit, says, "The feeling almost all of these kids have is that they've been discarded. They think no one out there wants them. And they may be right."[20]

What leads them to this conclusion is more than a single discrete period (or even many such periods) during which they are handed over to institutional caretakers. A thousand different experiences chip away at the rock of security and belonging that children cling to. Before the child can memorize the features of his father, he has vanished. Even as the child begins to test the authority of his mother, he learns that she is a fumbling adolescent whose own life is devoid of design and purpose. When home life crumbles, and the preadolescent turns to his grandmother for sanctuary, he typically finds a young woman, in her early thirties, burdened by poverty and parenthood, who has yet to clarify her life goals. While the child is trying to compose a singular and separate identity, the family retreats to public housing, where she may find herself part of an undifferentiated mass in which *everyone* feels abandoned.

There is nothing unusual in Linda's desire to leave, to put her memories behind her. Comings and goings are the staples of childhood. When an unmanageable crisis erupts—as opposed to pedestrian, everyday crises—the Puerto Rican families in Newark and Chicago dispatch their young to the care of relatives in the Island; the Hispanic families in San Antonio and Los Angeles send their children to kin south of the border; poor whites in Louisville and Cincinnati seek relief in the clans of Appalachia; and black mothers in New York and Houston discharge their youth to whatever family remain in the South, although now it's increasingly likely that the Southern branch of the family has dispersed, and the desolate teenager must find his nest in the cellars and the roofs of the block. These kids always have their bags packed.

Youth is a yo-yo. Up when you're nestled safely at home— except when the home is a battlefield—and down when you're threatened by abandonment; up when you adhere to your parents' control—an authority undermined by poverty and adolescent motherhood—and down when you're tempted by the turbulence of the street.

Discussing the crisis in poor black families, Eleanor Holmes Norton, former chairman of the federal Equal Employment Opportunity Commission, points out that in New York City in 1925 five out of six black children under the age of six lived with both parents. In the early 1960s, she writes, 75 percent of black households were husband-and-wife families. But now 43 percent of black families are headed by women. She attributes this phenomenon to the intergenerational joblessness of black males during the last twenty-five years, and to the self-devaluation that is a consequence of perpetual unemployment and finds expression in a subculture permeated by drugs, crime, and hustling. "Generationally entrenched joblessness joined with the predatory underground economy form the bases of a marginal life style," she says. "Relationships without the commitment of husband and father result."

When middle-class families fled deteriorating neighborhoods, Norton says, "blacks remaining were often trapped and isolated, cut off from the values of the black working poor and middle class—where husbands work two jobs, wives return to work almost immediately after childbirth, and extended families of interdependent kin are still more prevalent than among whites. The phenomenon . . . affects a significant portion of young people today, many of whom are separated economically, culturally and socially from the black mainstream."[21]

That is hardly breaking news; two days in the Seventh Avenue housing project in Newark or in Chicago's Cabrini Green will tell you all you want to know about the deterioration of poor families. But it wasn't until recently that the unraveling of family life and the childhoods of so many thousands of young men and women were discussed openly and publicly in minority communities.

One reason it wasn't discussed is that many middle-class blacks and Hispanics had worked their way up from poverty with the support of stable, sacrificing families; they, like Frank Martin in Detroit, had been cushioned against the assault of an uncaring and evil environment. Surely, in a decade or two, conditions couldn't have deteriorated as much as reports from the ghetto suggested. Their own ascent encouraged their disbelief.

Another reason was the feeling that this was family business— dirty linen—that should be kept hidden from the neighbors' eyes. Shhhh—the neighbors will talk. "Wounds to the family were seen as the most painful effect of American racism," says Eleanor Holmes Norton. "Many blacks and their supporters have regarded talk of black family weaknesses as tantamount to insult and smear."

Also, minorities have learned from harsh experience, to concede that some of the hurts of family life were self-inflicted would act as a disincentive to already reluctant public policymakers. If you could attach blame to poor families, you had a perfect excuse for ignoring them. It had worked that way before. The occasional example of welfare cheating or misuse of food stamps has provided public officials with a moral justification for reducing government assistance to all welfare recipients.

Something else camouflaged the deep decay spreading throughout the slums. A certain romance and perverse glamour colored accounts of growing up in poverty in the 1960s. It crept into the popular and academic literature and could even be detected in public policy analyses issued by foundations and government agencies. The romantic vision was that the manchild of the slums learned to be tough, to be resilient, to survive. He picked up cool and smarts from the streets. In the gutters and in the alleys, he sharpened his "survival skills." With modest reorientation, the gang member could hold his own at IBM or Harvard, according to these accounts. So some social analysts believed a black street gang like the Blackstone Rangers in Chicago or a Puerto Rican gang like the Young Lords in New York could be easily converted into legitimate profit-making enterprises. But street smarts were never easily translated into relevant and useful occupational and professional skills then, and they are not now. The truth is, as Eleanor Holmes Norton says, "The skills necessary to survive in the streets are those least acceptable in the outside world."[22]

Some children survive this forbidding terrain and cross over to the other America. (How they do it is a subject I will address later.) Many more don't. What might improve the odds? A valuable dividend of the new and open examination of poor families is the recognition that effective and lasting help cannot be provided by government alone. It must come from within and without. While new public initiatives are critical to the revitalization of family, so, too, is a mobilization of community resources—spiritual, material, and social.

The time I have spent with lost children and their families persuades me that there are untapped reserves of spirit and concern that can be marshaled within these communities. In an age of self-absorption, the will to sacrifice for other people's children is not easily summoned. But there is a growing awareness that nothing short of a new partnership must be negotiated between the public sphere, impoverished communities and youngsters, and their families. I shall have more to say about the specific terms of such a contract. But I want first to consider the mission and performance of a key principal in this essential alliance.

I refer to an institution that holds the keys to the prison; an institution that could, if it were so motivated, inspire these children to dreams of a productive life; an institution that could offer to its constituents, if it reconceived its mission, unimpeachable evidence that the world can be rewarding; an institution that has the power, if it were to exercise it, to transform lives. Tragically, it has done little of that. It has evolved as more of a custodian than a leader, more of a guard than a guardian. I refer, of course, to one of the principal caretakers of poor children: the American public school.

FOUR

School Days

The American Balance Wheel

Stebbins is a tiny dark speck on a sheet of white. Three or four hundred souls cluster here; the entire frozen tundra of Alaska is their backyard, the icy, wind-swept Bering Sea their lawn. Across the sea is Siberia.

    Modernity is marching across the tundra. Satellite dishes have sprouted in the ice, and on long winter nights Eskimo families in Stebbins huddle around the tube watching *Dallas* and *Dynasty*, learning how the folks in the Lower Forty-eight live, learning that without any apparent labor you can drive Rolls Royces, wear ermine, and eat caviar. I flew into Stebbins in mid-February during a spell of unseasonable warmth. It was only 20 degrees below zero. (The week before, my host told me, the weather had been "normal": "about 60 below.") At the end of the one long street in Stebbins a handful of kids were basking in the heat wave. They frolicked on swings, their red cheeks barely visible under the hoods of their fur-lined parkas. Behind them was a two-story building that doubled as an elementary and high school. As I walked in, I almost missed the small printed sign that had been posted on the front door. When it registered I stopped and did a double-take. It said: "If you show up drunk for school, go home."

93

The teenagers I spent the next few hours talking to were torn. They were torn between their loyalty to the culture of their parents and grandparents and their desire to achieve recognition and power and wealth in the mainstream culture of America. In the videotapes their teachers showed them, in their history and English and social science classes, in the books and newspapers they read, they had absorbed one immutable truth: To make their future, they would have to leave Stebbins and their class and culture behind. Stebbins was preserved meat and dried fish, powdered milk and stale, airlifted Twinkies. New York, L.A., Chicago, and Dallas were where you tapped into American success: filet mignon every night and brunch on Sunday.

Were they ready to embark on the grand quest? They could if they wanted to; they could finish high school in Anchorage or Seattle, they could go to college in Berkeley or Cambridge, they could line up for their interviews with recruiters from Wang or Apple. It was all out there for them, if they wanted to reach. That's what the modern scripture of American education taught them: Reach and you shall find. But did they want to reach?

They couldn't be sure. "If I go, I leave a lot behind," said one fifteen-year-old boy. "I'd hate to leave the ways of my people. The storytelling, the hunting, the fishing, it's our lives. I wouldn't want to live the way the other Americans live, but I'd want what they have."

"The big office, all those people sneezing when you tell them sneeze," a thirteen-year-old girl said, wistfully. "It would be nice." And then, as if she suddenly remembered where she was and who was listening to her, she added, "But I wouldn't want to disrespect my grandparents. I wouldn't want to break the chain."

"But . . ." I said, fumbling for a way to bring up the sign. "The old way is not all that good. I read the sign on the door."

The room was silent for a long time. Then one brave young man offered, "The winter is long. Once or twice a month the village goes crazy. Everybody is drunk."

"*Everybody?*" I asked.

"Everybody," the young man said. "The children, the grownups, the old people. The school says it's bad, we shouldn't do it. But it's hard to change the old ways in Stebbins."

Angrily, the thirteen-year-old girl interrupted him. "At least we're not on Fourth Street in Anchorage. We're not in Skid Row, sleeping in the gutter. We're drinking at home, with our mother and father, with our grandmothers and grandfathers. We trust them because they are our own."

"At least here we know who we are," the boy said. "Out there"—his faraway gaze took in all the images received by the satellite dishes—"out there you're all alone."

As I stood on the ice field, listening to the engines of the bush plane rev up, the girl who imagined a life where you could make your subalterns sneeze when you wanted them to came up alongside me and whispered, "The women in New York, do they wear dresses in the winter? Are they pretty?"

If she and her friends in Stebbins are really curious, if they want to embark on the great American quest for success and power and celebrity, they know that education will be their vehicle. If they decide to leave their familiar Eskimo culture behind and venture out into the unknown, the school will be the gateway to a future of promise. As so many millions of Americans in earlier generations have been told: Study hard, listen to your teachers, make the most of your opportunities, and you will be given a chance to succeed.

But the question has to be asked today: Does that still hold true? Does it hold true for the children of America's devastated slums, the children of Harlem and Watts and Stebbins?

From its beginnings, the public school was conceived of as a sanctuary where the hard experience of life outside would be diffused and softened as a young person's promise was nurtured. In 1848 Horace Mann, a Whig politician and the first secretary of the Massachusetts Board of Education, wrote: "Education, beyond all other devices of human origin, is the great equalizer of the conditions of men—the balance-wheel of the social machinery." Mann sounded the self-interested and unqualifiedly optimistic theme that would be echoed by reformers during the next 100 years. Education "does better than to disarm the poor of their hostility towards the rich; it prevents being poor."[1]

Mann believed that the schools would provide all youngsters, of whatever race or class, with *access* to power and prosperity. It was up to the individual to take advantage of that opportunity.

Has public education succeeded in carrying the outsiders into the broad main channel of American life? Has it equalized the conditions of men and women so that in their young adulthood they can compete on merit for the treasures offered by a rewarding world?

For many youngsters it has succeeded. It has brought them to the gate of the main arena. By 1982, more than 86 percent of all Americans aged 25–29 had graduated from high school. That was an increase of more than 50 percent over the 1960 rate. Between 1960 and 1982 the high school completion rate for blacks and other minorities more than doubled.[2]

Two sets of statistics demonstrate just how dominant schooling has become in the lives of American children and adolescents. A century ago less than 5 percent of the nation's sixteen-year-olds were enrolled in secondary schools; today more than 90 percent are. If they are staying longer in school, they are also beginning earlier. In 1970, 20 percent of all three- and four-year-olds were in preschool; by 1982 the percentage had risen to 36.4.*[3]

Those substantial achievements, however, mask a terrible failure by *some* students and *some* schools. The proportion of *all* students who graduate from high school dropped from 77 percent in 1972 to 74 percent in 1983, reversing a hundred-year trend toward higher rates of school completion. One in every four students who enrolls in ninth grade leaves school before graduation. In large cities and poor rural communities, approximately half of the high school students drop out. Officially reported estimates of the number of dropouts range from 750,000 to 900,000 a year. The actual total (for reasons I shall discuss shortly) may be much larger.

The prospects for earning a high school diploma are least promising for minority youngsters. In 1981, 79 percent of all white nineteen-year-olds had finished high school; but only 63 percent of black and 52 percent of Hispanic nineteen-year-olds had received their diplomas. In some of the largest urban school districts, the dropout rate for students at the greatest risk—pregnant teenagers, blacks, Puerto Ricans, and Mexican-Americans—reaches 70 to 80 percent.[4]

There is one other statistic that is particularly pertinent to this discussion. An estimated total of one million youngsters leave their homes every year. *Ninety percent of them never finish school.* [5]

It has been clear for some time—it may even have been clear to the realists of Horace Mann's time—that there are two classes

---

* Unfortunately, those children most likely to benefit from preschool are least likely to be enrolled. Only 19.2 percent of children whose families earned less than $10,000 a year were participating in preschool programs.

of children in American public schools. In one class are the youngsters—most of them from relatively secure and advantaged families and a few from severely disadvantaged backgrounds—who
will overcome whatever obstacles confront them. After 17,000
hours of schooling, they will be in a position to claim some of
the bounty America offers to its deserving young.

These are children who have the advantage of some stability
at home, of parents who have received enough education to understand the value of academic credentials, of families and communities that have achieved enough in America to believe that the
next generation can achieve more and do better than they did.
These are the children, some of them quite poor, who believe
they have a chance to succeed; they have been so persuaded by
their parents and their teachers.

For other children, the children I am writing about, Mann's
vision is a myth. Almost from the first day they arrive in school,
they are taught that not many adults expect them to make over
their lives. A few youngsters will defy the odds. A very few, through
acts of indomitable will, manage to overcome the expectation
of failure. Most don't. There comes a time, usually in high school,
when they finally accept the judgement of the jury and repair
to the familiar, as some of the children of Stebbins will. They
choose what they know best; the drugs and alcohol that suppress
their anxieties, the violent streets, the shattered families, the criminal associations, the dependency and self-abnegation. They submit to what is expected of them.

One observer, Edith M. Stern, wrote in 1937 after visiting
Harlem schools:

> The combination of poverty, ignorance and overcrowding gives
> rise to appalling environmental conditions and home backgrounds.
> In one school, of 1,600 homes, 700 had one parent missing. One
> little boy, when asked why he had fallen asleep in class, answered
> it had not been his turn to go to bed the night before. Eight people
> in his household occupied two rooms. . . . To all these difficulties
> the Puerto Ricans add those of language.
>
> Obviously, the school system is not to blame for Negro children's
> economic and environmental handicaps. . . . But it is responsible
> for not making heroic attempts to overcome their disqualifications
> by the best schooling money and lack of politics can supply.
>
> A typical Harlem school is like a prison, and a badly run one

at that. . . . Teachers, trying to cope with classes whose numbers average slightly more than even those in other overcrowded sections, with children who have eye defects and toothaches and empty stomachs, suffer frayed nerves and give way to harsh-voiced impatience. In this fashion New York's colored children are prepared for higher education.[6]

In 1984, Earline Levicy, recalling the classes she taught in a predominantly black high school is Detroit, said:

The bell rings. You've got thirty-eight kids in the class. If you have thirty, it's a teacher's dream. Fifteen of them are cutting up. Five of them are coming in late and you've got to handle paperwork for them, write out passes, or whatever. Of course, you don't have an aide. Of the fifteen who are cutting up, ten are ready to go on with the lesson. The other five need specialized help. You've got forty minutes, mind you.

So you deal with those fifteen behavior problems. Already you're seeing the minutes dribble away and you're getting frantic, so you start to scrap the lesson you've laid out. The ten who are ready to go on with the lesson are getting bored. The five who need help are lost. In the back of your mind you're saying, "I've got to cover X number of chapters."

Now you've got what—twenty minutes left. And you're thinking, "I'll try to reach that middle-of-the-road student." But then some smart aleck tries to mess with you and at the same time someone who needs your undivided attention walks into the room. Just when you realize you've got thirty books for thirty-five kids, *rrring,* the forty minutes are up, and a few minutes later a new class is walking in and the problems start all over. By the time you've gone through this three times in a day you are *tired.* So some poor kid who really wants to learn raises his hand and says, "Teacher." You spin around and yell at him, "What do *you* want?"[7]

Lest one conclude that Earlene Levicy is an unqualified teacher trying to blame the "system" for her own shortcomings, it should be noted that in 1983 she was cited by the Detroit public school system as one of the outstanding teachers in the city, who "works both attitudinal and academic miracles." But she no longer works her miracles at a conventional, mainstream high school; she now teaches in an alternative educational program conducted by the Detroit Urban League.

Under the kind of pressure Ms. Levicy describes, many teachers are tempted to give up on the "difficult" child when the kid isn't quick to respond to whatever attention and help are offered. In San Antonio in 1985, Linda Ramirez tutored a junior-high student whose troubled family life mirrored her own. The boy would act up; he would run through the classroom shouting and crying; he would distress the other children; he would anger the adult teacher. But after Linda would talk to him for a little while, sympathize with him, make him laugh, the youngster calmed down. After a month of tutoring, he began to show real progress in his classes. Linda took as much pride in the boy's progress as he did. It seemed to her that his success was proof that she could finish high school despite the continuing problems she had to face every day on the outside.

The supervising teacher informed her that her young charge had been removed from the tutoring program. "He's a problem child," the teacher told Linda when she protested. "He's a disruptive influence. He's ruining it for the other kids."

"Give me a little more time with him," Linda pleaded. "He's getting better. We understand each other. I know I can help him."

The teacher told her the decision was final. "That boy is trouble," she told Linda. "We can't reward him for his misbehavior. He's got to learn that he can't get away with everything."

Linda dropped out of the tutoring program. "I don't have the heart to keep on," she told me. "They are going to lose that little boy. He's just going to disappear. Don't they care about saving him?"

The same month that one boy was dismissed from a tutoring program in a San Antonio school, a national commission issued a report on the condition of Hispanic students in the public schools. Paul Ylvisaker, co-chairman of the commission and dean emeritus of the Graduate School of Education at Harvard University, told the author: "Schools usually do not offer the aid and comfort that would enable youngsters to overcome their personal setbacks. The important things in these kids' lives," he continued, "are not the curriculum or organizing the school day differently. What counts is caring. The students want to know, 'Are you interested in us?' We're not going to be able to substitute gimmicks, organization or money for a one-to-one relationship. The truth is that this society doesn't care enough about its kids and the schools aren't different in that respect."

The Sputnik Effect

When waves of social change coincided with the right demographics and urgent, easily understood issues (dramatized by popular, persuasive advocates), the nation could be mobilized to demonstrate its concern about *all* school kids. The 1960s was such a time. Then, education was an issue with punch.

In that decade, almost 40 percent of the population was under the age of twenty, and one-third was younger than fifteen. The baby boom of the late 1940s and early 1950s had created an enormous national education industry; it involved the full-time participation as students, teachers, and administrators of more than 30 percent of the American people. Reform, expansion and regeneration of the schools was not perceived then as an issue of concern only to poor and minority youngsters. In his 1963 State of the Union address, President Kennedy said:

"Never before have there been so many students who find the educational process wanting and abandon it; never before has the scholastic experience seemed so remote from what youngsters find real . . . so just plain boring. . . . The future of any country . . . is damaged whenever any of its children are not educated to the fullest of their capacity."

As Kennedy framed the issue, everybody had a stake in improving public education. The launching of *sputnik* by Russia gave the country an instant inferiority complex. Unless we rapidly improved the teaching of mathematics and science, we would lose the space race; suddenly, engineering became the hot new career. Lots of parents in the working-class neighborhood where I grew up were buying slide rules for their grade school prodigies. A youngster like me who had an interest in literature and writing was considered something of a drag on the national defense.

The country's internal peace and security also seemed threatened. The end to legal segregation, the civil rights movement, and the inner-city riots put the matter of equal access to a *good* education on the national agenda. Required reading in those times was a book by Harvard University president James B. Conant entitled *Slums and Suburbs*. Using a phrase that was to resonate through the 1960s, Conant wrote: "I am convinced we are allowing *social dynamite* to accumulate in our large cities." Conant was primarily concerned about the "plight of parents in the slums whose children either drop out or graduate from school without prospects of either further education or employment. . . . Leaving aside human tragedies, I submit that a continuation of this situation is a menace to the social and political health of the large cities."[8]

The disparity he found between schools in poor communities and more privileged schools went to the heart of the national debate on education. Conant found that in the early 1960s a wealthy suburban school spent as much as $1,000 annually for each student; in a big-city school the expenditure was less than half that. "The contrast," Conant wrote, "challenges the concept of equality of opportunity in American public education."

Some of Conant's recommendations for urban schools were woven into the larger fabric of education reform. Others stimulated national discussion and debate but were ultimately abandoned when they encountered political opposition. Rather than breaking down urban schools into smaller units responsive to community concerns as Conant proposed, many schools were consolidated into larger bureaucratic institutions remote from the needs and problems of city neighborhoods. The aloofness of massive school bureaucracies made it even more difficult for poor families to influence school policies.

The federal government did respond in a big way to Conant's central concern, the financial disparity between privileged and underprivileged schools. The Elementary and Secondary Education Act and Project Head Start, both of which were enacted in 1965 as part of President Johnson's War on Poverty, authorized substantial federal funding for education. Annual federal expenditures increased from $1.1 billion in 1964 to $19 billion in 1984.[9] The net outcome of that investment—whom it reached and how it affected students—is a matter of argument. With the possible exception of bilingual instruction, Head Start, a preschool program for children three and four years old, attracted the most attention of all the Johnson administration public education initiatives. There is still dispute about whether the gains achieved by Head Start students are lasting, but the program enjoys wide support among parents, educators, and legislators. Yet it never reached a majority of those children who could most benefit from it. In 1984, only 18 percent of eligible children were served by Head Start.[10] Of the 280 adolescents I interviewed, fewer than fifty had participated.

The centerpiece of the 1960s education legislation was Title

I of the Education Act. Twenty years after its enactment, Title I
had provided remedial and compensatory services to more than
5 million students at a cost to the federal government of more
than $42 billion. The impact of the program was substantial. In
1981 the National Assessment of Educational Progress found that
participating black students had reduced the gap in reading levels
between them and white students by 40 percent. Similar progress
was made in mathematics.

But again, Title I, like Head Start, never reached a majority
of the students who needed it. Even when it was most generous,
the federal government provided support for approximately half
of the children who were eligible for Title I services. Since 1981
support for Title I has been reduced by 20 percent in real dollars.[11]

Several reasons account for this decline in support. The
Reagan administration was not philosophically disposed to make
a high priority of the plight of poor, minority youngsters. Also,
the sense of urgency that stirred policymakers in the 1960s is
gone; the cities are not burning *now.* But I think there is a more
important reason for the declining interest: Passion ebbs as the
players change.

In the 1960s the achievement of equal access to a quality
education had universal appeal. Twenty years later, equal treatment in the schools was considered the particular problem of
the "special interests"—blacks, Hispanics, and some poor whites.
Many middle-class taxpayers could ask: What's in it for me? And
the answer: Not much. A 1985 study of the National Coalition
of Advocates for Students estimates that only 27 percent of adult
Americans have children in the public schools. Thus, 73 percent
of adult American taxpayers have no direct personal interest in
public education. The declining white enrollment is not a passing
demographic aberration. Between 1979 and 1992, the total number of high school students was expected to drop by 23 percent.[12]

As the overall public school population is reduced, the number of black and Hispanic students increases. Now, half of all
black families and 60 percent of Hispanic households have school-
age children.[13] With the flight of many middle-class white children
to suburban schools, the big city schools have become predominately brown and black. Already, two-thirds of all Hispanic and
black youngsters attend schools in which they are a majority.

With the fall in numbers of middle-class children and their
departure from the central cities, the urban tax base continues

to erode. Compassion wanes when self-interest is absent; national policymakers and legislators are unlikely to press for fiscal equality in the schools where there is little interest or demand from constituents. Meanwhile, federal contributions to local school districts declined from 9.2 percent of the school's total budget in 1979 to 6.2 percent in 1985. There is less money to pay for teachers, for special programs, for physical improvement of the schools, and for extra-curricular activities.

The disparity in resources and talent between suburban and urban schools, so alarming to James Conant a quarter of a century ago, may be sharper today. "There are two school systems in America," says Josué M. González, associate superintendent of schools in Chicago. "One is for middle-class and affluent kids. The other is a pauper's system."

Cute Kids, Ugly Adolescents

Two relatively unnoticed but critical policy developments have contributed to the calamity of disadvantaged adolescents. One is the heavy emphasis on programs directed toward preschool and elementary school students. The other is the lack of political accountability in the high schools.

When Title I was enacted, it was part of legislation that included both elementary and secondary schools. But in the years that followed, 70 percent of the funding went to elementary schools.[14] The investment in younger children has improved the teaching, the administration, and the general mood and atmosphere of elementary schools. When I revisited grade schools in New York, Chicago, and Detroit after fifteen years, they seemed warmer and more inviting places than I remembered. A scene I watched in front of a Detroit elementary school captured the changes that have taken place in many inner-city schools. A couple of teachers sat on the steps in front of the building. They were encircled by a group of kids who appeared to be about ten or eleven years old. The kids passed the time while they waited for their school bus, good-naturedly ragging the teachers. The teachers in turn kidded them about their hair and their clothes. I thought it a lovely example of how kids and adults can meet on common ground.

I don't mean to suggest that all elementary schools in poor

neighborhoods have become paragons of education. Many disturbing practices persist that undermine a child's confidence and sense of well-being. Too many schools still track children from the earliest grades, dividing them before they learn to read and write into classes of winners and losers. Too often slow-starting children who are not facile in English are dumped into classes for the mentally retarded. There is also the occasional teacher who disposes of a "problem" child, like Edward Armistead in Cleveland, by locking him in a closet.

In general, though, the outpouring of resources and the expression of concern about early childhood brought teachers and principals into the schools who are generous with their kindness and affection. My conversations with youngsters who had dropped out seemed to confirm my impressions. I asked them if they could remember any teacher whom they really liked. None of them could think of a high school teacher. A few recalled junior high school teachers they liked. But almost all of them remembered a special teacher, a kindred soul, in elementary school.

The Chicago gang leader Ralph Ortiz describes his high school teachers as "machines." "They were cold, they were uninterested in how you felt, or what you did and how you accomplished it. There was no encouragement, no nothing. It was like they were training you to be a computer. They feed in the information, and you spit it out."

Elementary school teachers were different. "My writing teacher, Mr. Tibbs, he was really *fun.* He cared about how you did your work, and if you didn't understand it, he would help you, give you information. Once I went to him about the gangs, the little-kid gangs, in the school, and you could tell it really worried him. He was getting gray hairs over it. He couldn't do nothing about it. But, at least, you could see he felt somethin', it bothered him."

The realization, for some youngsters, that the teacher who cared has left their lives is almost as painful as losing a parent. In Chicago, I met Carla, a black sixteen-year-old who had dropped out of school and was raising her two-year-old son by herself in Chicago. She told me:

> The most wonderful thing I remember was a real special teacher I was mostly crazy about. She was in the sixth grade. We'd sit down and she'd say, "How you doin', Carla?" I'd

say, "I'm doin' all right." She'd say, "You sure? Anything happenin' at home?" I'd say, "No, me and my mother are all right." We'd talk like that. She'd make me feel relieved.

She would take me home sometimes, like teachers take kids. Or take me out to eat. She knew my father was dead, and she worried about me and my mother. She didn't give me no break in the work, but she tried not to put me under a whole lot of pressure 'cause a doctor had called and told her how much pressure I was under. The pressure was mostly from not having a father at home to help me and my mother, a father or somebody to look up to.

And what hurt me and was another pressure, was this teacher got killed. Going home one day in a head-on collision. They came back to school and told us we would have another teacher, and our teacher was dead. I didn't want to accept it. I told them she would never die and leave me, like my father. The school seen I was takin' it real hard, so they made me stay at home for about a week and a half. I was real, real close to her.

Why are such relationships confined to the early grades? I don't think the entire answer has to do with the way high schools are organized and managed, although the fragmented, hectic, and impersonal environment has something to do with it.

The difference may stem from how young children and adolescents are perceived by teachers and administrators. Regardless of race or class, very young kids are seen as innocents, vulnerable and impressionable. They arouse maternal and paternal feelings. They represent raw material that can still be molded. They're also cute. While teachers do try to shape their futures, their efforts are not all directed toward the future. There's room in every school day for some fun, a few laughs. That doesn't happen in many inner-city high schools. High school is a serious business, a rehearsal for adulthood.

One teacher I spoke to had taught in both elementary and high schools in the Bronx. "When I walked into an elementary class, my heart went out to the kids. I'd do anything to make their lives better. When I walked into a high school class, with a lot of tough, angry black kids, my heart nearly stopped. If I closed my eyes I could imagine myself getting into an argument with one of these guys and getting punched out. After I had words with a kid and I'd see him in the hall or out in the parking lot, I'd think, Shit, here comes the switchblade."

Contemporary psychological theory profoundly influences how teachers and schools respond to students. There is a deep-seated belief among educational theorists that the important work has to be done when a child is young. As the twig is bent it will grow—this view continues to dominate educational policy. Offer the young child a sympathetic, compassionate environment and you give him or her a head start. That may be true, but the initial advantage is dissipated as the child becomes an adolescent. The unrelenting pounding of family and street life finally hardens and isolates children, unless the affection they received in their early years is sustained later on. The most tragic flaw in American education is that children whose promise was nourished when they were young are abruptly and callously abandoned when they are ten and eleven years old. For children who grow up in a hard world, the cold eye of the high school may be the meanest initiation into adulthood.

Peter B. Edelman, former director of the New York State Division for Youth and now a professor at the Georgetown University Law Center, has found that "people are most interested in prevention at a point where it is most easy to prevent problems. The younger the child, the more willing society is to invest in him. Most of the gains achieved in elementary school are dissipated by junior high school and certainly by high school.

"If you're a minority person who's been a model citizen, you get some opportunity to make it. If you've managed to stay in regular school, there's at least a place for you. But once you start in another direction—your family life is crumbling, you're in trouble on the street—it becomes much more costly to help, and because there's a disproportionate number of minority kids in difficulty, that makes them doubly unattractive."

Do affection and concern have to be wrung out of education when a boy or girl starts to grow up? The answer to that question really turns on the issue of political accountability. The issue is: To whom are high schools accountable? Who judges their success or failure?

As it now stands, teachers and administrators answer to one master—the school system. But schools also have a responsibility to students and parents. As public institutions they ultimately have an obligation to the tattered communities that they are supposed to serve and to the larger society that, in the end, will be forced to engage the youngsters they rejected. Schools will take the first step toward greater accountability when they determine the actual dimensions of the dropout crisis and begin to confront it. For too long, they have hidden the true extent of the problem from public scrutiny.

Playing the Numbers

For years poor parents believed that dropping out was a minor problem affecting a small group of incorrigibles, youngsters who couldn't learn, who were stupid, who were troublemakers, whose parents didn't care about them. Black parents read that on a *national* basis almost twice as many black students dropped out of school as did white children. Hispanic parents read that, *nationally,* *43 percent* of their children *never* enter high school.[15] But their local schools told them that only a few students drop out. In cities throughout the country, school officials estimate the local dropout rate at 5, 10, or 15 percent; thus, what on a national level is a momentous social issue on a local basis becomes the problem of a few teenage misfits.

Chicago is a prime example. Through the 1970s and early 1980s, the Chicago Board of Education reported a dropout rate of 10 percent or less for all of the city's public high schools. (The board did not report a dropout rate for junior high schools or elementary schools, although many youngsters were, in fact, dropping out.) In 1984 the Illinois State Board of Education after a formal inquiry found that the Chicago dropout rate was 50.7 percent. That was a revelation. But what was even more of a revelation was the public acknowledgement that dropping out was not the exclusive problem of blacks and Hispanics. The rate was consistently high among all students: 38 percent for whites, 56 percent for blacks, and 57 percent for Hispanics.[16]

The clear conclusion of the state report was that leaving school was a *systemic* failure. As telling in its conclusions was the fact that the report had been buried for two years in the state education bureacracy. It was made public only after independent investigations by community organizations found a much higher dropout rate than that reported by the city and the state.

The principal independent investigator was Father Charles L. Kyle, associate pastor of St. Francis Xavier Roman Catholic Church in Chicago. Father Kyle, who holds a doctorate in sociology from Northwestern University, concluded that the official dropout statistics were "vastly understated and were based on a bogus formula." He added: "A tremendous dropout problem in Chicago public schools has been glossed over and covered up since 1971."

The deception begins with statistical sleight-of-hand. In Chicago, as in other cities, students who leave school before graduation are grouped in a number of different categories. Only one category uses the specific term, "dropout." (The full title of this category reads: "Drop out—lack of interest and/or poor scholarship") Other categories, or "leave codes," include: "Lost—not coming to school", "entered verified employment"; "needed at home"; "married"; "transfer to a school outside Chicago"; "miscellaneous leave for involuntary reason (including pregnancy)"; and "cannot adjust." Only a small number of students who leave are officially listed as dropouts. In reality, those students who have left ostensibly because they are "needed at home," have got "married" or found a job, or are simply "lost" are just as much dropouts as those who are officially listed. But in the data collection center of the Chicago Board of Education they are not counted in the dropout rate. Using this system, it is possible to claim a dropout rate of 5 or 10 percent.*

There are other ways of playing the numbers. The Chicago system tabulates dropout rates for each school each year rather than reporting how many students who started as freshmen received their diplomas four years later. If 15 percent of the entering class drops out at Marshall High School, Chicago officials say there is a 15 percent dropout rate at Marshall. However, as Father Kyle observed in his study, 17 percent of that class may drop out in the second year, and 16 percent in the following year. "Dropping out entails at least four years," Kyle says. When after four years the students gather in the school auditorium to receive their diplomas, only half of the original class is still in school. "That school has a 50 percent dropout rate," Kyle says. "It's completely bogus to give any other figure."

One high school principal described to Father Kyle what happens when a student decides to leave:

"A youth comes to the counter and asks for a leave card.

---

* Similar accounts of the underestimation of dropout rates are reported in California, Texas, Michigan, and other states. A range of other practices are employed in school districts throughout the country, all resulting in the underreporting of the number of dropouts.

The youth is given a card for his/her parent to sign. The youth gives his/her reason for leaving. The reason is not checked. The youth then brings the card with the parent's signature and is signed out." The entire process, Kyle said, "relies heavily upon the whim of the administration and the student. . . . There are no checks as to the accuracy of the reasons given. When the school administrators were asked if the parent's consent was ever verified, they replied that they suspected that the students forge the parent's signature."

If the system makes little effort to verify the student's reasons for leaving, neither does it care much about what happens after he's gone. Using students' ID numbers, Kyle tried to follow up on 121 students who were listed as transfers to another Chicago public school. He found that forty-two (or 35 percent), who were being carried on the rolls of the school system, had not enrolled at any public school.

They don't only disappear from high school. Some disappear before they ever get to high school. Some Chicago school officials estimate that as many as 25 percent of the graduates from elementary school never show up at high school. Dr. Hamilton McMaster, district superintendant in the predominantly Hispanic Humboldt Park area of Chicago, says, "In this district one of every five kids who graduates from elementary school gets lost." And he adds, "In this district we have ten attendance (truant) officers for 23,000 youngsters."[17]

Some educators don't believe that the disappearance of children from the public schools is simply a result of bureaucratic inefficiency, of a kid falling through the cracks in a vast system. They believe that children who fail repeatedly, are frequently truant, and are disruptive in school are, in effect, invited to drop out. In San Antonio's Edgewood school district, where poverty, teenage pregnancy, drugs, and street violence are epidemic, James Vasquez, the district school superintendant, says: "My feelings tell me that a lot of kids who are labeled dropouts are really kick outs. In this state we have a dropout category called 'parent's request.' You get the kid to get his mother to write a letter to the school saying, 'Jose is withdrawing today because in the future we plan to move to Michigan.' That's the end of it. Gone, goodbye. There's no priority to finding out if that kid is actually in school in Michigan, because you don't want him in your school in the first place."[18]

Sometimes the implicit invitation to leave school is codified in the system's regulations. In Texas the age at which a student can legally leave has been dropped from seventeen to sixteen. In practice, this means that at the age of fifteen years and one day an adolescent can sign out—and nobody will try to stop him. "The attitude that prevails now in the schools is, If you don't want to stay in, then leave," says Vasquez. "What the schools are really saying to these kids is, You make our situation better by leaving. What really gets me is the deceit. Schools will never admit that they're encouraging the hard cases to leave. They pretend it's all the student's fault for dropping out."

Lowering the leaving age and various other regulations that encourage students to drop out reinforce an inequality of long standing: The average child from an affluent family gets four more years of schooling than the average poor child; Hispanic and black students drop out at a rate twice that of white youngsters.[19]

In California a public policy organization interviewed some 1,900 youngsters who had recently dropped out. One purpose of the study was to determine the actual dropout rate in the state. But the authors found that to be no easy task. Local school districts were not required to report how many students had left. To be accredited, a school has to fill out a form that includes enrollment statistics, but the researchers discovered that few schools bother to complete the form. "In California, no one asks the schools for their drop-out rates; there is little incentive for them to collect such data," the authors wrote. "Some school administrators express fear that such an investigation might uncover a 'can of worms' that the public might interpret as yet another indictment of the schools."[20]

Like many students, teachers and administrators have surrendered to the inevitability of failure. As one California educator said: "Of course, kids drop out, but it's not our problem. We have our hands full with the kids that are here in school. The kids on the street are someone else's problem. We just don't have the resources any more to bend over backwards and beg kids to come back to school."

As long as schools are not held accountable for the students who vanish as well as the students who hang in, the dropout rate will always be underestimated. That has serious policy implications. Until full disclosure is mandated by school systems and legislators, dropout prevention efforts will continue to be directed toward a handful of "troubled" students rather than the majority of the student body that will leave some schools before commencement day. Until the outside world learns just how many former students are out on the streets, no substantial effort will be made to reclaim them.

Statistically and politically, dropouts have no status today; as far as the school system is concerned, they don't exist. The only recognition that they once sat in a classroom, listened to a teacher, and read a book will be a dusty file buried in a warehouse where old school records are stored. The file will be stamped: "Whereabouts unknown."

Nelson Torres: The Pursuit of Class

Nelson Torres never struck a teacher, never fell asleep in class, and hardly ever missed doing his homework. The worst his teachers could say of him was that he was a "squirmer." After I met him the first time, about eight months after he had left school, I understood what they meant. Nelson, a dark-skinned kid with a little pot belly and round cheeks, just couldn't seem to sit still. He'd stretch his legs out in front of him, constantly turning his ankles one way and the other. When conversation bored him, he'd open and close his thighs faster and faster, until I thought I could hear his knees banging.

He came from a poor but tightly knit Puerto Rican family in Manhattan. A strong strain of loyalty ran through the family; if someone had problems, the others would pick up the slack. He was a grade behind in reading when he entered high school, but his math and science test scores were consistently in the low nineties. He was rarely absent in the fall and winter, but in the spring his work and attendance would drop off. In his freshman year, he missed forty-four days in the spring, and in his second spring he was out seventy-three days. In May of his second year he stopped coming to school altogether. He was ten days short of his sixteenth birthday.

Paul Levitas* was Nelson's guidance counselor. At first he had difficulty remembering Nelson—"There's so many, they keep comin' in and out"—but after he found his folder, he said, "A strange kid. He'd do well and then . . . He was not marginal,

---

* The staff at Nelson's high school agreed to speak to me on the condition that their real names not be used.

definitely better than marginal. Last spring, when he was there he hardly said anything. He just stared out of the window. It was like his mind was elsewhere. He wasn't angry or hostile. He just didn't seem to be here any more."

His dance teacher, Carol Green, perhaps knew him best of all of his teachers, which is not to say she knew him very well. "He didn't have a lot of talent," she said, "but he had tremendous enthusiasm once he got over his shyness at taking dance. His electricity charged up the whole class. Our first dance recital of the year was in December. He was the star. The parents loved him, the teachers loved him, and the girls, well, he got on the stage and they started to swoon." In the spring, he was just as enthusiastic. But the payoff was, he didn't show up for the big recital. No explanation. He just didn't show up.

"When I caught up with him, I said, 'Nelson, what's wrong?' All he'd say was, 'I'm sorry, I have things on my mind.' Then he transferred out of dance into gym. 'I'm afraid I'm gonna let everybody down,' he said. 'I'm gonna take a class where nobody's dependin' on me.'"

Nelson wasn't planning to take any class at all. A few weeks after he spoke to Ms. Green, he quit school. In fact, he had psychologically quit months before he actually left. While he went through the motions of being a student, his mind was on selling arroz con pollo and Budweiser at the baseball diamonds in Central Park and other parks in Manhattan. He was thinking about getting a cut-rate price on a hundred bottles of Schlitz and ten bags of charcoal. His mind was on work. Four or five days a week from the end of March to mid-October the Torres family set up their portable grills and shopping carts filled with food and paper plates and hot sauce and charcoal at diamonds all around Manhattan. The business earned the family as much as $4,000 extra a year, all untaxed.

Abe Melendez, for twenty years a youth worker on the upper West Side where the Torres family lived, says that in this enterprise Nelson was the main attraction. "The kid's a small legend. When he was eleven, people bought from him 'cause he was cute. You know, curly hair and a round face and dimples. Mucho cute. When he was older, they bought from him 'cause he was faster than any other vendor and the food was better and always, somehow, a few cents cheaper. In this neighborhood vending is a very competitive business. Usually, the Puerto Ricans buy from the Puerto

Ricans, the Dominicans buy from the Dominicans, the Cubans buy from the Cubans. The amazing thing is everybody bought from Nelson."

The year Nelson dropped out, his family had been having a hard time making ends meet. His father, a cab driver, got into an accident and had his hack license suspended; while he was waiting out the suspension he worked for minimum pay as a short-order cook. Nelson's mother did piecework in the apartment for a dress manufacturer, but her production fell off when arthritis reached her fingers. Her boss fired her. Nelson, the oldest child, became a primary provider. He did a lot of the shopping and cooking for the vending business and much of the hawking.

"Nelson came to me and said, 'I'm thinking of quitting school,' " Abe Melendez says. "I started to tell him how I was tempted to take shortcuts when I was young, how I could've gotten into stuff. But I could see he wanted to be told: Yes, it's okay to quit. He thought it was time he took care of business, stopped being a kid and go out and take on the world. To be honest, I didn't say no, stay in school, and I didn't say, yes, quit. I said, Do what you have to do."

Why didn't Nelson talk to his high school teachers or his counselor?

> Melendez knew me from when I was seven when I go swimming at the community center," Nelson says. "My teachers I didn't trust or not trust. In my history class, the teacher he say my name, *Torruss*. My English teacher, he say, *Terrissss*. They just don't know me.
>
> Oh sure, I coulda stayed two more years. But then what? Burger King? A mailroom guy? I know all about that stuff. I been workin' summers since I was eleven. I pushed a hand-truck downtown, ran a ton of mail to the post office every afternoon. So I gotta sit in class for two years so I can do some more of that?

I realize that as I write what he told me it makes him sound a little cocky or arrogant. That's not how the teachers at his school remember him. They remember that he demonstrated in school many of the same qualities that made him an effective entrepreneur on the street. Nelson seemed to know what a teacher wanted before she asked for it. "He was very good at picking up cues," says his dance teacher, Carol Green. "He'd give you back the right answer, but then he'd put his own special twist on it, his own brand. When I got his interest he'd look at you in a way that made you feel you were the most important person in the world. I thought he'd make a terrific salesman someday—or a psychiatrist."

Nelson's very quickness could sometimes work against him. An English teacher recalled how Nelson would rush through a sentence, skipping some of the articles, reversing words and letters. "But he always got the thought right," the teacher says. "If he didn't know a word, he'd figure it out from the context. He struck me as shrewd and clever, but not coy or manipulative the way some smart kids are."

Spending time with him on the street, I imagined that, with the right breaks, Nelson could be very successful in the business world. With his poise, intelligence, and sparkling personality, he could be climbing the corporate ladder two rungs at a time. But for that to happen, somebody would have to take hold of his life. Somebody would have to persuade him that a high school diploma would lead to more than a job at Burger King. There wasn't anybody around like that. He was merely another dark-skinned, impatient kid with an accent, a kid whose attention sometimes drifted away from gerunds and geometry.

After Nelson had been gone for a couple of months, he was forgotten. His parents received a total of two phone calls and a form letter from the school. There was no home visit by a teacher or attendance officer, no one to sell him on the long-term dividends of education. Maria Torres, Nelson's mother, says she didn't argue with him. "We said it won't be so easy, but if he wanted to stay in school we make out, we figure a way. But he was sure he wanted to stop. He didn't feel there was anything in the school for him. It was hard to tell him that maybe twenty years from now he'd be sorry, 'cause we're only taking care of business for today."

Nelson branched out from the vending trade once he left school. Once or twice a week he collected for the local numbers bank. The money wasn't great. (A good day for a runner is a $300 collection; Nelson, who gets twenty-five cents on the dollar, might pick up $75, working at full speed and efficiency.) But in the neighborhood running numbers is considered an apprenticeship, during which Nelson would have to prove that he was trustworthy, level-headed, tight-lipped, and smart. "No one like Nelson is gonna stay in numbers," says Abe Melendez, " 'cause no dark-skinned Puerto Rican kid is gonna become a banker, and unless you're a banker there's no money in it, and most important there's no class in it."

So Nelson adopted a strategy that has profited many corporations. He began to diversify. Vending and numbers are supplemented by other odd jobs: delivering liquor and food to late-night card games and running "errands" for neighborhood drug dealers. A year out of high school, a dropout, Nelson Torres earns from his various ventures close to $15,000 a year, tax-free. To the U. S. Bureau of Labor Statistics, Nelson Torres is an unemployed high school dropout. To his family, his earnings are not the difference between welfare dependency and solvency; but they are the difference between barely making it and making it with an edge.

As important as money is to him, he knows its value is diminished if it's tainted. "Like I been runnin' errands, deliverin' packages," he says. "First thing I asked was, Is it smack? No way I gonna get mixed up with heroin. It's low-down; the people who use it are low-down; the people who sell it are low-down. Most of the time I been deliverin' smoke. If people trust me, I'll be deliverin' coke. Coke is somethin' else. Rich people use it, stars. Coke is class."

Class. For Nelson there is no more powerful symbol of class than *the door*. The door cost $1,300 to construct and install. It's made of triple-plated riveted steel. It's wired with three different kinds of alarms. One night I waited with Nelson and the dealer he runs errands for outside the door. When it opened we walked into one of Manhattan's hottest private clubs for Hispanics who are part of the drug trade.

The main feature of the place is a sunken swimming pool. The night we were there no one was swimming. Most of the members and their guests were sitting around the pool on wicker chairs alongside marble-top tables. On each table was a lamp with a tassled shade. When we ordered drinks, no money changed hands. That wouldn't be classy. Here, the members pay a monthly tab.

That night the crowd was mostly Hispanics. There were a few blacks and even fewer whites. At a couple of tables some lines of cocaine were being laid out. "Conversation and a little coke," said Nelson's boss. "That's about it. Deals are discussed here, but nothing is transacted—no money, no stuff. Sometimes the police come by, just to see who's here. That's why the door was installed; it gives people a feeling of security. A feeling of privacy.

"Look around, there's people here in their forties," he went on. "They been doin' this twenty years. Do they look beat? Do they look spent? What keeps 'em sharp? It's the challenge. Every day you got to get up with somethin' different in your head. Your mind becomes so sharp and cunning. It's like this—" He takes a razor blade out of his jacket and holds it under the lamp. "Don't make any mistake—the members here earned their membership."

"Someday," Nelson said, "I'll be a member. Someday soon."

"Maybe," his boss said.

Maybe is the biggest word in Nelson's life. Maybe he will commit himself to dealing. Maybe he'll get tired of hustling and play it straight. When I met him, he was straddling both worlds. The people who know him well say his future is a toss-up, too close to call. His uncle, who is a district sales representative for a soft drink company, says, "I worry about Nelson sometimes, but he's got a fast mind, he's got personality, he's known in the neighborhood, and he doesn't like violence. I think he's got a shot.

"What would be his chances in a corporation like mine? I'm where I am because the company needed a light-skinned Hispanic 'cause we sell a lot of bottles in this market. A couple of shades darker, a little louder, and I'd be going door to door for three hundred bucks a week. A kid like Nelson, his skin is dark, the chances are a thousand to one against him that he'll make it like me, and he's just as smart."

In 1985, some middle-class parents were hiring private counselors at fifty dollars an hour and more to advise their fourteen-year-old children on what high school courses to take and how to tailor their applications so they could get into the best colleges. Nelson Torres has no private advisers to plan his higher education. He goes on his own instincts and what people he trusts tell him. "I won't stay in the neighborhood all my life," Nelson says, "but right now it's givin' me a start. I'm still young. I'm just lookin' for the openin'. And when it comes I'll be ready. I'm just waitin' on life."

If you asked Nelson why he left school, he would probably say, I wanted to get a job. When Hispanic organizations survey dropouts, they find that up to 40 percent of the males say they left to find employment.[21] But I'm not sure that the answer should be accepted uncritically. Finding a job is the socially approved reason for dropping out. It's better than saying, I was tired of school, or I just wanted to hang out, or I want to make a baby. Schools prefer to hear that a student dropped out to take a job, because it takes them off the hook: It's not the quality of teaching or disciplinary practices or lack of school interest in the students that makes them leave. Ostensibly, they drop out because they need to find the money to pay the electric bill. Advocacy groups also like the job answer, because it absolves students and families of responsibility; their thinking is that if poor families had jobs, students wouldn't have to drop out. And students who reach a deadend in school know that saying they want a job puts a positive sheen on a potentially disastrous decision.

But when dropouts are pressed, they concede that the job is not the primary reason for leaving. At Benito Juarez High School in Chicago, some 500 students, most of whom were poor and Hispanic, were asked why so many drop out.[22] Only 8 percent thought it was because they were looking for a job. Many more said the important factors were the attitudes of parents, the influence of gangs in the school and community, and the behavior of teachers and students. James Vasquez, the school superintendant in San Antonio, says, "In the 'thirties, with the bread lines, you could say, Yeah, there's abject poverty. But it's a copout to say that jobs are the primary reason for kids leaving in 1985. I don't believe that at all. I think what's crippled these kids is the attitude that's been drummed into them that they can't possibly achieve anything, that they will never be better than they are at fifteen."[23]

I think Nelson Torres would summarize Vasquez's analysis with one word: Class. Nelson hoped to find behind the $1,300 door the elusive, compelling something that meant more to him than money: the chance to move up, to gain respect, to become *somebody*. Nelson chased significance. In school, he thought he was indistinguishable from every other poor brown-skinned kid with no future. At least in the street, he felt he had a destination.

It's reasonable to inquire why Nelson thought he had to leave while some middle-class kids, who also feel confused and out of place in high school, continue to plug away. Permit a personal note that may help to clarify the difference. When I was Nelson's age, I felt maybe more frustrated in school than he did. I landed in a New York City public school for math and science prodigies, where I was surrounded by young men (it was then an all-male school) who planned to go on to college, graduate school, and a brilliant career. They also planned to win a Nobel Prize. (And some did.) My plans were more concerned with the immediate: Would I ever be able to pass mechanical drawing? In that subject, I received a final grade of 29 out of a possible 100. The teacher, a blunt man, asked me, "How the hell did you get into this school?" Damned if I knew.

The year I took the citywide entrance exam for Stuyvesant High School, the examiners must have felt charitable toward the "humanities" types. My reason for trying to slip into this incubator for future Einsteins and Salks was a lot like the reason Nelson Torres went out into the streets: I wanted desperately to climb onto higher ground. I viewed my Brooklyn neighborhood as a terribly materialistic place where people were so eager for wealth that they would sell their identities for the price of a Packard. My home life was probably more unsettled than Nelson's: It measured about 7.8 on the emotional tremor scale. My neighborhood high school was universally considered a graveyard for scholastic wrecks. I wanted out.

Every morning for four years I took the BMT subway to school in Manhattan. As my failures and near-failures piled up, so did my absences. Many days I checked into the home room class to be counted present and then ducked out a side door with a couple of other misfits.

Our announced purpose was to "find some girls." We never did, those being more innocent times, when young women were less likely to play hookey. (Maybe we just didn't know where to look for them.) We would spend the day gawking at the pool hustlers at Julian's, climbing rocks in Central Park, or swimming in what was advertised as the world's biggest swimming pool, in a hotel in Brooklyn. But for all my misfortunes in school and for all the days I missed, I never thought I would drop out. Neither did my parents or my teachers.

It was inconceivable to my mother, a master at inducing guilt, that her only child would drop out of school. Even to think such a thought was an unforgivable blasphemy. At Stuyvesant I finally found some English and history teachers who encouraged me in the belief that there was life after chemistry. They shrugged off my odd-man-out status at Stuyvesant as an ironic but hardly fatal twist of fate, a fish misplaced in the Sahara. They suggested that when I arrived at the promised land of higher education with its courses in sociology, political science, and literature, my true talents would be recognized. I believed them.

That is what sets my experience apart from Nelson's. In school nobody told him they expected him to rise out of his class. Outside, nobody pushed him to persist until, in a more fortuitous setting, he could shine. His class and caste marked him for academic failure. He heard, of course, that there was always the one-in-a-thousand case who escaped his background; somebody had to be class valedictorian. Nelson reasonably concluded that the odds were more favorable out on the street.

In *Elmtown's Youth,* the sociologist A. B. Hollingshead conducted what is widely regarded as the most incisive and exhaustive inquiry into adolescent class structure in America. In 1940 and 1941, he did his research in a small Midwestern city he called Elmtown. There he studied some 500 families and more than 700 teenagers. At the top of the social and economic hierarchy were what he called, Class I and II. At the bottom were Classes IV and V. Hollingshead wrote:

> Withdrawal [from school] is a complex process which begins in the elementary grade . . . it comes into focus in the upper elementary grades as the child becomes aware of the way in which he is regarded by his peers, teachers, and the community in general; from there on the process is intensified. If his family regards education lightly . . . or has a "bad reputation," the youngster develops stronger motives to escape from school than he does to continue.
>
> The teacher may help to keep a student in school, but if he comes from a lower class family the chances are against this. Moreover, the lower the position the child's family occupies in the social structure the less his chances of being helped by a teacher, and, equally important, of accepting the help.

Hollingshead found that high school education is outside the experience of Class V parents and beyond the expectations of most of their children: *"The principal ambition of the Class V child is to grow up and escape from the authority symbolized by his parents and teachers."*[24]

In "Elmtown" all of the youngsters Hollingshead studied were white. As more recent studies have found, the combination

of class *and* race can be a double drag. In his discussion of the
contemporary high school, Theodore Sizer, former dean of the
Harvard School of Education, said the stereotype in many urban
high schools is that "if you're black, you're poor. If you speak
English haltingly, you're stupid. If you're white, you have a future.
Blacks are basketball players. Blond is beautiful." Sizer concluded:

> The hard fact is that if you are the child of low-income parents,
> the chances are good that you will receive limited and often careless
> attention from adults in your high school. Most of this is realism
> that many Americans prefer to keep under the rug, of course; it
> is no easy task for the poor in America to break out . . . of their
> economic condition. But a change in status that is a matter of moder-
> ately poor odds becomes impossible when there is little encourage-
> ment for them to try.[25]

Paradoxically, class distinctions can be most invidious when
they appear in programs specifically designed to help poor youngsters. This has been true of school programs that try to find part-
time employment for students. A teacher trying to develop jobs
for students at a Scottsdale, Arizona, high school, asks, "If you're
trying to find some jobs in a bank or electronics company would
you send out a kid whose father is an alcoholic, a kid who's been
truant a lot? No, the school's going to send out a kid with the
best chance of sticking on the job, the kid who's going to make
the school look good." Of the twenty-three seniors I interviewed
in the program, seventeen said that they had planned to go on
to college before they ever enrolled in the program. They clearly
were not the most in need.

Eunice Elton, the employment and training director for the
city of San Francisco, says, "School counselors put the poorer
kids into public sector jobs. They worked in community organizations or in government agencies. The middle-class kids were
placed with the law firm downtown or with Standard Oil. Nobody
admits it's segregation, but it's segregation just the same."

How schools respond to different classes of youngsters is
also reflected in how much money they spend on them. One small
example: Kentucky is a state without large urban slums, but with
a lot of poor people. In Kentucky, $30,000 more per classroom
is spent each year in wealthy districts than in poor ones. Census
data show that Kentucky ranks as the worst among all states in
the number of people over the age of twenty-five who do not

have a high school diploma. Seventy-two out of every hundred high school graduates do not go to college; yet 75 percent of state funding for special programs is directed toward college-bound students.[26]

It is not only in formal programs that youngsters suffer the penalties of class. Class-consciousness charges the mundane, seemingly innocuous everyday experiences in school and outside.

Mark's Bag and Deezie's Hair

Mark Williams stood out among all the other students. When the teacher quizzed the class, he understood the question and was ready with the right answer while the other students were still chewing their erasers. Mark also looked different. A short, slender black kid with big glasses, he dressed like an undergraduate at an Ivy League college: a rumpled button-down shirt, gray slacks, loafers. Mark's bible was *Gentlemen's Quarterly,* a magazine that featured photographs of models lounging in Harvard Yard or leaning against the rail of a yacht, all warm and cuddly in their Irish tweeds and crew necks. "I'd always be crazy about the *GQ* look," he says. "In high school, all the kids were into Lees and Pumas, flares with the seam on the side, sneakers untied. But I wanted people to say, Mark, he don't look like every other nigger."

He was frank about why he had adopted that image: girls. In that respect, Mark was a conventional sixteen-year-old male. "If you're goin' after that special girl, that kind of girl she wants someone who looks like he has class. If you look good, they gonna want to sport you on their arms. It's nothin' about likin' each other. The girl's gonna want a guy and the guy's gonna want a girl who'll make their friends say, 'Wow!'"

I met Mark when he was a student at an alternative education program in New York for teenagers who had dropped out of conventional high schools. Most of the kids at the school had been in trouble with the law and had spent time in correctional facilities. But Mark hadn't, and I was never quite able to pin down how he got into the school; as quick and smart as he was, he clearly didn't belong. I surmised that his father had exercised a little clout to get him in after Mark was suspended from his high school for repeated truancy.

One day Mark walked into the classroom carrying an imitation Louis Vuitton bag. It was like wearing red in a bullring. The other kids didn't know a Vuitton from a Gucci, but they knew that bag was not something you carry when you're going to hang out at the arcade in Times Square.

"Hey, man, where you get that thing," sang out a kid who'd just come back from a year in an upstate lockup.

"Got it on 125th Street, from a Chinese guy. He said it was a real Louis Vuitton."

"How much you pay?" another kid wanted to know.

"Forty. They cost $120 in a regular store."

The class roared with laughter. When the laughter subsided, a girl who had just paid her dues at the Rikers Island jail snorted, "Loooooooie Veeet—what? Who the hell is that guy?"

"He's special," Mark explained. "All the rich guys buy his stuff. It shows they're special. They're not part of some big universal mob."

Considering where Mark bought it—on a Harlem pavement—the class decided that whatever a Louis Vuitton bag was, this couldn't be it. What a dumbo—dropping $40 out of your $65 weekly pay on a bag with washed-out colors and a pattern that looked like bad TV reception. And it wasn't even the real thing.

The teacher tried to mediate. "My wife sometimes buys an expensive bag to keep up," he offered. "It's an image of prestige. People think—If I carry that bag I'll be just like *them.*"

Somewhat chastened, Mark said, "That's all I wanted, really. The name. I didn't want to be like everyone else."

That didn't sway anyone. "Shit, man, that much money you coulda bought enough chiba to stay high all week," the parolee from upstate said. "You don't understand. You always gonna be what you are. No dumb bag's gonna change that."

After the class was over Mark reflected on the uproar. "I know I got gypped," he said. "I might get gypped again. But in a way I wanted that bag. When I bought it, it lifted me up. All my life when I try to lift myself up, there's somebody who pulls you down. They always say, You never gonna be any better, no matter how much you spend. I don't wanna believe that. I wanted that bag."

Mark's mother was fourteen when he was born. His father was sixteen. This is what Mark learned about his conception: "My daddy used a rubber and there was a hole in it. It was defective. That's how I got born. Mama got caught on her first try. That's why she was so shocked. When I was born my grandmother said she was gonna put me up for adoption, but my great aunt said she would take care of me and she did until I was thirteen, and my mother got remarried. When I was a kid sometimes on weekends I'd go to my mother. My father would never come and see me. Growing up, people told me so much about him that was bad—mostly about his problems with drugs."

The standard practices and procedures in inner-city schools are not sensitive to the personal problems of children like Mark. One of the big events of the school year is parent-student night. The memory of those nights still stays with me: My father coming home early from work, dropping off his sample case, changing into a fresh shirt, walking with me to school. I sat outside the classroom wondering what terrible things the teacher would tell him. When I was invited back in, both of them would be smiling, she saying, "Mr. Lefkowitz, Bernie is doing quite well," he squeezing my shoulder, approvingly. The adults had conferred, passed judgment. I was renewed for another year.

That didn't happen to Mark.

> On that night I'd never show up. I didn't have a father to bring. It would make me ashamed when the teacher would say: "Mark, did you tell your father he was supposed to come to school?" The next day the other kids would hear that my father didn't come. They'd say, "I know why your father didn't come. He's dead." And they'd hear I didn't live with my mother and they'd say, "Your mom is a prostitute on 42d Street." I'd go home crying. I didn't want to come to class and face the teacher and the other kids any more.

Even at the bottom of the social pyramid, there are different strata. In Mark's alternative school class, a class made up of dropouts, there was one young woman named Deezie, and she was at the bottom of the bottom. At the age of five she had been sexually abused by her father. "He was jealous that I was a nice-looking child and he abused me. My mother came and almost kilt him."

When she was nine her brother forced her to have intercourse with him. "He got his later. He killed somebody and went to jail for life." When she was eleven, her mother went to court and had Deezie judged a child in need of supervision. She was sent to a group home. "I didn't like it. I cried all day and all night. It made me feel bad, but I hadda handle it. Either that or I woulda been dead." At thirteen she was arrested when she beat and robbed a physician in his home. She was sent to Spofford, a juvenile detention home in New York City, and then to another juvenile facility on Staten Island. When she got into trouble there for fighting with the other kids and the guards, she was transferred to upstate New York near Elmira. In that secure facility, she spent a year and four months. "My trouble was I didn't wanna shut up when they told me to shut up. I couldn't follow the rules and regulations. They restrained me three times—some of the staff they hurt you, they really hurt you up there."

Now she was back in New York, and one condition of her release was that she attend classes in this alternative school. In the class, she had two strikes against her. On her first day I over-heard her telling some of the other students about her past. She talked about the crimes she had committed, she talked about how she had been a prostitute. Deezie, who was sixteen, boasted that she didn't go out with "nobodies. Older men understand more. The younger guys after they fuck you they'll talk about you. The older men know the score." The man she was spending time with now, she said, was thirty-two. "He's doing a lot for me. He buys me clothes, gives me money. He's married, but he's not with his wife. I never gave him my ass yet. I was brought up this way—don't give up your ass too soon. Check out the guy, check out what he's all about. I'm gonna wait for a month and a half. Or at least two months. If you can't wait that long you're in trouble."

Deezie was saying too much too soon. The boys who heard her took her preference for older men as something of a threat to their manhood. Her past as a prostitute was something they could use against her. She had let down her guard. That was strike one.

Strike two was her appearance. Her lips were thick. Her nose was broad. Her hair sprouted like a wild, tangled thicket. Her clothes were too tight for her chunky form, and their colors clashed. It's possible that sometimes she forgot to bathe.

I was an observer in Deezie's class, but sometimes she would ask me for help with her reading and math lessons. In return for my help she would draw a heart on a sheet of paper. The lines were made up of a series of connected stars. When I mentioned to her that I was married, she drew a smaller heart in the corner of the page and wrote inside of it: "With love to Bernie and Becky, your close friend, Deezie."

Deezie always maintained that white men could see the goodness in her behind her tough exterior, but black men only wanted to use her. Maybe it was because she believed that white men had the power to make things better for her, while black men thought that she had sunk so low that she deserved to be stepped on. Whatever it was, she would tell me, "White men gave me advice, and still gives me advice. I can learn more from a white man than from my own kind. All the time I been dealing with blacks, my own kind, they always took me up the ass, like that, you know."

I liked Deezie, but I was in a minority in the class. When the teacher called on her, or, in those rare instances, when she volunteered an answer, I could hear the others around her snickering. Mostly it was the boys.

Twenty years ago when kids put each other down it was called ranking. Now, particularly in the black classes I observed, it was called "snapping." Usually the snapping had an element of cheerfulness and good humor behind the wisecracks. But when snapping was directed at Deezie it was especially cruel and vicious. One afternoon she was reading out loud a composition—actually, it was only a few lines—that she had written. The title was "Addiction."

Deezie read, "I'm addicted to clothes—"

Behind her I heard a boy say, in a mock whisper, "How you be addicted to clothes the way you look?"

"—and I'm addicted to cigarettes because when you put it in your mouth it keeps you relaxed," Deezie went on, as if she hadn't heard him.

Louder now, the boy said, "The only thing you got in your mouth is a dick."

Deezie lunged across the aisle at him, knocking over a chair and scattering notebooks and pencils. She locked her arms around his neck and wrestled him to the floor. Then she reached into her pocket, pulled out a comb and raked his face. By the time the teacher could separate them, the boy's face was streaked with welts.

The teacher took them out of the classroom to cool down.

When he came back in, he didn't ignore what had happened. "Why," he asked the class, "do you think she went after him?"

After a long silence, one girl tried to defend Deezie. "I noticed when nobody was snappin' on her, she was real nice. But he kept going."

A boy said, "The first day she was talking about how she did prostitution. You don't tell that to strangers. After that everybody was snapping on her."

A second guy added, "She's so ugly. She's just a nasty creature."

"But consider where she's been," the teacher said. "She's been upstate, locked up. Away from the natural environment and the sun. A lot of guys come back from there bald. Suppose she went to the right makeup artist. She'd knock you out."

"If she makes money every week, why don't she get a haircut?" the guy said.

"Maybe she like it that way," said the girl.

"You see her armpit . . . hairy," the guy said.

"Remember she's been upstate for a while," the teacher reminded them.

"No difference," the guy said. "She went and sold her body to make money. Nothin' else you can say about her."

The class roared. The kids in that class had held up banks, pistol-whipped old ladies, robbed their mothers, and shot it out with the cops; now they had found somebody they thought was lower than they were. And there was no way anything Deezie could do would change their feelings about her.

When I asked Deezie about the fight, she said, "On the street I don't deal with all that off-the-wall bullshit. I just say, Mmmmm— and keep goin'. The trouble I had today was unnecessary. I was gonna ignore the kid. I didn't wanna listen. But I did listen— and it was too late. I couldn't hold myself back. Now on, they can say what they say and I ain't gonna do nothin' but close myself up."

A week later she dropped out of class. Ran. I like to think that maybe some of the girls in the class were right when they said that she probably went off with the thirty-two-year-old guy. Maybe he was making her laugh. Maybe he was buying her roses. Maybe. The last time I saw Deezie she told me, "I don't have it easy, but I'm not dead. I'm not in the ground yet. So maybe I still have a chance."

The teacher who taught Deezie's class was a middle-aged black man. He had been a prison guard and a counselor at a runaway shelter. He took on without flinching all of the issues that were of critical importance to the youngsters in the class: raising a child by yourself; hustling on the streets; peer pressure to break the law; gangs; "getting over"—making it from day to day without thinking of long-term consequences—and the never ending hostility between adolescents and their stepparents.

This teacher, as patient and understanding as he was, could not reach all of the kids in the class. He lost Deezie; he lost others who went back to the streets. Some were too far gone; he had come on the scene too late. But I couldn't help thinking that if they had met him three or four years earlier—before they were hardened by the public schools, by the streets and by the reformatories—he might have been able to save them. But the way the public education system works is that you meet teachers like him only after you get into deep trouble.

At about the same time that the teacher in New York was trying to save his students, a high school in Detroit was about to lose one of its best pupils. Through elementary and middle school, Irene Rogers consistently placed in the top 5 percent of her class. In her freshman year in high school, she had an A— average. "I liked school. I *loved* school," Irene says. "I just loved to learn. I would read anything I could get my hands on."

Irene made it very easy for schools to respond to her. She was everything Deezie wasn't. She was highly intelligent and extremely articulate. She was quietly attentive to and respectful of her teachers. She dressed attractively and carried herself well. Her mother had graduated from high school. Although Irene's father was not at home, her mother had supported three children by working at white-collar jobs. Irene was black and went to inner-city schools, but wasn't bound by her social and economic class.

Irene had only one problem: her mother. In the seventh and eighth grades, Irene's mother frequently kept her home to clean the house and take care of her brother and sister. After Irene's freshman year, her mother, in addition to working, became involved in religious proselytizing. She ordered Irene to leave school and, in effect, raise the other children while she pursued her religious calling.

Before Irene was forced to leave school completely, she had to stay at home for long stretches.

The school would call my mother and say, "Mrs. Rogers, your daughter hasn't been in school, she's never in school!" They'd send letters, and they'd come to my house and my mother would say, "Oh, Irene is too sick to go to school." I'd stand against the door of my room and hear my mother say that, and they'd believe her.

One time the school threatened to take me and my sister out of the home. I kept wishing they would, so I could go to school. But they never did anything. And then I hear about other people who complain that the schools took away their kids because they weren't doing right by them. And that makes me upset. The kids who really didn't want to go to school they take away from their homes, and the ones, like me, who really wanted to go, they leave in their house.

What most distressed Irene was that the school ultimately came down on her mother's side.

I made a terrible mistake. When my mother said I had to stay home, I told my counselor. I said to her, "My mother is keeping me home to watch my sister and brother." The counselor kept asking me all my secrets. She had me there crying in her office. I kept pleading with her, "I'll tell you everything, but don't tell my mother I said it. *Please.*" And before I got home that day, she had called to tell my mother exactly what I told her. And my mother just beat the shit out of me.

I decided after that talking to anybody in school about my life was an act of death. They never believe you, they never trust you. I will never, ever tell them anything again. And what gets me most, here they were always saying, "You're such a smart girl. You can go on and do something, don't just sit around." And when it comes to it, they go out and destroy you.

She could confide in a boy who was her closest friend in school. She told him that her mother was forcing her to leave school. "He said, 'This time next year you're going to be pregnant. And you won't be living at home any more.' I said, 'You're crazy. I bet you I'll find a way to get back to school, and I won't have a baby, and I'll still be at home.' But he was exactly right. He knew the future and I didn't. A year later I was pregnant and I was living by myself. And it didn't seem to make any difference to anybody, except to me."

Irene's story doesn't end there. She will not spend the rest of her life alone with her child in a housing project or welfare hotel. She is a fierce battler. Later, I'll describe how she won her battle. It's important to remember—certainly, Irene will remember—that she won it without the help of her school. If the school was unable or unwilling or simply didn't care enough to respond to a youngster who had so much going for herself, how, one wonders, does it treat a child who has fewer advantages, a child like Deezie?

Leaving the Hollow

James B. Conant, the Harvard educator writing in 1961, argued that American education should respond to the problems of poor youth, both inside and outside of the schools. "Big cities," he said, "need to bring the schools closer to the needs of the people in each neighborhood and to make each school fit the local situation." The responsibility of the school for the poor child, he said, does not end when a diploma is awarded. "The schools should be given the responsibility for educational and vocational guidance of youth *after* they leave school until age 21."[27]

Conant and other "reformers" argued that a child's parents, his home, his economic condition, his running buddies in the street—all of that determined his future in and out of the school as much as anything he would be taught in the classroom. To enable a child to learn and advance himself, someone, perhaps the entire staff of a school system, would have to accept the responsibility of stewardship: The school would act as a shepherd guiding the flock across the bridge of childhood and adolescence.

In the school hierarchy, that responsibility falls to the guidance counselor. In urban schools, there is a ratio of one counselor for every 500 students; in some school systems it is more like one to 700. Most counselors I interviewed say they have barely enough time to advise students on what classes they should take next year and how many credits they need to graduate. To probe beneath the surface of any one of the teenagers I met is to engage the unmanageable: drugs, violence, crime, divorce, adolescent pregnancy, self-hatred, and class shame. To try to manage the unmanageable is to sink into a morass of many different and mutually antagonistic bureaucracies: the child and adult welfare systems, foster care, juvenile justice, family planning, health, employment, and training. And then, of course, if you make one phone call, involve one outside agency in the welfare of a troubled adolescent, you risk exposing the school and its inadequacies to the scrutiny of a "nonprofessional." "To be honest, if a kid doesn't tell me about his personal troubles, I'm not gonna look for them," a Chicago high school counselor says. "You get involved in one kid it could ruin your schedule for the whole week. Besides, I don't want to have a thousand outsiders telling me how to do my job."

A middle-class youngster with problems in school will mobilize concerned parents and teachers who can tap a broad array of psychological and social services. The minority kid or the poor white kid in an urban school has only the counselor. And that, many educators acknowledge, isn't very much. "Basically, they're paper-shufflers," says Chicago School Superintendent Manford Byrd. "Most of them have no rapport at all with the kids."[28]

The intervention of a concerned adult cannot solve all the problems confronting poor families and their children. But what long-term intervention can do is establish a relationship based on sympathy and trust. The youngster has found someone who is willing to invest time and effort in his future. Now there is someone the young man or woman can be accountable to. A great many of the youths I met grew up believing that the only reward for doing well was escaping punishment. Do well and you won't be thrown out of school. Do well and you won't wind up in jail. Do well and your parents won't beat you.

Because positive intervention occurs so infrequently, there are no comprehensive studies that confirm its value. But there is anecdotal evidence that is very persuasive. In 1980 Eugene Lang, a wealthy executive, promised sixty-one Harlem elementary school students that he would pay $2,000 toward their college tuitions if they stayed in school. Five years later, the students, black or Hispanic and mostly poor, had all met the qualifications for admission to college. An important element in their success was the presence of a counselor whom Lang had paid to monitor their progress all through high school. "Sometimes you see what happens to your friends," said one of the students, "and you wish other classes and other kids had what we had."

In 1965, the federal government and New York University also offered a group of low-achieving youngsters from Harlem and Bedford-Stuyvesant a substantial inducement to continue their education. In the program, which was called Project Apex, sixty adolescents were brought into the freshman class at NYU. Those youngsters had completed high school, but all had finished in the bottom third of their graduating class; their average reading score was at the sixth grade level. They had managed to graduate as a result of the policy of "social" promotions.

Before they began their freshman year, they were required to attend what amounted to a summer camp. There they were closely supervised. Some of the most talented teachers on the NYU faculty participated. The result was that half of the group, thirty kids, improved their reading scores by three years in three months. "Boom—those kids jumped right to the top," says Professor William Kornblum, who supervised the social sciences section of the program. "It was the mentorship notion: 'Someone cares about me, someone who won't let me fuck up.' " Another quarter of the group advanced more slowly, but within a year at NYU they, too, were passing their courses. Only one-quarter of the youngsters "just didn't have it to get through college," says Kornblum.[29]

But the program did demonstrate that at least three-quarters of the participants, with enthusiastic support and certain rewards, could perform at the college level. "What proportion of kids hanging out in the pool halls and on the street corners of Harlem," Kornblum asks, "could achieve just like anybody else if you gave them attention and hope? I suspect at least 50 percent."

His estimate may be low. If hope is offered at the right time, that is, before a youngster believes there is no hope at all, I would guess as much as 80 or 90 percent of the nation's dropouts would have a fighting chance of growing up as decent, productive adults. That isn't simply a gut feeling, an intuition. And it isn't wishful thinking. I have seen it happen. I saw it happen in a tiny mining settlement in the foothills of eastern Kentucky.

In the early 1950s, David, Kentucky, in Floyd County, was a relatively prosperous company mining town, owned by the Princess Elkhorn Mining Company. Company films of that period show a self-contained community with a theater, Olympic-size swimming pool, scout lodges, ball fields, a school, and a church. But when Danny Greene trekked from Brooklyn to David in the late 1960s, a depression in the coal industry had ravaged the place. Half the houses were deserted; the other half were without adequate water or sewerage.

Greene was part of the wave of youthful volunteers who

poured into Appalachia during the Great Society era. Unlike many of the other idealistic newcomers, he stayed. A tall man with a long, somewhat mournful face, he says, in an accent that retains some of the rough edges of Brooklyn, "When I came I looked around at the hills and the sky and the people, and I thought, I can plant something here. I wanted to build something—and see it through."[30]

He built a school. He was joined by Joan Ford, a Catholic Servite Sister from Iowa; together they established the David School for youngsters who had dropped out of the public schools in Floyd County. Today the school, whose staff consists primarily of Catholic lay workers, claims a 90 percent graduation rate.

It hasn't been easy. The boys and girls who attend the David School, like their friends and relatives who went north to towns like Newport, Kentucky, have grown up hard. The hills covered with spring flowers, the rushing streams and clear brooks, offer natural consolations. But nature cannot conceal the poverty you can find here in the tiny hollows just off the blacktop roads, in the shadows of the abandoned coal tipples and in the scattered settlements that still cluster around closed mine shafts. For all of the attention devoted to Appalachia during the War on Poverty, assistance to the poor is not exactly generous. The federal-state AFDC program provides a maximum of $235 a month for a family of four in Kentucky, or $2,820 a year. The program does not raise any Kentucky family's income up to the national poverty level of $10,000 for a family of four.

It's mostly white kids who live in David and the surrounding area. But they feel the impact of class discrimination in education as deeply as black and Hispanic kids in Chicago and Detroit. Parents and their offspring talk bitterly about a school board at the county seat dominated for generations by the same small group of wealthy families; about school officials who socialize regularly with the most powerful families in the area, who dine at their homes and are their guests at private clubs.* They complain about

---

* The domination of Appalachian schools and school systems by powerful families has been a persistent problem in the region. Harry M. Caudill, in his definitive book on Appalachia, *Night Comes to the Cumberlands,* describes how in the 1920s competent teachers and administrators who had roots outside the region were ousted from their positions by local political machines. "[T]here were other applicants for the job who could point to dozens of first and second cousins and a small army of uncles and aunts. The politicians could not long resist the temptation to profit from this situation. One by one the competent teachers from outside the plateau were dropped from the rosters and the sons and daugh-

a system of nepotism that provides sinecures for favored kinfolk, from the public school janitor to the principal. "The kids from influential families get the attention in the public schools," says Danny Greene. "The other kids get what's left over."

What's left over isn't very much. Myra Robertson, who now attends the David School, lives in a remote hollow about 10 miles from David. Five other families, all related, cling to this notch, which, in addition to their houses, contains the rusting skeletons of many old cars and trailers. When it rains, everything sinks into a sea of sludge. The Robertsons' house, a sagging white structure, has seven rooms; all but three are sealed off, because it costs too much to heat the entire house.

When Myra took me there on a rainy, wind-swept morning, her parents, Mac and Celia, were sitting on straight-backed chairs in the front parlor; the only light in the dim room came from the old black-and-white television. Her mother was a heavy woman whose coal-black hair was streaked with gray. Celia Robertson was in her late forties, but she could have passed for sixty. Myra's father, Mac, rocked back and forth in his kitchen chair; his bony frame was wrapped in a flannel shirt, two sweaters, and a lumber jacket, although there was only a slight chill in the air. Four years before he had suffered a stroke, and now he spoke slowly, slurring his words. He was in his early fifties, but he could have been taken for a man of seventy. A very tired man of seventy.

Myra stopped going to school the day after she received her grade school diploma. She was thirteen. One reason was that the high school bus stopped only infrequently where the Robertsons lived. But the real barriers were her father's stroke and her mother's loneliness. "Mom was real lonely," Myra remembers. "She wanted me to stay with her. She's always been with somebody, first her grandparents, then her parents, and now Daddy. But after Daddy got sick I think she was afraid to be alone."

Mrs. Robertson leaned forward and said, "I'd probably go crazy if I was separated from Myra." Myra's mother worried about something more frightening than being left alone. A strict Baptist, she worried that the immoral world outside the hollow would corrupt her daughter, her only child. Throughout her conversa-

---

ters of local citizens assumed their duties. . . . They were willing to see their employment as a political job rather than as a high and honored professional calling . . . too many performed their work simply as tasks to be gotten through with no great outlay of effort."

tion she interjected warnings of the evil that tempts the innocent; in that she didn't sound very different from Edward Armistead's mother in Cleveland, who tied her son up to keep him off the streets. "Myra's cousin, she has a six-year-old boy and she don't care if he goes to school, 'cause she's on dope. I worry my girl gonna get ahold of dope," she said. Then, as if she saw a connection, she went on to another misfortune: "My brother he married a young woman out there, she got tired a' him, and had him killed for another man."

When all of this came together—the fear of the outside world, Mr. Robertson's illness, Mrs. Robertson's loneliness, and the difficulty of finding transportation to school—it seemed a lot simpler to keep Myra home. Besides, there was no indication that the school cared very much whether Myra showed up or not. "Nobody in that school ever said they wanted me anyway," Myra said. "And I saw myself as no good. I had but one pair of pants all through grade school and two shirts, and there was no hot water, and the kids teased me about it."

> And some of the teachers weren't that terrific, either. I remember one time we had special reading and I was coming back to class and there was this teacher, she's real fat, and she looked at me and said, "You did real well on the test." And I looked at her and said, "I did?" And she looked at some of the other girls, and they were talking and laughing. And the teacher said, "Yeah, you got a zero."
> The kids who didn't have money, they weren't popular. The other kids made fun of them. The people that were rich were real popular with the teachers and the principal. And the poor kids drop out and go work in the mines. It's a cycle vicious. It made me feel useless. Finally, after the eighth grade, I got fed up with it, and I thought, "Well, I'll just quit."

A part of Myra just wouldn't quit. All her life Myra had had a lively curiosity. "I always thought when I was a little kid I knew exactly what the grownups were talking about, and I got furious with them because they wouldn't let me in on the conversation. I thought I was grown up enough." And when she got older— "I always wanted to see the cities and do this, and go to the movies, and all that."

So for the three years when she was shut in, when her world was bounded by the overflowing creek and the mounds of old tires and the junked cars, Myra sustained her own secret fantasy life. And there it is—in a tiny windowless room behind the parlor. Three hundred or more books, arranged alphabetically on wooden planks supported by piles of bricks. Three hundred romance novels, stories of girls who fell in love with dark, handsome strangers, who were spirited away in jet planes and limousines, who lived in lush splendor in places like Paris and London and New York.

Whenever an old classmate or friend or relative saw a book they could buy secondhand, he or she contributed it to Myra's library. Every day, when she was done with the cooking and washing the dishes and sweeping the floor, she would slip away into her special room, prop herself up against the wall . . . and dream.

But then the book ended, and Myra would still be there; no limousine waited outside to carry her away. She'd climb into bed and stare at the ceiling and think. "She wouldn't get up and go outside," her mother said. "She wasn't sick, she was just losin' her strength by sleepin' all day in bed." Her father recalls, "She was paler and paler. You could hardly tell her from the sheet she laid on."

Her father decided this had to stop. A neighbor had told him about the David School, and he insisted, despite his wife's misgivings, that Myra had to give it a chance.

This time Myra had no problem with transportation. One of the buses sent by the David School would be waiting outside her door every morning. Once she got to the old coal company building that now housed the school, she found herself in a partnership based on mutual effort and trust. Only forty-five students attended, and the ratio of faculty to students was one to five. What happened during class seemed less important than what happened between classes. The teachers helped Myra brush her hair. They taught her to apply makeup—a bright red lipstick that contrasted with her creamy complexion and dark eyes, and just a trace of eyeshadow. "Just a little eyeshadow," I overheard one of her teachers telling her. "You're so pretty you don't need too much of that."

When there was no hot water at home, her teachers arranged for her to shower at the school. "Our whole family are a bunch of uglies, and I'm about the only one that turned out pretty," Myra said, with newfound pride. "They're shocked I'm so pretty now. They say I look like Mona Lisa. So I have to keep it up, 'cause I don't want to disappoint them."

As you might guess, the David School is very different from the public schools she once attended. In the public school she felt she was a stranger bused in for eight hours a day and then trucked back home. It wasn't her place. At the David School she feels the pride of ownership, a feeling she had earned by helping to cook the students' lunches, by cleaning the gymnasium, by painting the building's exterior with a coat of white twice a year to cover the layers of coal dust, and by earning some money as a clerk in the convenience store operated by the school.

It's not a one-way deal. Whatever she gives to the school, the school pays back to her. Twice a week it sends out an extension teacher to the hollow to teach Celia Robertson, who left school after the eighth grade, to read and write. "I didn't want Myra gettin' too far ahead of me," says Mrs. Robertson. "I weren't too old to learn."

The home teacher also helps out when Mr. Robertson has difficulty getting his monthly disability payments. "Before I could only make my mark," he says. "Now they learned me to write my name."

Regardless of what they've accomplished, Myra's parents are most proud of what *she* has been able to achieve. As I sat talking to them, Celia Robertson, bent over with arthritis, pushed herself out of her chair, reached over to the shelf beneath the television, and brought over a dictionary, which she placed in my lap. "I bought this from a feller from Ohio for thirty-nine dollars," she said, "to help Myra with her words." Mac Robertson, not to be outdone, left the room and returned with an encyclopedia. "For Myra's lessons," he said, and put it on top of the dictionary. By the time I was ready to leave, the books had piled up to my chin.

After we left the house, Myra confided, "I don't really use big words around my parents, 'cause half the time they don't understand what I'm talking about and they might think I'm different, like I'm too perfect, or something. I try to go slow when I'm home."

I asked Myra how she had been changed by going to David School. She said it reminded her of a story she had read about a blind man. "He wouldn't accept he was blind. He tried to do everything else normal people do. Like when his daughter was drowning, he went and saved her. I don't accept that I'm dumb any more. I think I can do anything."

"Anything" included college, perhaps Berea, an outstanding school in Kentucky, or even an out-of-state university. She is thinking about a career in teaching. "When I told my mom I'm thinking about college, she stuck her nose up. She didn't like it at first; she's not used to me being away yet. I told her I'd go someplace where I could come home weekends. That's the first step, getting her used to it." And then? "Then I'd like to live in New York sometime. Or California. I guess I'm just curious. I want to see what's there over the mountain."

Why does the David School succeed with dropouts like Myra Robertson when the public school fails? Public school officials would be quick to point out that the enrollment at David is low, freeing the teachers to devote themselves to the individual student. But I think the real reason for the school's success has more to do with the staff's sense of mission and its relationship to the people who live in Floyd County.

David is a nonsectarian school. But most of the people who work there are lay church workers. They come to this hardscrabble country from Baltimore and Cincinnati and Dubuque prepared to give a year or more of their lives to Floyd County's young people and their families. They are not motivated by money, professional status, or even skill enhancement. What drives them is a faith bordering on the missionary, that good work and earnest commitment can make a difference in the lives of these kids.

Public school teachers and administrators are geographically present in their students' communities during their work hours, but they are socially, emotionally, and culturally detached. David's faculty is not a force acting *on* the community; it is part of the community. No parent has to make an appointment to see a David teacher. If parents have something to talk about, they simply show up, during school hours and after. The entire staff lives within walking distance of the school. Hardly a night goes by when some teacher or staff member at the David School doesn't visit a kid or a parent who has some problem. It could be a father who just has been laid off from the mines. It could be that two kids have gotten into a fight, and the family on the losing side has sworn to dynamite the house of the kid who won. Sometimes the problems concern a student at the school; just as often, the problems affect somebody who doesn't have a child in the school but simply happens to live on this patch of Appalachian earth. "If there's one kid or one family in this community whose life we don't know about, we feel we have failed," says Jean Ford, principal of the David School.

The success that the David School achieves with its public school castoffs and dropouts is directly related to the teachers' understanding of and feeling for them as individuals and for their families. Don't get the idea that the David School coddles its students. Teachers respond to their pupils on a case-by-case basis. When I visited one class, the teacher introduced me to a tall, hulking young man who was sitting in the back of the room. The boy looked, and indeed was, two years older than the others in the class. "This here is Rico," the teacher said. "If you don't get a chance to talk to him, don't worry. He's probably gonna be here for another three years."

When I seemed a bit disconcerted by what I took to be a rather cruel remark, the teacher told me the student had been arrested after he belted his public high school principal. He had been involved in half a dozen brawls at local taverns. He had raised a half-acre of marijuana behind his house. "This is one tough kid," the teacher said. "We don't want him to get the idea that the school is a place for him to hang around in because his father and the cops are putting pressure on him. We want him to know that we expect him to finish school, to graduate, and to get on with his life. If we have to talk tough to get the message across, we know how to do that."

Going, Going, Gone

Why do public high schools seem incapable of educating the very youngsters who are being educated at the David School? If there is one answer to this question, it has to do with the school's expectations. The teachers and administrators at the David School believe, as an article of faith, that each student has the capacity to progress. They recognize that some students are more intelligent and gifted than others. They don't harbor the illusion that simply because students earn high school diplomas they will find jobs in this economically depressed region, or their marriages will be stable, or they will do a wonderful job raising their children. But they are convinced that within the limited purview of the school, young people can taste their first bite of success. And they hope that will inspire them to strive for other successes once they have left. At least they have made a beginning.

The public schools, by contrast, operate on a worst-case scenario. As a class, poor children, the schools believe, will be difficult
to teach. Liberals and conservatives, however disparate their social
and political outlooks, agree on one point: Whatever the school
can do for students, however hard it tries, the kid, more often
than not, will fail. He will end up an uneducated dropout, headed
for jail, welfare dependency, or an early grave.

The expectation of failure paralyzes the attempt to teach and
to learn in a public school where the students are poor. It is
like a nerve gas that deadens everyone—teachers, principals, and
students alike—numbing them to feeling and hope. In its punitive
practices, in its regulatory controls, and in its guarded isolation,
the school comes to resemble a penal institution, with the students
as inmates, the teachers as guards, and the administrators as war-
dens.

Is that too strong? Does it overstate the situation? Consider
what happens in public schools in Kentucky, not the most educa-
tionally progressive state, but not the most backward, either. A
survey conducted by the state department of education estimated
that in a school year there were almost 35,000 suspensions from
all schools—elementary, middle, junior high, and high school—
with most occurring in high schools. More than 1,100 students
were expelled.[31]

High school principals reported that they spent 20 to 30 percent of an average school day disciplining students. Junior high
school administrators estimated that they spent up to 40 percent
of their day disciplining preadolescent youngsters.

Suspension and expulsion are fairly drastic measures for controlling misbehavior. It would seem to follow, then, that suspended and expelled students were guilty of the most serious
offenses. That wasn't what the Kentucky survey found. The leading
reasons for suspension from high school were, ranked in order
of frequency: defiance of authority, chronic tardiness, chronic absence,* and profanity/vulgarity. Some of the *least* frequent offenses were violence and stealing. The policy of suspending
students—particularly disadvantaged students who have no one
with clout to stand up for them—for relatively minor offenses is
practiced throughout the country. A national study by the Chil-

---

* Increasingly, schools are punishing students who are absent by suspending them.
In Texas, for example, a new law provides that five unexplained absences in a school
year are grounds for suspension.

dren's Defense Fund, a child advocacy organization in Washington, concluded that there is a "pervasive intolerance of children who are different . . . the incidence of suspension is more a function of school policies and practices than a student's behavior.[32]

A report by a Kentucky youth advocacy organization observed: "Suspension from school is used frequently as punishment for non-serious, non-threatening behavior."[33] Rather than trying to find out why a student is misbehaving, the school gets rid of the student and the problem. Only 45 percent of high schools in Kentucky said they had established an in-school program as an alternative to suspension or expulsion.

The suspended student doesn't always spend his or her time away from school sleeping late at home or watching television. "Children are frequently taken from school to court and placed in adult jails or in juvenile detention centers for truancy or minor infractions," the advocacy organization said. Some of the teachers and principals I interviewed concede that jail probably isn't the right place for students who cause "problems" in the schools, but dumping a kid in the correctional system is one way (suspension and expulsion are other ways) of exorcising a problem; by locking a kid up, you transfer responsibility from the schools to the courts. While many white youngsters are banished from the schools, this is a punishment that is inflicted disproportionately on minority children. Data gathered by the U. S. Office of Civil Rights show that black students throughout the country are more than three times as likely as white students to be suspended.[34]

Banishing students to the streets is not regarded by many educators as an effective means of changing attitudes and inculcating a love of learning and education. As one Massachusetts organization concerned with educational reform notes, "Suspended and expelled students end up in a nonsupervised, noneducational atmosphere outside of school, increasing the risk of their becoming involved with crime and the criminal justice system."[35]

The practices designed to control and punish troubled and troublesome students *inside* the school aren't much better. Two of the more popular ones are beating them and isolating them.

Getting beaten never did seem natural to Charlie Ayres. What was natural was having fun. Fun was skipping out on school, picking up your best friend, Buddy, heading out to Fish's Packing Company outside Louisville, and dragging the stream that ran alongside it for worms. "Make us fifteen or twenty dollars an hour or so, selling the worms," Charlie says. Fun was piling into his cousin Tom's pickup, busting out all the cylinders, gas pedal down to the floor, zipping across the Indiana state line, doing 80, 90 until you hit Beal's Five Lakes. "And then you lay back in the sun, relax, throw out the line and wait for the fish to bite. Hey, that's fun." Fun was sneaking out of school right after home room, ambling over to Uncle Frank's, lighting up a joint, chugging a few brews, and settling in to watch the ball game. "My people always said if you're going to smoke dope, it's better to do it with your folks than out by yourself."

Charlie and his whole family—aunts, uncles, grandparents— had come across the state from Harlan County to Louisville about ten years before. The neighborhood the Ayreses settled in, south of the Ohio River, was mostly white, mostly Appalachian, mostly poor, and mostly uneducated. Charlie's kin found irregular work fixing cars, repairing machinery, working in the brewery, and sometimes selling things that didn't belong to them. City life didn't change Charlie that much. Like the kids I would meet later in Floyd County, Charlie hated to be cooped up. He loved the outdoors. Fun and sun. "Trouble was, every time I'd go have a little fun, I'd end up getting my ass whupped," Charlie says.

Through junior high and in high school, Charlie developed something of a reputation, not all of it undeserved. He pulled his C's, and sometimes when he got interested even a B, but all the teachers knew he was trouble. If something bad was going on in school, just look out for old Charlie. Even if you punished him for something he didn't do, it just evened out the score, because he'd probably gotten away with a lot that nobody could pin on him.

On the climactic Tuesday morning Charlie was in the third-floor boy's room with a bunch of the guys, gabbing and smoking. In walked a school guard rumored to have had a brief career as a semipro football player. He was on one of his four daily "sweeps," inspecting the halls, bathrooms, locker room, and slop closets—all the hiding places where students shouldn't be but often are.

After smelling Charlie's breath for a whiff of tobacco smoke, the guard marched Charlie down to the administration office. There, along with that morning's lineup of other miscreants, he sat for a half-hour on a wooden bench. It was a scene not entirely unfamiliar to generations of high school students: the boys sitting at the edge of the bench; the school secretaries tapping away at their typewriters, occasionally peering over their glasses at the rogue's gallery. A name is called, and a student walks into the assistant principal's office. There is silence behind the frosted glass of the door, then *thwack,* followed by "ooow!" The boy walks out, face red, head hanging. The voice of authority calls out, "Next."

Now it was Charlie's turn. Standing in front of the assistant principal's desk, he asked, "Don't you want to hear my side?"

The school official was already reaching into the file cabinet for his paddle. "I know all I want to know," he said. "I know you been smokin'."

He walked around to the front of the desk and told Charlie, "Take everything out of your pockets—the change, your wallet, your comb—I want everything out." After Charlie complied, the assistant principal said, "Now touch your toes. Get ready for your five whacks."

Punishment administered, Charlie dismissed, the assistant principal dictated a letter to Charlie's mother, explaining why he deserved and got five "whacks" that morning. In most schools there is no consultation with parents *before* students are beaten.

This was only one of 25,000 times a year that Kentucky school students are disciplined with corporal punishment.[36] It's happened to Charlie many times before, so it was a little hard to understand why he was feeling so aggrieved. Maybe it was the cumulative effect. He's had so many run-ins with the school authorities; he'd been reprimanded and punished so often. School and Charlie simply don't seem to get along.

Whatever the reason, Charlie's blood pressure was rising when he and the school guard squared off again in the bathroom, later that afternoon. They glared at each other and after a few minutes of fierce silence, the next thing you knew they were rolling on the floor, the guard trying to get a choke hold, Charlie kicking him in the head. This time there were no whacks. This time the assistant principal delivered a sterner sentence: Three weeks' suspension.

Two things happened during the three weeks Charlie was out of school. He turned sixteen, the legal age to leave school, and his uncle offered him a job unloading beer trucks. On one side of the scale was money, independence, manhood; on the other side, what? More fights, more humiliation, more suspensions, and all for what? For a piece of paper that says he stuck it out for four years and he's now qualified to unload a beer truck? The scale's unbalanced; all the weight is on one side. The decision has been made for him: Charlie's school days are over.

What happened to Charlie happens to thousands and thousands of high school students. Beatings, threats, and humiliation are instruments of educational policy in public and private high schools today, as they have been throughout this century. Only eight states in the country have prohibited the use of corporal punishment to discipline students. (Hawaii, New York, Rhode Island, New Jersey, Massachusetts, Maine, Vermont, and New Hampshire.) In his recent study of American high schools, Theodore Sizer, former dean of the Harvard Graduate School of Education, says: "The stick is firmly in place in American schools."[37]

Some school administrators argue that threats and beatings are effective in "clearing the air." But Sizer had doubts about their effectiveness. "A school that relies on threat for its motivation eventually provokes unrelenting, hostile reactions by students," he says.

As a problem-solving technique, beatings may have long-term implications for already troubled youngsters. If beatings are accepted as a legitimate means of resolving disputes in school, why shouldn't they be used on the streets? If authority figures in school beat minors, why shouldn't these youngsters use force when they become parents? (Which, in many cases, will happen very soon.) "Corporal punishment teaches that violence is a way to solve problems and contributes to the concept that it is all right to do what you want to do to children," Irwin Hyman, professor of psychology at Temple University in Philadelphia, says.

The schools call it *in-school suspension* or *detention*. But in various parts of the country kids have different names for it: in Louisville, they call it, The Cage; in San Antonio, it's The Hole; in Newport, Kentucky, it's the Rubber Room, as in padded cell. But everywhere it looks pretty much the same.

It's usually an open room; that is, a room with sliding walls on rails, or it's part of the school auditorium. When it's an enclosed room, the door is left open so that other students and teachers may see who has been sent here for punishment. Students who have misbehaved are sentenced to detention for periods ranging

from several days to several weeks, although some students may
be required to spend part of the day in detention for as long as
an entire school term.

Detention time is spent doing make-work exercises. Sometimes this work is assigned by the students' regular teachers. Other
times it is given by the teacher/guard who is assigned to watch
them. Usually the work has little relation to what is being taught
in their classes. Occasionally, they do their homework from one
of their regular classes, but these assignments are not discussed
or corrected during the detention period.

The students are not allowed to talk to each other. They
are not allowed to ask questions of each other or of the supervising
teacher. They are not allowed to turn in their seats or to look
around. They are not allowed to stand up or stretch their legs.
In some schools I visited, if the students turn in their seats or
stare out the door, they are cuffed on the back of their heads
by the supervising teacher. Frequently, they must eat their lunches
in the classroom.

Detention is a punishment meted out for a variety of offenses:
uttering an obscenity, cutting classes, fighting, not doing homework. In all the cities I visited, the practice of detaining students
had three common characteristics: Parents were informed only
after the detention went into effect; there was no right of appeal;
the penalty of detention was imposed without concern for or an
investigation into the student's personal background or private
circumstances.

Some adolescents are clearly disruptive and make it very difficult for a teacher to maintain a semblance of order and organization in the classroom. There are times when they have to be
removed; but it is doubtful whether sitting in silent isolation, staring at a wall, gets to the heart of *why* a youngster rebels or succeeds
in changing his behavior.

No one I spoke to—his parents, school officials, friends—
including Charlie himself, defended his conduct in school. They
all thought he had brought the school's wrath down on him by
persistent misbehavior. Even though he was provoked, they
thought he should have backed down when he was confronted
by the school guard. Charlie acknowledged—as did many of the
people who know him—that he contrived to bring matters to a
head so that he could justify breaking out of what he considered
a prison.

For two years Charlie felt that he was being pushed into a corner; the space that was his own, that he could feel easy and natural in, was shrinking. As he talked about his school days, I could almost hear him gasping for breath.

> My first year in the school we were able to go outside for lunch. This past year we couldn't even go out on the street. Everybody's inside. Keeping all those kids in is dumb, 'cause they need some air during the day. It gets heated up, and everybody gets heated up inside. Everybody wants some air, so everybody tries to sneak out of the building. I understand why they closed the building up. People around the neighborhood were saying like the kids made noise, caused trouble, so they got it like everybody's closed in and stuff.

Before he got to high school, he says, he never felt that he was being held under lock and key. "In grade school they seemed to think your mind was on what you were studying. In high school they thought you were always scheming to get out. Not everybody; just the kids they got their eye on that they call the bad ones."

After the school threw everything it had against him—beatings, detentions, suspensions—they would call his parents. Do something about your kid, the school said. *Control him.* His parents tried to do what the school couldn't. "My father wouldn't hit me or nothing. He's just keep me inside the house. He'd take away my privileges, like going outside Friday and Saturday with my friends. He'd say, You can't go outside for one or two days. So I'd stay in the house, not doing nothing. Just like in detention, not doing nothing."

The circle was closing. The more time Charlie spent in school, the more he tried to get out. The more times he tried to get out, the more time he spent in detention. The more time he spent in detention, the more time he was locked in at home. It's hard to know who precipitated the fight between Charlie and the school guard. Certainly it wasn't planned. But deep down Charlie knew it would take some unimpeachable proof of his incorrigibility to put an end to what he considered a never ending cycle of resistance, accusation, and detention—at school and at home. He thought he was old enough to exert some power over his own life.

As a kid, Charlie wasn't as engaging and moving as some of the others I'd met; certainly I wasn't drawn to him as I was to Nelson Torres, the master vendor of the baseball fields, or to Irene Rogers in Detroit and Myra Robertson in David, Kentucky, both of whom I considered victimized by their parents and the public schools. But with Charlie I did feel a great sense of waste. At the David School, they would have had him outside part of the day, cleaning up an old fishing pond or repairing a school bus. They would have made him feel he was earning his way, doing real work, and winning his stripes as a grownup.

But for a school to do that, to adjust to a student's unspoken needs, requires some understanding of what's going on in the kid's private life. Typically, that understanding is not there. The gap isn't breached between what the school expects of the poor adolescents it's trying to educate, and how the youngsters see their own evolving future.

Two-thirds of the boys and half of the girls I interviewed had been penalized repeatedly with in-school detention and suspensions before they decided to drop out. Would they have stayed in if other means had been used to alleviate their problems? I can't say yes for certain, because so many different in-school and family pressures contributed to their sense of worthlessness, but I do know that the policies of threat and reprisal did not induce them to adhere to the school's rules and to persevere in their studies. When they were beaten, quarantined, and suspended, they concluded, reasonably enough, that the schools had quit on them. School officials may contend that it is not their intention to chase students away, but that is the result, and it's always been the result. In the mid-1970s, the Children's Defense Fund in Washington found that at least 25 percent of all dropouts had been suspended before they dropped out and that another 20 percent had been designated as "behavior" problems by their teachers.[38]

In the past, efforts to reform the public schools have involved the expenditure of vast amounts of money, the introduction of new technology, and the hiring of various experts, so-called learning specialists. "Throughout the 'sixties and 'seventies, we did lots of things, but we never stopped to ask, Why?" says Billy Reagan, superintendent of the Houston Independent School District.[39] "Why are achievement scores going down? Why are kids getting pregnant? Why are they dropping out? Why can't they find a job? The whole emphasis was on process. Someone came up with the idea of new math—here's another process to apply to the issue. No one stopped to ask about the product . . . about the children themselves."

It's much easier to tinker with the process than to change the existing balance of power in the public schools. What needs to be changed is the overall relationship between the people who work in the education industry and their clients—students, especially poor students. To address the needs of the abandoned half of the school population will require a reexamination of all of the social, cultural, political, and economic assumptions that control the treatment of poor children and their families by the schools.

Officially sanctioned punishments—detention, beatings, suspensions—are only the most visible and severe manifestations of educational policies that reinforce existing social, economic, and racial inequities and are effective only in fulfilling the expectation of failure. There are other, less conspicuous practices that may be even more pernicious. Yet they are hardly ever debated and almost never challenged.

I am thinking here of something that happened to Bill Craig, the kid who left home when he was just ten years old and spent most of the next four years surviving in the streets, basements, abandoned houses, all-night restaurants, and railroad sidings of Newport, Kentucky. While Bill was a confused and disturbed youngster, he was clear-minded and tenacious about one thing: He wanted to stay in school.

For three years, he showed up almost every day in junior high, then high school. He passed most of his subjects, a few with B's and A's, his school record showed. Bill says that what kept him in school for so long was a promise he and his fellow wanderer, Johnny Bayley, had made to each other. "I didn't fail because I had Johnny pullin' for me," he said. "Johnny told me, 'Hey, you can't quit—you can't be a bum all your life.' Our friendship kept me goin' to school. We said, We're gonna be somebody. Even with all the drugs I was doin', I still had a mind. We always thought, We're gonna reach the top."

If Bill's perseverence went unnoticed, it was because of a lack of money. In his Newport high school, students were required to pay an annual school fee of $45. They also had to pay to rent textbooks—at a rate of $4 per book. Students who didn't pay the fee and the book rental were punished: They did not receive report cards. "The other kids could get their report cards and show 'em off and say, I got A's and B's. Nobody believed, nobody 'cept Johnny, that I was nothin' but a dopehead."

At the end of each term, the final grades were posted on a wall near the principal's office. That's how Bill would find out how he had done. After a couple of years, the school authorities caught up with Bill. Come up with the money, they told him, or we'll call your parents.

"I don't have the money," Bill told his teacher.

"That's no excuse," the teacher said. "The school needs the money. We'll have to talk to your mother."

That was the last thing Bill wanted. If they called home, they would find out that he had been gone for a long time. They might force him to return. He stayed out of school for a week, and when he came back, he had his friend Johnny call the school and pretend he was Bill's father. Johnny said that Bill's family didn't have the money to pay the school fee. The school authorities compromised; they let Bill stay, but he had to borrow the textbooks from other students or use the ones in the school library. He couldn't take books home to do his homework. And he would never receive a report card.

On the first day of his junior year, Bill Craig got a bill for $187. "I looked at the piece of paper for a long time," Bill remembers. "I thought, Shit, they don't care whether I pass or not. They don't care that I'm still comin' to school. All they care about is the money."

If Johnny had been around still, he might have talked Bill into staying in school. But by then Johnny was gone. "I just got tired of tryin'," Bill says. "I didn't have the money and I didn't want to fight with them no more. What was the point in stayin'?"

Getting Even

Not many of the youngsters I met got themselves kicked out of school by fighting with teachers or other school officials, although in the weeks and months before they dropped out, they were frequently involved in "incidents" with adults that stopped just short of a physical confrontation. But three-quarters of the boys and half of the girls said just before they left, or soon after, that they would "get even" with the school by committing an act of vandalism.

In the year that Charlie Ayres dropped out, Kentucky education officials reported an estimated total of $1,434,000 in damage to school property. In urban schools across the country, the destruction inflicted by vandals costs many millions of dollars every year. Windows are smashed. Fires are set in waste containers. Mimeograph machines are wrecked.

When I questioned dropouts about crimes they committed on the street, almost 80 percent of the males and approximately half of the females said the first time they broke the law was not on the street but when they vandalized their schools. I knew for a fact that wasn't true. Some had been picked up by the police for robbery and selling drugs while they were still students. But I thought it was revealing that they remembered the destruction they had caused in school as their first criminal act. I think their vandalism left such a deep impression because it was a different kind of crime from the ones they committed earlier or later on the streets. Their street crimes were for thrills or profit. What they did in school was a crime of passion.

In 1959 a Los Angeles youth counselor found a clear pattern to adolescent crimes:

> They started out by breaking into schools. They went to the junior high that most of them had attended. They went into the rooms and they were starting to swipe things there—typewriters—and they would throw things around and just mess it up in general. . . . Then from there they learned to get into businesses from roofs. . . . They get bolder and bolder and they start doing things. . . . This really spread.[40]

Ten years later in Newark, the pattern hadn't changed. William Sosa, who was later to become a youth worker in Newark, had moved to the city from Perth Amboy. He was almost sixteen in 1969 and in his first year of high school after being left back twice in the eighth grade. In his freshman year, he had been absent about seventy-five times. He had been picked up several times by the police, who suspected that he had participated in robberies and because he wore the colors of a gang that had been involved in a lot of street fights. Willie Sosa remembers:

> I been on the street for a long while, doin' things, B's and E's and things, and then I found the sex scene. Instead of goin' to class we'd go to a girl's house. The mothers and fathers

were working, and we'd have a party—drink, pop pills, sex, and the whole bit. The reason I enjoyed it like hell was because there was no violence. You could do bad things and have fun, but nobody was breakin' heads.

Nobody I ever met in school tried to do anythin' about it. One teacher, he used to call to me, "Hey, man, you got a chill on you? You're one bright kid, and you're just ruinin' your life. You bein' like everybody else. Where you goin' to be twenty years from now?" But they were just words. He didn't do no more than talk.

Inside I was really hurtin', although I didn't want to admit it. I was hurtin' my mother. I was hurtin' myself in the streets. I was hurtin' all over. I just didn't want to be part of that any more. I wanted to escape, I wanted to change my life. The first semester of high school I scored very high in my class. But I couldn't see myself continuing up to the twelfth grade. I was saying, I'll be nineteen when I get out of here, twenty. So I wanted a way out—and the school and me, we worked out a way.

One day me and my buddies went outside after one of the classes and bought some Gypsy Rose from bums and we started drinkin' and drinkin' and drinkin' and drinkin'. We got drunk and went to class. You could smell our breaths all over class. And the teacher was gettin' up and we caused a ruckus. And they had to throw us out. But I didn't give a damn about that. I was fed up with it anyway. And my boys, the guys I hung out with, they were fed up with it, too.

That night it hit me. The school was over and I was out on the street and my mother would go crazy and what did I have? What was I goin' to do? Three guys we knew, they were a couple of years older, they'd spent time in reform school, and one of them said, "Let's do somethin' to that school of yours." I was really mad, crazy mad, and I went with them. I'd never broke into a school before, but this night I wanted to. We got a window open and got inside and went crazy. We ripped the arms off the phonographs. We stole cameras. We found the money they kept for the school trips, and we took it.

And then I went to the room of the teacher that threw me out that morning. I pulled my pants down. I opened the drawer of his desk. And I took a gigantic crap. It was like I unloaded everything inside of me.

When we got out of the school building, we couldn't stop. We took trains all over Jersey that night. We went city to city

looking for schools to bust into. We did a chain of nine schools
that night, and when we got back I had $125. When it was
over I was jittery. I'd never done that before. I was saying,
Wow, this is too much. But there was another part of me that
didn't give a damn. I was striking back at the educational system
and it felt good. I could be just as tough and rough with them
as they was with me.

Edward Armistead in Cleveland; Ralph Ortiz the gang leader
in Chicago; Deezie, the girl who was reviled in the class in New
York; Irene Rogers, the bright young woman whose mother kept
her out of school in Detroit; Willie Sosa rampaging through the
schools of New Jersey; Charlie Ayres, the Louisville kid who
wanted to get out in the sun; Myra Robertson, who lived in an
Appalachian hollow where the school bus never stopped; Ruby
Howard, the perpetually enraged teenager in Newark who went
looking for her father; Bill Craig, who couldn't afford the price
of staying in school—all faces in a crowd. Black faces, white faces,
Hispanic faces. By the end of the century there will be four and
a half million youngsters like them—already on the streets or
on the verge of dropping out.
　　Their departure won't even be a matter of record, because
the deceptive data reported by the schools will hide the fact that
they dropped out. Educational "reformers" will contend that they
simply weren't intelligent enough to meet the new, elevated standards for academic success. They won't say anything about
whether the schools encouraged them to stay in or whether they
tried to do anything to repair the damage these youngsters had
suffered at home and in their neighborhoods. The qualities of
compassion and empathy, absent from their educational experience, will not be noted. No one will recall that the schools gave
up on them before they gave up on themselves; that, in their
last days, the instruments of control and containment—detention,
suspension, expulsion—obliterated whatever was taught in the
classroom.
　　It will be hard to remember that all of these kids once looked
to the schools to lead them on the long climb out of poverty,
dependency, and social chaos. There will be no photographs of
Ralph Ortiz stiffly marching into assembly in his white shirt and
red tie; no photographs of Ruby Howard performing in the school
orchestra or of Irene Rogers beaming when she got her "A" in

history. Who will recall that these youngsters, much like the Eskimo kids in that tiny frozen village of Stebbins, once reached out for that other America they read about in their schoolbooks and saw every night on their television screens?

The saddest loss of all—but one the children of the poor learn to expect—will be the denial of distinction. Grouped within the category of "School Failure/Dropout," they will all be seen by the outside world of seekers and doers as inert matter—one compressed mass. Yet each of them leaves school as much an individual as when they entered. There is Nelson Torres, who has won the title of wizard purveyor of arroz con pollo on the baseball diamonds of Manhattan; there is Irene Rogers, who knows she is as smart as anybody in that Detroit school; there is Ruby Howard, who never doubts that she will be acclaimed as Newark's Diana Ross; there is Charlie Ayres, who the Louisville school says can't be taught but who knows how to take apart and put together a car engine in less than half an hour; and there is Myra Robertson, who the public schools of Floyd County, Kentucky, are sure can't read above the third grade level but who has already consumed three hundred books in her dark, cold hideaway.

When the schools deny that the dropout is an individual with special assets and singular ambitions, all they're doing is looking ahead. They assume that with a little time in the streets the dropout will be consigned to yet another category of failure: Irene Rogers, Unwed Mother; Ruby Howard, Welfare Recipient; Nelson Torres, Drug Dealer; Bill Craig, Juvenile Offender. Schools aren't stupid; they know failure begets failure.

That certain prophecy of failure can drive a kid a little nuts. It can make you do something really crazy just to prove the school's wrong. This is what Eddie Armistead was thinking about: doing something really crazy to show them he wasn't just another sadsack flunk-out. Eddie, whose mother had tried to tie him to a chair to keep him off the streets, whose elementary school teacher locked him in a closet to punish him, had been kicked out of school two weeks before. Now, he was standing in the parking lot of his high school in Cleveland. It was Prom Night. Eddie watched the dressed-up kids filing, hand in hand, into the auditorium. Eddie wasn't sure why he was there. Maybe he'd try to pick up some girl who'd had a fight with her date. Maybe he'd sneak a drink from somebody's bottle. Maybe he'd pick a fight with some fancy dude and score his wallet. Eddie weaved between the lines of parked cars, waiting for something to happen.

Inspiration struck. There it was: a red and tan Nightrider Camaro. Mrs. Levinson's Nightrider Camaro. The same Mrs. Levinson who had thrown him out of English class, biting off the words: "You are not going to ruin one more day of my life."

Eddie quickly arrived at an estimate—it would take thirty seconds, a minute, no more. It was an expert estimate. Eddie had been picked up by the police three times on suspicion of auto theft, although he had never been charged. Too slick. Friends had told him that the police in the station house near the housing project where the Armisteads lived, had hung Eddie's picture on the wall. Eddie could imagine the caption under the sketch: Eddie Armistead, the best car thief in Cleveland.

He took a piece of a plastic Venetian blind slat out of his pocket and tickled the lock on the car door. Ten, fifteen seconds and he was inside. *Bust it down, pop the pin.* Twenty seconds and Eddie was moving. He spun the car around, aimed for a couple, guy in a white jacket, girl in a frilly dress, and made them jump to get out of the way. Eddie took a turn on two wheels. The tires squealed. He gunned the motor. Eddie roared across the parking lot, narrowly missing a couple of parked cars, then sideswiped somebody trying to park his father's Buick.

Now where to go? What to do? He could leave the car parked on the other side of the city. He could take it over to the Puerto Rican who ran a chop shop out in the country, strip it down, and come home with 150 bucks in his pocket. He could do that, but who would know what had happened? He didn't want only to steal a car. He wanted to leave his mark. He wanted to make a statement.

It came to him. At the back of the school building a concrete bunkerlike extension jutted out from the wall. The extension housed the school's auto repair workshop. Eddie stopped the car about 20 feet from the shop, slipped it into drive, floored the gas pedal, and jumped out. The car bounced off the wall, crumpling the front end, smashing the headlights. A plume of smoke rose from under the hood. *Now, that's something to keep the school busy—a thousand dollars in bodywork on Mrs. Levinson's Camaro.* Eddie walked away.

A few hours later a couple of cops were pounding on his

apartment door. After they roused him from his bed, one of the cops said, "We know you did it, Eddie. We know you busted up her car just to get even with her."

Eddie said, "I don't know what you're talking about. I'm not even in that school any more."

"Don't get smart with me," the cop said.

"You got the wrong guy. I'm not smart enough to do somethin' like that. I'm just a dumb guy who got kicked out."

I wasn't there when Eddie said that, but I imagine the expression on his face was the same as when he told me that story. He was grinning broadly, the jack-o'-lantern grin of victory. But I could have been wrong. It could have been the grimace of defeat.

FIVE

Street Life

Running in Place

I once spent time with the young nomads of Brazil. They were streaming south, by the thousands, from the sertão, the parched interior of the northeast. One of Brazil's periodic droughts had struck the backlands, turning the region into a gigantic dustbowl. The young, some no older than seven or eight, clogged the roads, hitching rides on trucks and vans, riding mule carts, walking a thousand miles. They carried all of their belongings on their backs.

They were trying to reach Brazil's great cities—Recife, Salvador, Rio de Janeiro, and São Paulo. Some died on the way. The strongest ones finally found a place in one of the poor *alagados* of Salvador, neighborhoods built on stilts over swamps filled with raw sewage, where one of every two children contracted tuberculosis before the age of two. The hardiest among them managed to make it to the *favelas* of Rio, where they lived amid the clotted mass of humanity clinging to the mountainsides overlooking the gleaming pink and white city.

In the cities, some of them would move in with a family friend or a distant relative. Others, not so fortunate, would band together with other children, living in drainpipes or shanties or sometimes just out in the open. They would spend their childhoods scavenging for pennies to purchase food, clothes, and water.

A government report in 1985 estimated that some 7,000,000 Brazilian children were living alone, severed from their families; in the international argot of social scientists, they were termed "marginalized" children. The report also said that 60 percent of Brazilians under the age of eighteen—36 million people—were living in poverty, and one-third of all the children in the country between the ages of seven and fourteen did not attend school.[1] It seems strange to say of children in danger of dying of thirst and starvation, but I think they were animated by a greater sense of purpose than the children who roam the streets of America.

The Brazilian kids were headed somewhere. They had a destination. Some of the youngest and most innocent shared a naïve faith that the glitter and glamour of the big cities would somehow rub off on them, if God smiled. The more knowing of them did not expect an economic miracle at the end of their journey, but they hoped to find the sustenance they needed to keep them alive. Hope transported them.

Most of the American kids I met weren't going anywhere. Some exceptions, most of them white middle-class and lower-middle-class youngsters, left towns like Bakersfield and Modesto in California, and landed in Los Angeles and San Francisco.* A scattering of poor teenagers who lived in remote rural communities—Appalachian mining settlements, Indian reservations in Oregon and Washington, migrant workers' camps in Texas and Michigan—struck out on their own or with a friend in the direction of the big city, where they thought they could find a hustle or a job. A few kids who lived on the fringes of large metropolitan areas bounced back and forth between their home towns and the city—Newport, Kentucky, kids could walk across a short bridge to Cincinnati.

The youngsters who took off for another part of the country were often motivated by romance or fear or both. Typically, they had become involved with a boyfriend or girlfriend whom their parents disliked. If they stayed in their old neighborhood, their parents or other adults might try to break up the relationship.

---

* The most mobile kids I met seemed to be on the West Coast and in some smaller Midwestern cities like Topeka. They were kids who had grown up in a car culture, where it was common to drive at eleven or twelve, and where for a hundred dollars or less they could buy and repair an old car. With a couple of days' work, they could make it run long enough to get them where they wanted to go.

In the first forty-eight hours after arriving in a new city, they were often picked up by the police, who held them until their parents reclaimed them.

Despite the recurring image in popular literature of great waves of runaway youngsters rolling across the country, the preponderance of adolescents I met hadn't ridden the rails or hitched hundreds of miles as some hungry and homeless castoffs did during the Depression of the 1930s. They weren't drawn to Haight-Ashbury in San Francisco or the East Village in New York, as self-styled rebels were in the peak of the 1960s drug culture. More than 70 percent of the 230 black and Hispanic young men and women remained, when I met them, in the same city where they had grown up. If they had moved to a new neighborhood, it had pretty much the same ethnic, racial, and economic makeup as their old one. Black kids in New York City took a subway from Brownsville to Bedford-Stuyvesant; Hispanic youngsters in Chicago caught a city bus from Humboldt Park to Pilsen.

Although they were living in neighborhoods familiar to them, they had made a change in their lives that was much more serious and frightening than dropping out of school. At least when they left school, they could fall back on some structure, organization, and routine within their families. They knew they had to get out of bed. They knew there were certain duties they had to perform— washing the clothes, straightening the bed. They had to answer to somebody in the family.

The rules were suspended when they hit the streets. They had no place to retreat to, no place to hide. Brute strength and animal cunning were their only defenses against the ever present danger. They communicated in a shout. They walked with a swagger. They zapped strangers with a murderous glare. Yet, even with their armory of guns and knives, they knew they were as likely to become victims as they were to be victimizers.

Those street kids could talk about how much they wanted to be independent—free from the school and welfare bureaucracies, free from the strictures imposed by their parents. But their claims to freedom and independence were fatally compromised by their own deep foreboding. No matter how tough they thought they were, their vaunted freedom and independence could be snuffed out in one sudden, final eruption. You can brag about freedom all you want, but out on the street no one controls his own destiny.

The bravado they assumed was also sapped by a feeling of

personal guilt. While the Brazilian youngsters attributed their misfortune to natural calamities beyond their control—drought, starvation, pervasive poverty—"marginalized" American youths
blamed themselves for their plight. They had failed at school.
They had failed in their own families. They had failed because
they couldn't win their daily bread.

Having failed in school, they had an even lower status within
their families than their younger brothers and sisters, who could
still identify themselves as students. They had nothing to attach
themselves to, no identity. Besides, as dropouts, they had little
chance of getting a job and contributing to the family income.
They were excess baggage. Implicitly or directly, their families
had sent them a message: If you can't produce anything of worth,
you might as well leave. Some youngsters tried to persuade themselves that if they left, they could find a way to gain respect and,
ultimately, return as self-sustaining, contributing adults. But they
knew they weren't likely to rehabilitate themselves on the street.
Still, what choice did they have? Where else could they go?

Once separated from their families, they didn't want to be
reminded of how they had screwed up. So they didn't hook up
with kids who were still in school or with adults who had a straight
job. They sought out other kids who had already dropped out
or were about to. Often they were a little older, a little more
streetwise, and they had some experience living by themselves.
Youths who were now out on their own found young people who
shared their guilt, their frustration, and, particularly, a generalized
suspicion and hostility toward the controlling institutions of the
community: schools, intact families, the welfare and juvenile justice systems.

Those alliances formalized relationships that had existed before they had left home and school. The friends they made on
the street were commonly people their parents had warned them
against: adolescent sisters and cousins who had been cast out
by their families because they had become pregnant and were
raising children on their own; youngsters who were known in
the community—even if they weren't known by the police—as
delinquents; kids who shuttled between shelters, foster homes,
detention facilities, and correctional institutions. By associating
and identifying with those outsiders, the youngsters I met had
begun to dissociate themselves from their parents even before
they actually moved out.

You might say it was a case of pariahs seeking out pariahs, except that these kids lived in neighborhoods where almost everybody functioned on the fringes of American society. They had been raised and were coming of age in communities where the dominant industries were numbers and drug-dealing; where the official unemployment rate exceeded 15 and 20 percent; where more kids dropped out of school than graduated, and where adolescent pregnancies, single-parent female-headed households, and welfare dependency had now become *the* traditional family. The youngsters, who had dropped out of school and left home, blended right in.

Sticking close to home turf was a practical and rational decision. They knew who had the power. They knew who might protect them if they got into trouble. Although they had distanced themselves from their families, they wanted to stay close enough so they could get an adult relative to show up if they found themselves in a police station at midnight. A key to survival was thinking ahead.

They also knew that life wouldn't be any better for them if they moved to a new city. Brazilian kids might hope for manioc and beans and a corrugated tin roof in the city, but the American youngsters couldn't see any improvement in moving from the slums of Detroit to the slums of Boston. If anything, they would be in greater peril alone and unprotected in a strange place. The white kids seemed much more prepared to uproot themselves. If they were slick, articulate, and attractive, they might find a protector, figure out a hustle, even pick up a straight job. The black and Hispanic kids knew better. So most of them stayed put.

Living by the Code

What do you do when you're waiting to grow up? How do you kill time, how do you kill three or four years when you're out on the street? The stock answer—repeated almost word for word on Eighteenth Avenue in Chicago, on Lyons Avenue in Houston, on Woodward Avenue in Detroit, on Avenue D on the Lower East Side in Manhattan—is: There's nothing much to do. Richard Wilson, a black seventeen-year-old I met in Tompkins Square Park on the Lower East Side of Manhattan, has the stock answer down pat:

Everything's the same. The first thing when it's warm you wake
up in the morning and go outside in the park. You drink,
smile a little bit. That's the main recreation—just gettin' high,
gettin' drunk. I used to run drugs, numbers. If you have a
bag of herb, you make a few j's, make a few dollars dealin'.
Right away, you blow the money.

When it's cold out, you watch TV, you try to get laid,
you hang out with the home boys, in the cellar, in somebody's
crib, wherever some one'll let ya, and ya scheme for Friday
night. You think about gettin' an ounce of herb for the party
Friday night, so a little girl'll think you got somethin' goin'.
Can you hustle up a new pair of jeans? Can you hustle up a
new piece of gold so you show a little flash when you hit on
the little girl?

Sometimes when I'm just sittin' here on the bench and
nobody's around, I get to thinkin', I'm just another hangout
artist. I'm sayin' to myself, Aaaah, another day, aaaah another
day. And then I'm thinkin': There's only one way I can go—
down.

Richard isn't down yet. He's still thinking about what he's
doing, what's happening to him. When I think of down, rock-
bottom down, I think of another bench in a vest-pocket park in
Pioneer Square in Seattle. The park is situated on the original
Skid Row in the United States. Loggers once rolled their logs
from the top of a hill to the waterfront. Today Skid Row runs
from Seattle's commercial center, past the revitalized Pioneer
Square area to the flourishing Pike Street market. At nineteen,
Martha Rainwater, sitting there on a bench in the park, has almost
reached the end of Skid Row.

Martha was sitting next to a faded denim laundry bag contain-
ing all of her possessions. A bottle of wine inside a paper bag
rested on her lap. It had showered earlier, and her coal-black
hair was matted against her scalp. The temperature was in the
sixties this gray September afternoon, but Martha was shivering.

Martha was a Kwakiutl Indian. She left her reservation school
when she was fourteen. She doesn't talk much about her family.
Her brother was serving a seven-to-ten-year sentence for armed
robbery. Her mother had disappeared. Her father had drunk himself to death. When she was eleven, her father raped her.

There are two people she remembers when she thinks of
the past, which she doesn't very often except when she dreams,
and her dreams are frequently set in that small reservation school

and in motel rooms. In school she had a teacher who taught her to sew. "She thought I was very nimble-fingered," Martha recalls, her words trailing off. "I don't remember how to do it any more."

The other person she dreams about is Rodney. He picked her up one night when she was hitchhiking near Olympia, Washington. For a year, she says, they stayed together. They would target medium-size towns in Washington and Oregon, usually located near military bases. Martha would pick up a serviceman in a local bar and go to a motel room with him. Rodney would follow them, slug the guy, and take his money. "We had some good times," Martha says. "We stayed in some nice hotel rooms. But he left me one night. I was losin' my looks and I wasn't makin' all that much money for him. An' he found someone younger."

The longest she held a job was for three months in a leather-tanning factory. "The chemicals made me sneeze and throw up. Besides, the foreman was always wantin' me to fuck. If I had to fuck, I could do it on the street and make more than in that lousy place."

On nice days Martha spends a lot of her time on a park bench. If she's up to it, she works the tourist trade in Pioneer Square for handouts. "I do better when I do my Indian talk," she says. "But I'm not doing so good since my hair started to fall out." What she manages to hustle goes for wine or for a room in one of the flophouses that have escaped urban revitalization. No more nice motel rooms for Martha. She often steals food at the Pike Street market. Martha isn't interested in hearing about schools and jobs and government programs. The time for that has passed. She's nineteen and old. All she wants from me is to be paid for her time. "Two dollars for an hour," she says. "The price of a bottle. That's the minimum wage, isn't it?"

Martha Rainwater gives the word "underclass" precise meaning. I am an optimist, but I don't know if she can be saved. As I got to know many youngsters, listened to the descriptions of their schools and families, and watched them cross off their days on the street, I had to fight against the premonition that even the most spirited kids were trapped in an irreversible decline, a disastrous slide from that park bench in Tompkins Square to that park bench in Pioneer Square. I had to struggle against the conclusion that there was no way out for any of them.

It wasn't so much what they said about their lives on the

street, but how they said it that distressed me. Everywhere I went, I heard the echo of Richard Wilson's flat monotone, evoking his adolescence as an unbroken chain of defeat—"Aaaah another day, aaah another day"—leading inevitably to a condition of total help-lessness. After a while, I learned that Richard and many of the other youngsters I met were instinctively tailoring their responses to what they thought I wanted to hear. I was in my forties, with graying hair, fumbling as I changed the casettes in my tape re-corder. I'm sure many of these kids thought: Why should this guy be any different from any of the other adult authority figures I've met in my life? (The black and Hispanic kids were probably thinking: *White* authority figure.) They assumed that I agreed with the judgment of their parents and teachers: They were incurable screw-ups, destined to end up like the stagnant pool of kids behind the liquor store in Fort Lauderdale, like Martha Rainwater hustling the price of a bottle of Thunderbird in Seattle.

It was only after I spent some time hanging out with them—not questioning them so much, but listening and watching—that I realized to some extent they had bought the view of adults who proclaimed them failures and outcasts. After all, they had been getting that message for a long time from a lot of people who seemed to know what they were talking about. The subgroup that resisted that judgment was composed of white, middle-class kids. Many had received considerable affirmation in school and at home. They had been exposed to a smattering of psychological theory, and some had undergone therapy when they began having difficulties. Their view was that they were going through a hard time now, but it was only a passing phase. The minority youngsters didn't think their troubles were temporary; everything everybody said persuaded them that the present was rotten and the future wasn't going to be much better, and it was this barren perspective that they were feeding back to me now.

Despite that deep and sometimes immobilizing pessimism on the most basic level they resembled so-called normal young-sters between the ages of twelve and nineteen, those who were still in school and at home. They were all trying to invent their lives. Experimenting, innovating, improvising, they went about the business of becoming *somebody*.

Self-change, psychic tinkering, personal reevaluations—these are very popular activities in American culture. For a time in the 1970s it seemed that half the corporate executives in the country were planning to go to Vermont and open an inn. But they had already achieved some personal goals—established families, held responsible jobs and succeeded in their first career. Street kids who searched for alternatives to their past failures were starting from scratch. They had no track record of past achievements and no confidence that they were competent at anything but running.

And they lacked something else. They lacked time. The college-bound high school graduate is also under pressure to make a preliminary decision on vocation and career, but he may change his major in college, may shift to a new graduate course of study, and once out in the work world may reconsider his vocational direction many times. But the dropout learns that making a commitment to a future occupation or vocation may be a life-and-death matter. The longer the dropout drifts on the street, he finds, the shorter his life-expectancy. Every straight adult he meets tells him the same thing: Decide; decide now; lay out the rest of your life; tell me what you're going to do and how you're going to do it.

From within and without the kid is under terrific pressure to define his future. Based on what he's experienced in his street life, he tries to come up with some answers. He says, I want to have fun. He says, I don't want to be bored, I want an exciting job. He says, I want to believe in somebody, I don't want to be alone any more. Those responses may sound like the fuzzy yearnings of a typically muddled adolescent, which, to some extent, they are. But they also represent the rational extensions of the basic themes that have shaped the youngster's life on the street. These themes make sense only if we understand what the kid's been through.

In their unhappy years at home and in school and in their struggles on the streets, certain needs and values are dominant:

- These youngsters want to live melodramatically. They are still drawn to the danger, excitement, and volatility of adolescence.

- They want to find a place in a community that accepts them.

- They want to complete the unfinished business between them and their parents—but on their own terms and in their own time.

- They want to separate themselves from the public bureaucracies that they depend on and that seek to control them.

- They insist on adhering to a personal code that values honor, courage, and fidelity; but in the Darwinian culture where they are trying to grow up, these virtues have been corrupted into justifications for violence and destruction.

- They seek a companionship, a kinship with peers and adults that is, at once, both nonjudgmental and directive. They don't want to be told about how they have failed. They do want to be told how to succeed.

These themes give a rough shape and order to their disordered lives. They are not peculiar to estranged adolescents. Secure and reasonably well-adjusted teenagers and not a few adults embrace them. What these needs and values mean and how they're expressed can be very different, depending on whether a teenager is on Main Street U.S.A. or in the alleys of the South Bronx. On Main Street, loyalty may mean lending a little money to a friend who has lost his job. For a kid in the South Bronx, it means coming up with an alibi for a buddy who's been charged with breaking into a liquor store.

Can the controlling themes of the street be reshaped so they apply to life in the mainstream? That's the million-dollar question for youngsters who want to break with their past and for the adults who are trying to help them. Can a concerned and sensitive mentor persuade a street kid who's drawn to the excitement of the gangs that it's also exciting to master a skill and excel in a job? Can you persuade a kid who's learned that trust is rewarded with a knife in the back to put his faith in a mentor, a teacher, a boss?

Getting a kid to suspend the suspicion and hostility that are his natural defenses on the street is a tough sell. It's especially tough because kids know that there's more to making it in the mainstream than shedding your personal liabilities. You must also circumvent the enormous barriers of racism and class prejudice. But in those rare instances when a teenager is shrewd or lucky enough to overcome the obstacles of race and class, he or she must still have the courage to reject the code of the streets. Otherwise, the street code, by which they have lived for so long, will drag them down to the depths of a Martha Rainwater, playing out the string on a park bench in Seattle. It will cut them off, destroy them. That is the strange and bitter fruit of growing up alone in America.

Courting Danger

I was raised by protective if somewhat hysterical parents. So I looked around for an occasional adventure to break the routine of growing up. Adventure for me, as for most children, involved a certain element of risk. If you weren't a little scared when you were doing something "bad"—if there wasn't a chance that you might be caught—it wasn't very exciting. So I refused to step aside when I ran into a couple of kids from the School of the Transfiguration during the height of the Jew-bashing season, although I knew I'd be bringing home a black eye for dinner. I stole *Classic Comics* from the corner candy store, certain that if I were caught, Ruth, the owner, would be on the hot line to my mother, demanding twenty years in the slammer for her hoodlum son.

I allowed myself those few cautious acts of rebellion because I could be reasonably certain that, on the whole, my life was pretty safe. A welcoming haven awaited me after one of my sporadic transgressions. I also knew that my parents had put me on the conveyor belt to a respectable adulthood: bar mitzvah, high school graduation, college, a vocation. I might take a few chances along the way, but I wasn't going to wander far.

The path followed by the young people I have been describing doesn't lead in any clear direction. There are no landmarks to measure progress toward the goal of secure and sane maturity. In their lives, drama takes the place of progress. The drama that unfolds at home and on the street is so much more exciting and involving than the calibrated crawl offered in school or in a sheltered middle-class household.

Tears for the social worker in the morning. Shooting up in the afternoon. The sound of gunshots in the night. The sudden departures: Papa's disappeared; sister's run away; brother's been sent to jail. That is their melodrama of childhood and adolescence. To sustain interest, you have to bet more, invite greater risk, court disaster. Without danger the drama is empty. The tension is in the uncertainty. Can you get over for one more day, improvise to survive one more deadly encounter—and live to talk about it tomorrow?

Now rationally, logically, Marta Albert shouldn't be here at all. She should be back in Bedford-Stuyvesant, where she knows people. She shouldn't be in Brownsville, feeling for the wall, inching her way along this dark hallway in Brooklyn, climbing the creaking steps to the fourth floor, where she's been told she can buy some dope. Marta's been around. She's fifteen now, and she's been on her own for more than two years. She's boosted clothes out of the downtown Brooklyn department stores, jostled handbags and wallets, done a few other things. In that time, she's developed a sixth sense. She can smell danger. Here she is, a pretty young woman, wearing the gold chains and bracelets favored by young people in her native Guyana. Here she is, alone, in a strange building, going to do business with strange people.

Breaking all the hard-learned rules of self-preservation, she climbs the stairs. The moth finds the flame. She knocks on the door. An eyeball inspects her through the peephole. Marta knows the drill: slip twenty bucks into the slot, out comes the grass. But not this time. The door swings open, and three men encircle her on the landing. Behind them she can see maybe a dozen other men in the room.

"What are you doin' here?" one man wants to know.

Marta presses against the wall. Her mouth is dry. She has always suffered from a stammer; now she can't get a word out.

"Now that's pretty," says one of the men. Is he talking about her or her jewelry? He yanks the chains off her neck. Holding her arm, he pulls off her bracelets. "Now," he says, "how about you?"

Marta has heard that question before. "I didn't sleep around like the other girls who were on the street," Marta would say later. "Even though I was bad, doing other things, I was very shy. I used to give the guys a hard time, so they gave me a hard time. They'd call me a bitch. But I knew I was never a bitch. All they wanted was for me to sleep with them, give them lays."

Only a few weeks before this encounter, she had narrowly escaped being raped. She had been held at knife-point in the apartment of a guy who she was sure was safe, because he was romancing her girlfriend. "This guy took a big knife out for me, and told me to pull down my pants. I was crying and I said, 'I'll take it off, just WAIT, WAIT, WAIT.' And I jumped out the window, right through the glass, and landed in the alley downstairs. I'm nice at conning people. Nobody ever raped me, 'cause I always got the intelligence from somewhere to con them out of it."

Except now, in the hallway in the Brownsville tenement, Marta can't come up with a con. Three guys drag her into the room, rip her blouse off, tell her exactly what they want her to do. Marta whispers through her tears, "No, no. Just kill me, I ain't gonna give it up."

They pull her up a flight of stairs, take her out onto the roof, march her out to the edge. "Just kill me," Marta screams. "Throw me off the roof. Then when I'm dead you can do to me what you want, 'cause I'm not giving it up."

"You think you're so good," says one guy. "Girlie, we'll show you how good you are."

One of the men grabs her ankles, another pushes her. She is held dangling over the edge. It's an eight-story fall to the pavement. This time she won't be as lucky as she was when she jumped out of the window and suffered only a sprained ankle. This time, she thinks, I'll die.

Just then a man she knows from her neighborhood, who has also come to the building to buy drugs, hears her screams, sees her on the roof. He shouts up, "She's my girl. You hurt her, you get hurt." Maybe the guy has enough weight to stop the men on the roof; maybe they never intended to kill her, only to terrorize her so that she would submit to them. For whatever reason, they free her. Marta has gotten over—she'll live to talk about it tomorrow.

And tomorrow she thinks: *This is not me. It's not right for me to be out there on the roof with those guys. I need help. I need to change myself.*

But the fear that forces self-examination fades quickly in the maelstrom of the street. Her bravado is restored when she tells her friends about how she survived her latest brush with death. A few months later, Marta is arrested when she's caught burglarizing someone's house. She's sent up for a year in a juvenile detention center.

After she served her time, Marta returned to New York, to her old haunts and to her home girls. A condition of her probation was that she had to participate in a program that combined remedial education and a part-time job. I asked her whether she thought she would complete the program. She didn't answer the question. "I'm tougher now," she said. "I'm quicker than before. I learned from being sent away, if you know how to take care of yourself, you can make it out there." Out where? I wondered. Out in the

job world, in the straight world? Or out on the street? I got my
answer a few days later: Marta disappeared. She was out in the
jungle again, sliding in and out of danger, risking everything—
and, I hope, living to talk about it tomorrow.

"When you start the day hanging out," Marta told me, "you
never know how it's gonna finish." If you come into this world
from a secure place it's almost impossible to comprehend just
how dangerous simply "hanging out" is. In a two-week period
in 1983, researchers interviewed 118 boys and girls, equally divided, under the age of seventeen, who had been admitted to
youth shelters in New York City. Twenty-five of the girls said
they had been raped. (Ninety-three percent of those interviewed
were black or Hispanic.) The number of actual victims may be
much higher; some of the victims may not have wanted to talk
about it.

Rape was not the only peril they feared. One-third of the
young women said they had been pregnant. Sixty percent of these
young men and women said their parents had been convicted
of a crime, took drugs, or drank excessively. Half of those interviewed had been abused by one or both parents. Two-thirds of
them felt they could not return home again. Seventy-eight percent
of the boys and 47 percent of the girls reported "contact with
the law." Thirty-seven percent of the males and 19 percent of
the females had been charged previously with an offense, usually
assault or robbery.

Living dangerously, unsurprisingly, took a psychological toll.
The researchers reported that by "using a number of different
criteria it seems that mental health problems are present in between 70 percent and 90 percent of the youth." One-third of
the girls and 15 percent of the boys said they had attempted
suicide. Many of those who hadn't actually attempted it said they
were thinking about it. Altogether, two-thirds of these teen-agers
had tried or given thought to destroying themselves.

"Shelter users have a psychiatric profile," the researchers
observed, "largely indistinguishable from adolescents attending
a psychiatric clinic."[2]

Kids who turn up in shelters may be more unprotected and
vulnerable than others in the depressed urban communities of
this country, who have some place to stay and are still involved

in social and educational programs. But the specter of fear and danger follows all of them through their adolescence. They never feel safe. Dodging catastrophe becomes *the* city game; everybody plays, and almost everybody loses.

In the small town of Danby, Vermont, Susan Curnan directed a training program for impoverished young women. They often told her that they were upset because men made suggestive or obscene remarks to them on the way to their training sites. For a while, Curnan served as an adviser to a training program for young women in Harlem. The women in Harlem were as poor as the women in Vermont, but there was a difference. All sixteen girls in the New York City program told her that they had been assaulted or raped *as they traveled to school. These were not street kids. They were school kids.* "The severity of their lives was so much greater," Curnan says. "The kids in New York have just been more severely damaged."

Crimes of Complicity

Everybody knows that street kids commit crimes, but not everybody is aware that their silent partners in crime are sometimes the decent, hardworking, upstanding pillars of the community.

These people commit crimes of complicity.

Eddie Armistead is the young man in Cleveland who jumped out of the window of his apartment after his mother tied him to a chair to keep him off the streets. He is the kid whose teacher punished him by locking him in a closet and by having him mop the floors of the school. He's the kid who rammed his teacher's car into his high school building. When his mother finally despaired of controlling him, she had him placed in a juvenile training institution.

When I met him, Edward was working, mopping up at the Garvey Community Center, a job that his counselors hoped would "rehabilitate" him. But Edward's real boss was not the center. He worked for the man who drove the Rolls Royce. The second day I came to the center I noticed the car in the parking lot. You couldn't miss it; it was a gleaming ruby in a nest of dusty, dented Chevys and Fords. The owner of the car was a tall black man in his mid-thirties. He was elegantly dressed in a dark overcoat with a fur collar, a wide-brimmed velour hat, and shining black cowboy boots.

I visited the center for five days in a row. Every day the man was there, every morning, afternoon, and evening. He always stood in the same place, staring out a window, perhaps 20 feet from the main entrance. He nodded pleasantly to the old people who came to the center for senior citizens' lunches. He talked to the little kids who attended the day care center there. He traded jokes and slapped skin with the black teenagers who passed him on the way to the gym, one flight below. When I returned to the center two months later, he was still at his post at the window.

The man is a gangster. His assignment was to watch a candy store across the street that was a center of drug traffic in the Hough. I couldn't find out whether he represented a rival drug faction that wanted to move in on the trade, or whether he was there to make sure the drops and pickups went smoothly. Three times a day Edward left his mop and bucket in the slop closet and took a walk. He told me that his walk took him, roughly, on a half-mile radius of the center. When he got back he reported to the gangster whether he had spotted any unusual police activity in the area: police cruisers, uniformed cops, obvious plainclothes cops. For that he was paid $100 a week. For mopping up the place, the center paid him $46.50 after taxes.

I asked Edward what he thought of the man. "Hey, man, he's heavy," he said. There was no doubt about the man's status with the other kids at the center. When he favored them with a wink or a smile, they would break into a wide grin.

I thought that maybe I should find out why the center staff lets a gangster use the building as a lookout post. Claude Robbins,* the assistant director, was not a complacent man. He worked hard to find jobs for teenagers; he involved them in social programs; he has organized parents to pressure the schools to do something about the high rate of truancy in the Hough. I asked Robbins how he thought the man influenced the kids who came to the center.

"They see the Rolls Royce and it's a positive image to them," he said. "Now this is a guy who probably doesn't have a second grade reading level. And he's dealing in all kinds of illicit, illegal activities. The young kids see him as somebody who's made it, somebody dealin' with a lot of money."

* A pseudonym.

Does he think the man should be allowed to use the center as a business place?

"I think he has a lot to offer," Robbins said. "He's an intelligent person, and maybe he has more to offer than some people who go through the straight nine-to-five routine day to day."

"But he's a gangster," I said.

Robbins glanced over at the minister who was visiting his office. Their eyes communicated in a private code. "We understand that it's incorrect for a man like that to be here," Robbins said carefully. "If I move on the man, and I'm not really ready to move on the man, well, I won't be here tomorrow. I don't mind dyin'. Dyin' ain't no big thing to me. But I do ask myself: The police come around that candy store at least twice a month and they can't break it up; should it be up to me to do somethin'? Should I do somethin' they can't or won't do?"

Later I asked Mrs. Armistead how she thought her son was making out now that he was back in the community. "Real fine," she said. "I'm sure glad he's workin' at the center. It's a real fine place, a lot better place than the streets. That boy don't have no control over himself before. But I do believe, I *know,* that center's goin' to straighten him out."

In Eddie Armistead's case, the complicity of the community in his crimes was passive. The community center director didn't encourage Eddie to break the law. He chose to ignore the problem, a strategy apparently adopted by the police as well. They simply didn't bother the drug dealers, except for an occasional drive-by patrol. Edward is quick to analyze this pattern of avoidance. "If they don't care, why should I care?" he says. "What I do don't make no difference to nobody but me."

Adults asked about youth crimes often blame "bad influences," by which they mean a kid's teenage friends. They rarely indict the "good people" in the community who passively or actively encourage youngsters to commit crimes. Although these adolescents may be living out on their own, there is no more powerful urge moving them than to find acceptance and approval. Business people in their community, who condone and profit from their crimes, grant them legitimacy. They form with the kids a partnership of conscious wrongdoing.

The key word is conscious. Both the kids and those legitimate entrepreneurs are conscious of what's going on. The income generated by these tacit understandings should be differentiated from the cash that flows through what's called the underground economy. Much of that money derives from legitimate transactions. It's just not reported for tax purposes. Waitresses don't report their tips; a mechanic repairs somebody's car and pockets the cash.

What I'm talking about here is dirty money. Dirty money was a significant part of the economy in every poor urban community I visited. For illustrative purposes, I am going to focus on Newark, but the system is pretty much the same in cities all over the country.

In Newark I spent most of my time in the area served by La Casa de Don Pedro, the community organization represented by Willie Sosa, the youth worker. Approximately 5,000 people live in this area, 60 percent of them Hispanics (mostly Puerto Ricans), 30 percent white, and 10 percent black. In 1984, La Casa received a grant from the Eisenhower Foundation to study the community's attitudes about crime. Two hundred people were interviewed in the study.

About one-third of the people interviewed said they or someone else in their household had been robbed or attacked on the street, and one-half said they knew of someone else who had been victimized by street crime. Almost 30 percent reported break-ins or attempted break-ins at their homes.*

The fear of street crime along the main shopping thoroughfares kept many people at home. During the day, half of the people said they felt unsafe, and at night *over 90 percent* thought they would be in danger on the street. More than two-thirds of the respondents said they avoided going out at night alone because of crime.

When people in this neighborhood discuss crime, they often mention youth as both victims and victimizers. More than half of those interviewed ranked teenage loitering as a severe problem. At the same time, almost 70 percent identified adolescent unemployment as a major community concern. This is a neighborhood with a large population of the young. Nearly all Hispanic households and two-thirds of black households had at least one person

---

* It is interesting to note that one crime repeatedly mentioned was arson. Many residents believed that people were being burned out of their homes by landlords for the insurance money.

under the age of nineteen living there. While adults were very concerned about youth crime stemming from the use and sale of "illegal drugs," at the same time "nearly every parent said he/she was 'very worried' for the safety of their children in their neighborhood. These levels of fear of crime are very high compared to other sites [studied by the Eisenhower Foundation], and especially to the nation as a whole," the study noted.

Residents were asked what could be done to prevent crime in the community. Two-thirds of the people expressed "dissatisfaction" with the way the police handled their calls reporting a crime and urged an improvement in police protection. Others suggested forming an anticrime community organization. But the most common response was that nothing could be done. "A majority of residents expressed a general feeling of 'helplessness' when asked if they felt people could avoid becoming crime victims," the researchers said.[3]

When they discussed the causes of crime, no one in this survey mentioned the complicity of some straight business people in the crimes committed by street kids. No one except for the kids and the business people.

Manuel Velez, who was fifteen years old and looked twelve, had left his mother and his ten sisters and brothers about a month before. The immediate reason was his mother's refusal to allow him to visit his older brother, Roberto, who was serving a two-year prison term for armed robbery. One of Manuel's teenage friends told me, "Manny feels like Roberto was his father. He thinks if he can spend a little time talking to him all his problems will go away." Mrs. Velez was apparently unwilling to admit at all that her son was serving time. When I asked another of Manuel's brothers, eight-year-old Frankie, when Roberto would come back home, he said, "In a little while. He's working out in the country. He's gonna come back when he makes enough money to buy Mommy a Cadillac."

A few times a week Manny would drop by La Casa to check in on his brothers and sisters and to talk to Willie Sosa. When he was younger, Manny had played on La Casa's baseball team, which had been managed by Willie Sosa. Manny was running wild on the streets now, but he didn't want to burn all his bridges. He knew he might need somebody straight to talk to if he got in big trouble.

After he heard that I was writing a book on street kids, Manny would seek me out. Most of the time he didn't say much. When he did talk, it was to challenge my credentials to write on the subject. "Suppose I steal this radio," he'd say as we sat in an office at La Casa.

"That would be stupid," I'd reply, trying to appear stern, but feeling a ripple of fear.

"You know I could do it," Manny would say.

"I know you could do it. But it still would be stupid."

I guess my answer satisfied him, because a few nights later he opened up.

We were standing on a street corner a couple of blocks away from La Casa. It was a still, humid night in early September. We were talking about how few jobs there were for out-of-school teenagers in Newark. "And how do you think you're gonna support yourself, now that you're not home?" I asked him.

"I'm doin' crime," he said.

I let the declaration hang there for a few minutes. "For how long?" I asked him.

"Coupla weeks ago was the first time," he said. Another long pause. And then, as if he'd been waiting all along for the right time to confess, he told me about it.

It was about nine at night. A few blocks aways. There's a corner, a grocery store and a bar across the street. I had a gun I bought just that night from a dude on the street. A gun and a knife. We were standing there, my friend and me, and we see this old lady, I don't know how old she was, least she had gray hair. I was *scared*, but my friend, he was younger, thirteen maybe, he says, "Let's do it."

When she came around the corner, I pulled the gun out and said, "Give me your money." My knees were shakin'. She gave me the money and I take it but it was only a few dollars. I look inside her bag, and I see all these food stamps. So I put my hand inside her bag—I was shakin' 'cause I was nervous—I was standin' there and talkin' to the lady and the other dude was sayin', "Come on man, run, run, run." She was askin' me if this was the first time doin' it, and I was saying, "Yeah, yeah, the first time." I really didn't know what to do. I was tryin' to remember how my brother used to do it before he got sent up. I seen him a coupla times do crimes.

I remembered. I tell her, "Stay there until I get half way down the street." Be tellin' her, "Don't run, just walk away." I started to walk away, fast like, but not runnin'.

I asked Manny how he felt when it was over.

"A little scared for an hour, maybe," he said. "But then I knew I got over. I really didn't care. After the first time, I do it again, four, five times. One day I rob two people. I ain't scared no more."

What, I asked Manny, was he going to do with the food stamps he had stolen from the woman?

"My friend, the dude with me, he knew the guy who owned the grocery store the woman was comin' out of. The guy in the store tole my friend, 'If you take somebody's food stamps don't come straight to the store. Hold them for a while.' He say, 'When you bring 'em, don't pull 'em out in front of a lot of people in the store. You just wait 'til we go to the storeroom in the back and I'll give you the cash for them.' "

I asked Manny, "Have you sold the stamps to the guy yet?"

He stuck his hand into his pocket and pulled out a fist full of food stamps. "Eighty dollars of stamps," he said.

"When are you going to do it?" I said.

He stared at me, as if he were trying to decide something. Then he said, "Okay, c'mon with me. But don't stay near me in the store. Make like you're lookin' for somethin' to buy."

We walked together for four blocks. When we came to the grocery store, Manny walked in first, and I followed him a few minutes later. Manny was talking to an older man wearing a tan butcher's apron, standing near the cash register. A younger man, who I assumed was a clerk, stood next to the man in the apron. I bent over pretending interest in the selection of pork rinds and Frito-Lay snacks. I saw Manny and the older man walk to the back of the store. The clerk was minding the register.

A few minutes later Manny sauntered by, glanced in my direction, and gave me a broad wink. He walked out of the store. I took my purchases up to the counter. As the man in the apron was ringing up the sale, I said, "Why did you buy the stamps from the kid?"

The look on the guy's face said: Cop. "I don't buy no stamps. The stamps was for the food his mother buyed yesterday."

"No," I said, "the stamps were stolen. He took them off one of your customers. A lady."

I think he heard the tremor in my voice and decided I wasn't a cop after all. "What do you want?" he said. His tone was belligerent.

"Why do you buy stolen stamps?" I persisted.

"Not my business," he said.

He dropped the change from my purchase on the counter and looked over my shoulder at a customer who was wheeling a food cart down one of the aisles. "Don't come back," he said. The clerk standing next to him, who had been silent and impassive as I was talking, reached under the counter for something—a baseball bat? a gun? I backed toward the door. "An' don't come back to this neighborhood. We don't want you here, lookin' for trouble."

Outside the store, Manny stuck out his arm, opened up his fist. In his palm were two twenties and a ten. His take for $80 worth of food stamps.

A few weeks later I was standing on the pavement outside of La Casa, talking to a couple of kids, when an old blue and pink Ford pulled up. An older youth, perhaps eighteen or nineteen, was driving. Sitting next to him was Manny. He stuck his head out of the window and yelled, "Wanna go for a ride?"

"Where you going?" I asked.

"Gonna do some business," Manny said.

I got into the front seat next to him. In his lap I saw a tape deck. "Where'd you get that?" I asked him.

"I took it off a Firebird last night," he said. "Sold the car for $200 bucks."

A little while later, we passed a gas station located no more than a ten-minute drive from downtown Newark. "That's my man," Manny said. "He sez, No more '81s. All he wants is '83s, '84s. I find him a Porsche, he give me 800 bucks."

We stopped in front of an appliance store on a main shopping street in the neighborhood. Manny got out, carrying the tape deck. A few minutes later he returned. "Shit, that guy's cheap. He gave me forty for it. Shit, I know I sell it on the street, I make ninety, easy. But"—he rolled his eyes— "on the street, you never know who's buyin' it. Could be a cop. Could be trouble."

We rode for another fifteen minutes and pulled into the parking lot outside a motel. The sign outside the motel said: "Disco dance tonight, till 4." "Gonna check in here for a coupla nights," Manny announced. "Gonna buy some wine, find some fine pussy."

"Chill-out time," said Manny's friend. They left me to call a cab to take me back to La Casa. In the cab I imagined Manny, a fifteen-year-old boy who could be taken for three years younger, checking in. Did the motel clerk wonder what a baby-faced kid was doing with a fat roll of bills? Did he ask what he was doing there? Did he care? Did anybody care?

A month passed, and I heard that Manny had been picked up for robbing and pistol whipping an elderly woman on the street. He was being held at Newark's Youth House, where juveniles are detained while a decision is made whether to press charges and go forward with a trial.

I arranged to visit Manny with Willie Sosa. When we met Manny he was sprawled on the floor of the third-floor day room, watching a soap opera with a half-dozen other boys. We walked down a couple of flights to a cubicle where visitors can meet with inmates. "What now, Manny?" I asked him.

Manny didn't look upset or frightened. He rocked back in his chair, crossed his arms, and said, "My first time, so maybe they don't do nothin'. But if I do get sent up, it's gonna be Janesburg. So I'll be with my brother. We take care of each other. For sure."

Reuniting with his brother: that was something to look forward to. I reflected on the descent of Manny Velez. Willie Sosa and other staff members at La Casa had tried to help, tried to talk to Manny, to bring him together with his family, to offer counseling. But they had so much working against them. Manny's mother was confused and desperate. The other kids in the family were half-wild. The only person who could make Manny listen was in a prison cell, and he wasn't likely to be a positive influence. Then there were the other people in the community, the respectables. They were the ones who told the researchers that they feared for the safety of their children; they were the ones who were afraid of going out at night; they were the ones who said they felt "helpless" to do anything about the crime that was devouring the neighborhood. Most of them had stood on the sidelines as the struggle was waged for Manny's future. They were observers, like the community center director in Cleveland who closed his eyes to the gangster at the window; like the motel clerk who checked Manny in during his chill-out phase. And some were Manny's tacit accomplices: the grocery store owner who paid him for his stolen food stamps; the appliance store owner who bought his stolen tape deck; the gas station operator who stripped down his stolen car.

Manuel Velez was not a very sympathetic character. In the few weeks I knew him he impressed me as a very dangerous individual whose rage and violence throbbed close to the surface. But there are many unsympathetic characters, and they carry with them a full charge of pent-up hostility—yet they don't pistol whip old ladies. Could anybody have caught Velez on his long fall? La Casa and Willie Sosa tried, but their resources were limited, and they had no shortage of emergency rescue operations. But where were the others? Where was the spine of the neighborhood—the barbers, the undertakers, the doctors, the liquor store owners, all those who made their livelihood, and sometimes a very good livelihood at that, from this shattered community?

Early on, when I first met Manuel, we talked about the scarcity of jobs for youngsters like him. I don't know whether he would have taken a job if it had been offered to him. I don't know whether employment would have diverted him from the destructive path he was following. But I do know that that alternative never developed.

Across the country, there are a growing number of minority activists who are relatively young but who have put in a lot of time trying to help lost youngsters. While they are critical of deficient and ineffective public programs, they also fault an uncaring community that stands aside as young lives fall apart. When I. Roy Jones, a black man who is director of a youth shelter, describes the devaluing of life and property in the slums of Detroit, he might well be talking about Newark and all the Newarks in the country:

It's time that we begin to accept some responsibility. Any black person who is successful enough to own a business and doesn't hire a number of impoverished black youths is a threat to the community—*and needs to be removed.* People who are struggling, who find themselves encased in poverty, almost have to adopt an attitude that only we will care about ourselves. Therefore, all of our energy, and all of our resources, must be circulated within our own society.

Yes, it's time. The people who care about the community, who care about how children grow up in the community, have to make a statement about what they feel is socially acceptable behavior, things that will manifest themselves positively over the long run. But the statement is only the beginning. We have to commit ourselves as a people to reinforcing the statement. That means we don't purchase stolen items. That means merchants don't allow the use of food stamps to purchase other than what they were intended for. We don't let kids not have a proper learning environment.

Now, let's get real. The reality is we have families that do not have the internal capacity to prepare their young to grow up, to make it in America. There are some reasons for this, there's been poverty and neglect and racism for a long time, and I'm not going to go into all that. But the responsibility falls to the people who are making it, who are living off the community, the responsibility falls to them to teach the lessons of striving, competing, rising in this country. If they can't teach that, or are unwilling to, then we have to replace them.

If a community is indifferent, if it is unwilling to teach these lessons, then youngsters—estranged from their families, rejected by their schools—will seek an alliance that offers excitement and affirmation. They will join up with somebody as desperate and out of control as they are. They will find a partner.

Home Boys, Home Girls

All sorts of relationships can develop on the street: the pimp and the prostitute; the drug dealer and the addict; the numbers banker and the runner. One relationship is more binding and enduring than all the rest: It is the tie between two young people who have in common race, neighborhood, poverty, domestic turmoil, educational failure, and street life. When kids talk about their home boys, they don't mean recent acquaintances. They mean kids who've traveled right along with them for a very long time: They knew each other in grade school; they got kicked out of high school and broke with their families at roughly the same time; they used drugs and passed their nights together in subways, arcades and shelters; they broke the law together, got busted, took the same "bid" (sentence), went to prison, and maneuvered themselves into the same cottage or cell block. Finally, they floated together back into the old neighborhood to start the cycle all over again.

There are practical benefits to such alliances. Street partners share the effort of finding shelter and money, and they offer each other a little extra protection. But the advantages are as much psychological as pragmatic: You have somebody who'll tell you what you're doing is right; you have somebody to make you black coffee and keep you on your feet when you've OD'd; you have somebody to tell you to can it when you start to talk suicide. The home boy connection is indispensable, because every street kid has to fill an enormous emotional void that is almost never filled by traditional family and school relationships. That is the need to be true to someone, to believe they care as much about you as you care about them.

In Bill Craig's mind, the only reason he was able to survive *his* adolescence in the underground of Newport, Kentucky, was the solemn covenant he and Johnny Bayley had sworn to each other. They would share equally their money, their drugs, their punishment. One would never sacrifice or exploit the other. They were the home boys of Newport, clan brothers reinventing the Appalachian myth of tribal fidelity.

While they loved each other as brothers, they exhibited no brotherly love for strangers. For most of four years they lived as outlaws, prowling the streets of Newport and nearby Covington and sometimes venturing across the bridge to downtown Cincinnati, to seek out their victims among the Christmas shoppers ambling along in the indoor malls and the bystanders listening to the festive carillons.

They mugged old people, broke into houses, stole cars, dealt drugs. Just as Manny Velez had no trouble selling his stolen goods, Billy and Johnny found plenty of takers in Newport. "We'd steal a car stereo and just walk down the street and somebody'd buy it. Once we broke into this lady's house and stole a TV. They had this auction every Saturday. So we brought the TV in and nobody asked a question 'bout where we got it. They auctioned it for seventy-five bucks."

They would agree to draw the line at some crimes, but the line was elastic.

> We weren't out on the street very long, and we saw this old lady carrying her packages. Johnny and me, we'd look at each other and say, "We'll do it, and that's it." We needed money for drugs, and nothin' else was as important as that. I was scared, but I came up behind her and put my hand around her neck, and Johnny grabbed her purse.
>
>   After that I was still scared. We talked about going to the south end and doing more muggings. But we said, "Never

again." Yeah, that's what we said, but when we didn't have money, we'd do bad stuff again. On the street it's hard to live up to your promises. You feel guilty for a while; you forget about being guilty the next time you need something.

At different times Billy's mother found him and got him to return home. Bill's price for remaining with her was that Johnny had to come and live with the Craigs. June Craig agreed, and in return Bill entered a drug rehabilitation program. But those truces were short-lived. The conflict that had made him leave home in the first place hadn't gone away. Bill still felt that his mother was more concerned about his stepfather's welfare than she was about his. Bill thought his mother treated him as though he were a malignancy, eating away at their family ties, ruining everybody's happiness, especially his stepfather's. When Bill was born, his natural father left the family; sometimes Bill read into his mother's hostility an unspoken accusation that just by being born he had driven his father away. Now they were rehashing the same arguments they had had five years before: She accused him of destroying his stepfather's health, already made fragile by a heart condition; he accused her of treating him as a problem, a burden that she couldn't get rid of. Always there in the corner, leaning against the wall, staring down from the second-floor landing, was Bill's main man, his home boy—Johnny Bayley.

During yet another quarrel with his stepfather, Bill blurted out the forbidden thought: "I hate you. I hope you die." Which his stepfather did, two days later. Officially, the cause was heart failure, but unofficially, as Mrs. Craig put it to Bill, "We know who's to blame, don't we?"

In the funeral parlor, June Craig shook a trembling finger at her son and cried out, "You're the one who killed my husband."

Johnny Bayley, there by Bill's side, fulfilled his oath of fidelity. He said, calmly, "Mrs. Craig, I have no disrespect for you, but Bill ain't killed nobody."

"You stay out of it," June Craig shouted at Johnny, "you're as bad as he is."

Bill and Johnny spent that night at Johnny's parents' home. But Johnny's mother was as furious at them as Mrs. Craig had been. Before dawn they left, finally settling in where they always did when there was no other place. "White Castle, the back booth," Bill remembers.

It was where we went when we first split from our folks. But it seemed different this time. Before, it was our first time on the outside, alone—we didn't know what to expect. It was some kind of great adventure. But we'd learned something in four, five years: There was only trouble out there, trouble and more trouble. We were drinkin' coffee and starin' at the table, thinkin', We're sinkin' fast and we got nothin', except each other, to hold onto.

It is a night like so many nights in Newport since he had left home. A dozen boys and girls sitting on the floor, leaning against the walls, smoking dope, popping pills, drinking whatever booze was around. Sleet raps against the window panes. Not too many tourists will skid across the bridge to sin city on this raw winter night. Around midnight, somebody says, "Hey, who's gonna get some munchies?" Johnny Bayley slowly gets up, swaying back and forth. He looks at Bill Craig, who's flat on his back, a girl's head resting on his chest. "Wanna go with me, Billy?" Johnny mumbles. "Naaah, it's too cold outside," Bill says. Another guy stands up and says, "That's okay, Johnny, I'll keep you company."

Twenty minutes later, the door bursts open. The guy who left with Johnny is standing there. His eyes are wild. Breathlessly, he says, "We just been in a car wreck. Johnny's a mess—we bounced off this telephone pole and hit a wall. It's all fucked up."

"Oh, shit," says Billy, rushing out the door, followed by the others. The car wreck is only a block away. The windshield is cracked. Johnny's lying on his side, on the seat behind the wheel. His face is covered with blood. Billy calls an ambulance from a phone in a convenience store; it takes almost half an hour to arrive. The emergency medical aide checks Johnny's vital signs. He looks up at Billy, says, "I think your friend's had it. You better call his parents."

Billy follows the ambulance to the hospital. Billy's mother and Johnny's mother are already there. The two families have known each other since Johnny and Billy were babies. The doctor confirms what the ambulance aide already told him: Johnny is dead.

Johnny's mother stabs Bill with her look. "If he hadn't been with you . . ." she starts to say. Bill spins around, runs down the hospital corridor, stumbles out into the street. He walks alone for hours. It is almost morning when he rings the doorbell at his mother's house.

"Why're you cryin' for?" she asks.

"Why?" he sobs. "Why? We was our best friend. We showed each other love and nobody else would. He taught me, I'm not alone."

They talk for a while and Billy's mother says that she thinks it might not be such a great idea if he went to Johnny's funeral. The Bayleys have enough grief already. They're blaming their son's death on him. There might be a scene.

Zombie-like, Bill goes upstairs, runs the water in the bathtub, climbs in, swallows a handful of pills. His mother finds him as he's about to black out. She rushes him to the hospital, where they pump out the pills. "You know," she says to him a few days later, "I think both of you made each other crazy."

Much later, Bill Craig would look back at that time and say, "I don't know what's crazy. All I know is that Johnny was all I had. Even now, I still have nightmares—I wake up sometimes and I'm shakin' and cryin' and holdin' my hands up. I tell myself, Johnny's comin' back. He just went away to give me time to grow up. But he's comin' back."

In their choice of companions, street kids are like most people. They want their friends to accept them and approve of them as they are. Since many of these kids were torn in a dozen different directions, they were attracted to other "marginalized" adolescents who *seemed* strong, who *seemed* to know what they wanted and how to get it. During their period of greatest confusion and turmoil, they were not prone to deep reflection about the consequences of their lives on the street. They wanted to be around people who acted without a lot of ambivalence. What Kathy Andrews hated was a person who spent all of his time thinking and none of his time doing. The kind of people she went out of her way to meet weren't going to guide her out of her confusion. If anything, they were going to double her trouble.

Kathy Andrews didn't grow up terribly poor in Detroit. Kathy Andrews wasn't black or Hispanic. Kathy Andrews wasn't abused by her parents. Kathy Andrews didn't fail in school. But Kathy Andrews was running. She was sixteen, had quit school, and was out on the street looking for a connection—for a home boy and a home girl. She knew what she was running from. In a word:

boredom. And she knew where she was running to: (1) wherever she could find black kids and (2) New York.

At this stage in her adolescence, Kathy desperately wanted to be accepted by people who acted decisively, even if their actions exposed her to great danger. To her, that meant black kids. "What I like about them is their favorite thing is just to speak their mind," she says. "So everything that comes in their mind, they say. That's not like white kids. White kids spend all their time thinkin': Is this good? Is this bad? I'm at home with kids who don't think—they do." Kids like Kathy never shrink from generalizations.

Kathy had left her home in a lower-middle-class suburb of Detroit about a month before I met her. She was staying in a temporary youth shelter in the inner city of Detroit where most of the kids were black. ("My sister ran away a couple of years ago and the shelter she stayed in didn't have heat, so they sent her here. She said I'd find a lot of black kids in this one.") The shelter staff was trying to persuade her to talk to her father, but Kathy was resisting. "I don't want to talk to my dad," she said. "They say, How are you going to get things straightened out if you ain't talking? But I lived with the guy for sixteen years. It's not like I haven't tried to talk to him plenty of times."

Kathy doesn't want to talk to him because she's pretty sure what he's going to say: If you keep going the way you're going you're gonna be in a helluva lot of trouble. Kathy's dad had his share of trouble. His wife moved out of the house three years ago and left him to take care of two teenage girls. He worked nine hours a day as a machinist in an auto parts shop to bring home enough money to keep his kids in jeans. And what's his reward? His oldest daughter becomes pregnant, drops out of school, moves out of the house with the baby, and goes on welfare. Then there's Kathy: maybe 98 pounds, with a book bag strapped to her back. Half the time she's got a racking cough and a runny nose. Thirteen, fourteen years old, she's already missing school, she's already doing enough pills and grass and coke to send her off to the moon.

And Kathy's father knows what she's doing when she's not in school. She's downtown at one of those street fairs or rock festivals. She's not there for the music or the dancing. She's there to meet black kids. He's not imagining this stuff; he knows. There was that afternoon when he came home early from the shop.

Kathy was leaning against the closet door in her room. He pulled the door open and there were two black guys—not kids, nineteen, twenty years old, big guys. He chased them out of the house, down the street, around the corner. When he got back, Kathy was sitting on the bed. All he can say, all the words he can think of are, "You damn nigger lover. If I was back in Texas with you and you was like this, the KKK'd catch you and they'd know what to do."

So what was the point of her talking to him? He was going to say what he always said: They're setting you up, you're a mark. That's not what she wanted to hear, because she knew, in a way, that he was right. She found that out for herself a few months ago.

She had been in southwest Detroit with her white girlfriend and two black guys. One of the guys made a pass at Kathy and she punched his leg. He told Kathy he'd take her girlfriend home but not her. The guy's friend offered to give Kathy a ride, but when she got into his car, she saw five other men in there.

> We were driving and I said, "This ain't the way home." And they said, "We're gonna get some beer first." So we went to the store, and I got out of the car. I said, "No, I ain't going any further."
>
> Then they all got mad. But I knew what they were up to. They think white girls are stupid, they think they can use them. Sometimes I'd say to myself: Be careful—you be careful. Well, this time, I wasn't so careful. When I got out of the car I recognized a guy who was in my friend's band. He's black too, but there was just him and his friend. And it's better to go with two guys than six. So I started to go with them but I didn't know them very well.
>
> I got in the car and they went the wrong way. On purpose. Then they pulled up behind the railroad track, and I knew what was going to happen, 'cause that's where black guys all take their girls. They was talkin'. I thought, Oh, no! I'm in trouble. Then one came back, and he grabbed me, and he went to throw me in the back seat, and he hit my head on the door. I said: "Wait. I'll cooperate, I don't want to get hurt or nothing." 'Cause I know how rough they can be. So I said, "Okay," and I cooperated with them.

Afterward, sitting perfectly still in the car, staring straight ahead, she remembered what she used to think about before she started to go with blacks: "Oh, my God, what if I got raped by a nigger? It'll be a trauma. The rest of my life I'll probably be going crazy or something." But she wasn't tearing her hair out or screaming, or crying. All she felt was this absolutely frigid block inside of her: cold at the center. Later, she said, "It was no big thing—I mean it was, but I didn't make no big thing out of it."

She could have reacted in two ways: to recognize the horror of being raped or to minimize it. Kathy chose to block it out, because she was not prepared to separate herself from her companions of choice, from her home boys and girls. The night after she was raped, she spent several hours with a friend, a white girl, describing her experience. The girl lectured Kathy: "You know what they are, you know the only thing they want," she said.

Kathy responded, "Yeah, I know how they are. But I just gotta get used to it, because I don't want to go back to white guys. That's just how it is."

A few hours before I met Kathy, she got permission from the supervisors at the shelter to go, with another girl, to a convenience store a block away. It was only a few weeks after Kathy had been raped by a couple of guys she hardly knew. "I didn't really want to go with this girl, because she's only thirteen," Kathy told me.

> I like to be with girls my age or older because they know the score. There was a cute guy in the store, and he's black and he says, "C'mere, white girl." So I was going to go over and talk to him. The guy's lookin' and everything. The girl grabs me by the coat and says, "Girl, we ain't talkin' to no strangers. Oh, Lord, let us get out of here."
>
> So we walked out of the store and the guy goes, "Bye," and I go, "Bye," lookin' back at him. And all the way back to the shelter, the girl's going, "Well, am I going to tell on you!" And I'm thinking, Why did she have to be with me? If I was by myself, I coulda met him—and who knows what would have happened?

The issue, of course, is not simply meeting black people. The real issue may be how to fill the emptiness of her childhood.

> My parents were divorced when I was thirteen. My dad would always be gone. They'd both been very strict. All of a sudden

all that strictness was gone. I was never spoiled with money, but, I guess you could say, I was spoiled with doing whatever I wanted to. I practically lived by myself. Oh, my sister lived there for a while, but she'd go out and do whatever she wanted to, so I would go too. I was kinda young to be on your own, you know—thirteen years old. I didn't know how to handle the situation. But I thought I did.

Everyone would say, Kathy, when are you going to grow up? I always wanted to have fun. They'd say, But you're so immature. I didn't care because—I don't know how to explain it. I always had to have fun, I always had to be doing something. If it was being immature, or getting into trouble or whatever, but I always had to be having fun. I'd be doing drugs and everything, and it got to a point where even that got boring. I ran out of things to do. Then I'd start a new challenge, start dating black guys. And not only black *guys*. Since I started to date black guys, I started to meet black girls. And they're just as much fun as meeting black guys. They'll say anything. They'll do anything. I never got bored hanging around with them.

Kathy never wants to look back—boredom might be gaining on her. "When people say, Kathy why don't you grow up? I say, You know it will be a long time, because I really don't want to grow up."

When Kathy is out in the street, she is always looking for guidance. Her guides are not black youngsters who are still in school, who are planning to go to college and begin a vocation and a career. The guides she selects show her a city within a city, a city that bristles with guns and knives. A city governed by raw greed and brute force. It is a city that rocks to the refrain, "Happiness is a warm gun . . ." Whether you use it or not, cocaine sets the style. Miami Vice in the Motor City. All the surfaces are as smooth and slick, and as cold and unfeeling, as plastic. Here, action is severed from responsibility and morality; there is no repose, no contemplation or reflection; it's a jumpy place, all tics and twitches. Make a wrong move, and *zap*, you're dead. You survive by anesthetizing your emotions. The paradox is that no matter how much you try to cut off your feelings, you do want to feel. The only object of the game is finding the next kick, turning up the juice, feeling the jolt.

What's next? I ask Kathy. Where does the next kick come from?

"I get bored so easily," she says. "There's nothing that challenges me any more."

No challenge? At sixteen?

"Okay," says Kathy with a laugh stifled by a hard, dry cough. "You name something."

Press her, and Kathy can name something else, another challenge. It's called New York. When she turns eighteen, Kathy wants to go to New York with a friend, a white girl. "She's like me. She's the only white person I hang around with, and she dates only black men." Why New York? "It's glamorous, there's excitement. You can meet all kinds of people."

There's the minor matter of what she's going to do in New York, how she'll survive. It's unlikely that Mayor Koch will greet her at the Port Authority Bus Terminal, although there may be a few other men who will be eager to show her around the big city—home boys. "For a while I thought I'd be a model, like in *Playboy* magazine. But everyone says, You're not beautiful, they want those perfect women. They're right, so now I been thinking, I'll be a go-go dancer. But you've got to be developed, and that I'm not. But they say they have some flat-chested go-go dancers in New York, so maybe I'll use my personality and I'll act when I dance, and everything else. I mean it's exciting, but—"

But? "That's why I get high blood pressure. Hey, it's a challenge, New York, excitement and all. But after I live it up and everything, I'll be nineteen years old and there will be nothing left for me to do. It will be so bo-o-ring. I don't know, I might have a kid."

In the course of a long conversation with a kid, I sometimes ask a question that doesn't have anything to do with what the kid has just said. It simply pops into my head. What popped into my head, when I was leaving Kathy, was this question: Do you use any protection, any kind of birth control?

Kathy Andrews, sixteen, shook her head. "No," she says. "I never had my period."

You may feel lonely on the street, but at least the buildings and the faces are familiar; at least you still know who you are and where you are. But there's another kind of loneliness. It's that sinking, drowning sensation you feel when you've suddenly been taken from your family, pulled out of your neighborhood, severed from your friends, removed from your school, and deposited in a faceless institution—all because of circumstances beyond your control.

Children thrust into the care of institutions feel as if they are *abnormal.* They have nothing but memory; the memory of a pet dog, an ice cream truck that used to park on the street, a few feet of pavement where they once skipped rope. The only palpable sign that these children are still normal, still human, is a friendship. Children in institutions seize the first sign of interest, the first gesture of affection and concern, investing it with enormous significance. Someone pats you on the shoulder and squeezes your hand, and you take it as a pledge of undying friendship and never ending loyalty. When you are truly alone, as children in institutions are, you devote yourself to inventing your very own home boys and home girls.

At the same shelter where I met Kathy Andrews, I had a brief encounter with a sixteen-year-old black woman named Luann Harris. I did much of the talking, because Luann had a painful toothache.

Luann had been sexually abused by her father. Repeatedly. Abused and beaten. For several years. Her older sister urged her to tell her high school counselor. A few hours after she told the counselor, he called her into his office, where her father was waiting for her. "Is this your father, Luann?" the counselor asked her.

All Luann could think of saying was, "Oh, hi, Dad." Her father said: "Give me your house keys. If you're gonna tell lies about me, I don't want you home." As she got up to go back to her classes, her father whispered to her, "You let your sister get you into a lot of trouble."

At home that night, her mother made her repeat everything she had told the school counselor. Then her mother said: "You get this straight, little girl. You want to live here, you live with me *and* your father. You don't like that, you go find yourself some other place to live, because your father's staying right here."

The next day Luann went to school, but it was hard to concentrate on American history. She was confused. What had she done wrong? Could she muster the courage to go to court and accuse her father? If she repeated her charges against him, would she be taken out of her home? Where would she live? What would happen to her? She had a fierce headache when she left the school building at lunch hour. Then she saw her father leaning against a car, tossing a set of keys from one hand to another, staring at her. Luann ran back into the building, crying. A hall monitor took her to the principal's office. There, she remembers, the principal asked her a lot of the same questions that the counselor had asked the day before. When Luann was done telling her story, he said, "You're not supposed to leave this building with your father."

The principal made a call. When he hung up, he told Luann, "Get your book bag. I'm not letting you go home again." Escorted by a security guard, she was taken to the temporary youth shelter, where a few days later I met her. Luann wasn't sure where she would wind up. A counselor had told her that she might be placed in a Lutheran facility in Detroit. Another staff member had said that they were thinking of moving her to another institution in Bay City, Michigan, away from the reach of her father. It was all very uncertain and terrifying to her. "I don't know. I don't know . . ." she said. "Should I go to court and press charges? What'll he do to me if I do that? The worse thing is I miss my sister. She's so tough. She stands up to my father. And she doesn't even know where I am."

I had been so caught up in listening to her story that I neglected to tell her what I was doing there. She must have thought I was another counselor or somebody from family court. I explained that I was planning to write a book about youngsters who had been separated from their families and were growing up on their own.

"So am I," she said.

I thought I had misheard her because she was having difficulty talking with her toothache. I started to get up. She reached across and tugged at the sleeve of my jacket. "No, no," she said. "I'm writing a book, too." I sat down again. "It's called *Pages from the Heart.*"

I didn't know quite what to say, so I asked her how long she had been working on it. "Four or five days," she said.

"What's the book about?" I asked.

"I want to let other people in the world know that they are not alone," she said. "I want people to get to know what was happening in my life, the hard times I'm going through. I want to tell kids, If this happens to them, they should get away, tell someone this is happening. I waited so long . . ."

I went off somewhere and had a few shots of bourbon. It wasn't enough to put Luann out of my mind. I expected never to hear from her again. But a month later, when I was back in New York, there was a letter from Luann. The return address on the envelope had the name of a Detroit social agency for young women. (Apparently she had been sent neither to Bay City nor to the Lutheran home. Displaced kids find that plans for them are always changing.) She told me she was working on her book and would send sections of it to me soon. Generally, she said, she was fine, but in the next paragraph she wrote, "In fact, I am not doing too well. I am sick, but I will work out of this sickness. I wish you had the transportation to get to Detroit so you can come and see me."

She described a friend she had met at the institution: "Her name is Karen and she is fifteen years old, and me and her are getting along just fine, except when she is depressed and in pain, plus when she wants to kill herself. I talk her out of it too, but other than that we're just like sisters." In a postscript she added, "Me and Karen just can't stand the people or the girls and the noise they make. It's just too loud for us. . . . It would be nice to have some kind words of wisdom from you to cheer the two of us up. Karen's working on an autobiography book, too."

In my letter to her, I urged her not to give up. I said that the best of institutions could be very unpleasant places. I knew from talking to so many youngsters who were in difficulty that it's very hard to grow up in the United States, particularly when you're poor and black and you're not getting support from your family. But I was sure that someday she would make an important contribution to the welfare of kids like her. I closed by saying that I never wanted to hear her talking about suicide again, because she and her friend had a great deal to live for.

Five weeks later I got another letter from Luann. She thought that with the help of the staff she could "make it through the confusion and noise. It has been very rough and hard for me, but I can manage it." She was trying to banish the thought of suicide from her mind. "You won't hear that dreadful word no more, because I am feeling okay now and I am not thinking about that word. I am not giving up either. I know what contributions I am going to give the world with this book I am still working on." She did concede that sometimes her determination faltered. "It is most certainly hard to face life by yourself and with no one to help you, no place to go to either."

It was a little harder, too, because now Karen was gone.

The clouds did seem to clear up when I met Karen, and me and her were the best of friends and I helped her overcome her problems and she helped me, too. But she wasn't feeling too well at all, and she just couldn't make it through. So she just ran out the door. I haven't heard from her since the day she ran. I don't know if Karen is still working on her book, but wherever Karen is, I hope she is thinking of you and me.

As one friend vanishes, another appears. Luann's new friend is Sarah. "She helps me with everything and she makes me laugh too." When she talks to Sarah about her experiences it makes Luann realize that "what happened to me is not bad at all because it has happened to other people too." Another relationship is developing, but this one is a little different, and Luann is approaching it with some caution. "I have a boyfriend, too, and his name is Harold Lincoln and I like him and *he loves me too much.*"*

That was the last I heard from Luann. I called the foster care facility where she had been living, and a staff member told me she was "gone." He wouldn't say where. "Her files are confidential." He didn't treat her departure as exceptional. "Kids come and go all the time," he said.

All adolescents search for fidelity—for someone who will offer them a purpose and a place in the world. The search is pursued with a feverish intensity by the 250,000 youngsters who spend a large part of their adolescence shuttling from one foster care institution to another. In the absence of parents and families, they improvise: Adult strangers (like me) and transitory friendships and brief romances substitute for a nourishing home life. But substitutes and surrogates can't compensate for the absence of unqualified love and uncalculated intimacy. They arrive at the legal age of adult responsibility weighed down by the burden of incompleteness. They are expected to be responsible citizens without knowing who is responsible for them and to whom they are supposed to be responsible.

"Reassurance is what I need no matter who or what it's coming from," Luann had written in her letter. This is the lament of all "abused" children. In some sense, all the children I have described are "abused"—they suffer the "abuse" of poverty and

* My emphasis.

neglect and abandonment in their schools, communities, and homes. But the sexual abuse inflicted by parents and relatives— the natural sources of uncompromised affection—cuts so deeply. The National Institute of Mental Health reports that there are more than 2 million children so victimized. Children who are denigrated, humiliated, debased. In their longing they dare not question the motives of those who bear the gift of reassurance. It can be so easily withdrawn.

Ultimately, they understand that the hit-and-run relationships that develop in institutions and on the street are not enough. They need to account for what happened to them and why. They always come back to the unfinished business between them and their families. But returning may be much harder than leaving was. What they find is that those caretaking institutions whose stated mission is to bring children and families together again do not casily surrender their possessions.

Home Away from Home

In the later years of childhood and in early adolescence, the experiences of children from different economic backgrounds diverge. In public junior high schools and high schools, middle-class and more affluent youngsters take courses and belong to social organizations that prepare them academically and socially for higher education. If they need pocket change, they are likely to work after school and during the summer for private employers. Their recreation and leisure-time activities often involve family members or friends who are traveling along the same upwardly mobile track. Vacations, weekend excursions, family visits expose them to the world beyond their immediate communities; they are infused with a sense of possibility and growth.

Middle-class parents of children who experience learning and developmental difficulties may have to sacrifice, but they often find the money to pay for private assistance—private counseling and therapy, private tutoring and instruction, private camps and career-preparation programs. Middle-class as well as poor adolescents are exposed to the violent, get-rich-quick images transmitted by the popular culture of television, movies, and music, but in more privileged families financial, intellectual, and emotional resources offer at least a partial corrective.

All along the way their progress is accelerated by the support of helpful individuals—parents, relatives, friends. As they grow older they are comfortable trading on personal friendships and private relationships. That is what's normal and natural to them. They don't have to entrust their welfare to public institutions, with the exception of the school system. Even before they select a vocation and embark on a career, they are integrated into the private sector economy.

Poor children are raised by two sets of parents—the ones at home and the public bureaucracies that exercise real control over their everyday behavior and mold their expectations. Much of their development takes place within systems. Sustenance is provided by the welfare system. Recreation is provided by public community organizations, responsible to a philanthropic and governmental system of funding. If teenagers have children, their babies will be taken care of by a public system of child care (when it's available). If they want to or have to work, their jobs, until recently, were most likely to be in the public employment system.

Their work experience is a telling illustration of how dominant public institutions are in the development of poor adolescents. In the summer of 1979, before the Reagan administration killed the CETA program, 45 percent of all poor, minority teenagers were enrolled in a public employment and training project. Public sector employment accounted for 14 percent of all jobs held by sixteen- to nineteen-year-old black youths. During the life of the CETA program more than 2.5 million mostly, but not always, poor youths held public jobs.[4]

The objectives of the public youth employment systems were very different from the experience of work in the private sector. In the private sector, even the lowliest job shared a common objective with the best-paying and most important position: to increase the income earned by the enterprise. The kid who worked part-time sweeping up the grocery was helping to maximize the employer's profits; if the store was clean, it would presumably attract more customers. That wasn't true of a public employment program, whose real purpose was to meet a quota of participants enrolled, of assigned jobs, of money spent. The primary objective of the public employment system was not to improve the young workers' skills and efficiency or to inspire enthusiasm and zeal on the job—all prerequisites for achieving success in the private sector. The key objective was simply to be present, to show up.

How the youngster performed his job, what happened when he returned to school, whether his work experience led to other and better jobs—those were secondary considerations, if they were considered at all.

The effect of that experience was to persuade poor youngsters that they were "different." They were not part of that great river of adolescents flowing naturally into the broad channel of American life. Impoverished children were a maundering stream that led to a foreign and isolated backland. Just as kids like Luann Harris knew they were different because they didn't have families or communities but had to grow up in institutions, so, too, did kids who were directed into special public employment programs.

I remember spending a day in August with a crew of teenage workers who were raking leaves and picking up trash in the Boston Commons. The park was filled with tourists and city hall employees dining al fresco. Not far from where the CETA crew was working a group of rowdy, bleary-eyed Irish street kids had encircled a bench where two proper Bostonian ladies were sitting. The kids were trying to muscle the women for a handout. A few feet beyond the bench a couple of park employees, dressed in green uniforms, were doing pretty much the same work as the CETA kids.

During breaks in the raking, the CETA kids would sneak looks at the Park Department workers and at the kids hassling the bench-sitters. To which tribe did the CETA kids belong? I wondered. The hell-raising desperados or the sinecured civil servants? Each of the crew members had been outfitted in an orange T-shirt with "CETA" printed over the pocket. "So we can keep track of who shows up," the CETA supervisor said. Then he thought for a moment and added, "To keep 'em separate from the regular workers."

The CETA system had decreed that participants weren't part of the conventional workforce, although the work they did was as conventional and as hard as the work of regular adult Park Department employees. Public bureaucracies serve to separate youngsters from the mainstream, not to integrate them.

Critics may charge that public systems dealing with underprivileged children perpetuate and reinforce a caste system, dividing insiders from outsiders, projecting the judgments of success and failure into adulthood. But at least it might be said in their defense that most public systems do not consciously seek to break up families, to separate the young from their parents. (Some might argue that an exception is the welfare system, which forces adult male breadwinners out of the household.) That is true as long as juveniles stay in school and remain at home. It isn't true when they drop out and leave their families.

The youngster out on the street is likely to come under the control of two primary systems: juvenile justice and residential care. Reformers have long maintained that the goal of both systems, except in the case of serious criminal offenders, should be to reunite the adolescents with their families and communities whenever possible. The National Council on Crime and Delinquency observed in an unpublished discussion paper:

> Services to troubled youth and families must bear in mind that the development of close ties between child and responsive adult is essential to healthy emotional growth. . . . Only in a very extreme case should a child be separated from his or her family. . . . The monies spent paying others to care for young people could, for the most part, be better spent providing services to them and their families in the natural environment of their own homes, schools and communities.[5]

Approximately 55 percent of all people arrested each year are under the age of twenty-two. Some studies have found that as many as half are charged with "status" offenses; that is, acts that would be legal if committed by adults.[6] These include running away from home, truancy, possession of alcohol, and "sexual immorality." As one federal study noted, "Jails, detention centers and training schools are filled with youth whose only crime has been disobedience or unruliness."

Many of those picked up on criminal, rather than status, charges have not committed serious crimes. "In the mind of the public, the term 'juvenile delinquent' brings up the feared image of a huge, cruel, youthful predator," says William E. Gladstone, a circuit judge in Miami. "There are such delinquents, but it is very important to realize that they make up an almost minuscule percentage of the delinquent population. . . . Only about five percent of all arrested delinquents are, by any definition, violent."[7]

In the last spasm of reform policy, the Law Enforcement Assistance Administration attempted in the early 1970s to divert status

and nonviolent offenders away from the criminal justice system
and back to their communities and families. The deinstitutionaliza-
tion policy established youth service bureaus in local communities
to rehabilitate youngsters. In general, the result was that white
youths from middle-class families were returned to their homes
and communities. Minority youngsters were kept locked up. As
one youth policy analyst points out:

> Unfortunately, these neighborhood-based alternatives to incarcera-
> tion were developed, for the most part, outside the minority neigh-
> borhoods that needed them most. Most youth service bureaus were
> created in suburban areas by people alarmed by the growing num-
> bers of drug abusers and runaways among their youth. Today, you
> would be hard pressed to find 10 of the 500 bureaus run by minority
> neighborhood organizations.[8]

I visited six youth detention facilities directed by the juvenile
justice system. In each of them, youths can be held anywhere
from a few hours to six months awaiting disposition of the charges
against them. I was struck by two elements common to all of
the facilities. One was the predominance of black and Hispanic
detainees. The other was the across-the-board acknowledgment
by officials and youth counselors that little was being done to
rehabilitate incarcerated youth. "Oh, there's some lip-service to
counseling," said a former counselor at Newark's Youth House.
"Maybe an hour a week. But this is basically a place to isolate
and punish kids. And it doesn't make a difference if they're guilty
or not. The attitude is, If they're here, they're guilty."

My impressions were supported by national data gathered
by the federal Office of Juvenile Justice and Delinquency Prevention (OJJDP). In 1985, James Wooten, the OJJDP administrator,
reported that while minority youths account for 28 percent of
all juvenile arrests, more than half of all youths held in detention
centers and 48 percent of those sent to reform school were members of minority groups. Twice the proportion of blacks versus
white youths were sent to adult courts, where they would be dealt
with more harshly. Each year some 480,000 juveniles are held in
about 8,800 adult jails, detention centers, and lockups. "When
reasons for arrest are held constant," Wooten says, "minorities
are more likely to be arrested, more likely to be formally referred
for court processing, more likely to spend a longer time in the

system, and more likely to be held in a detention center or jail."[9]

The decision on whether to release a youth back into his family and community is a judgment call. The judgment is most often based on the likelihood of recidivism. What prefigures recidivism? In the instant judgment of probation officers, who in New York City have an average caseload of 225, two of the most accurate predictors are family stability and employment. White middle-class youths are more likely to have come from "stable" families, where the parents are employed and have the means to find jobs for their children. Minority youngsters who have been arrested will more frequently come from broken families marked by high unemployment rates and welfare dependency. If you play the averages, you will refer a white youth for treatment to the community; you'll keep the black youth behind bars. "Those deemed treatable are diverted and provided with services," concludes administrator Wooten. "The others—and those are the minorities—stay in the system and go to court . . . Kids who have a lot going for them will get more help. Those who do not, will not."

I understand the need to lock up kids who commit serious, violent crimes. That's what jails are for. But there are many other institutions that assume responsibility for youngsters whose only offense is that they are alone on the street. The federal government estimated that there are between 730,000 and 1 million "runaways" in the United States—a term that refers to a youngster under eighteen "who absents himself or herself from home . . . without the permission of parents or legal guardians." The government puts the annual number of "homeless" youth at 500,000; approximately 150,000 of those receive services provided by federally funded facilities. Some 60,000 of them are actually sheltered in facilities funded by the federal government.[10]

But the youths who are served by the federal runaway and homeless program represent only a thin slice of the vagrant adolescent population. There are 250,000 adolescents, half of them minority juveniles, who spend time in short-term or extended foster care. There are kids in group homes supported by private donations and philanthropies. There are kids in drug treatment facilities, in psychiatric institutions, in training schools, in multiservice centers, in residential employment programs such as the Job Corps, and in sectarian or religiously oriented facilities. Some of these programs are inspected and supervised by public agencies; others are answerable only to themselves. In some programs, kids spend only a few hours; in others, they spend days, weeks, months, years.

Most of the programs that provide relatively short-term shelter say their objective is "to reunite children with their families . . . to strengthen family relationships." But that's not what most of the youngsters who had been there told me. They said that shelters and other residential facilities were good for a hot meal and a temporary roof over their heads. But only five of 142 teenagers who said they had used these services thought that they had helped to resolve the differences that divided them from their parents. There were only two who said that the staff followed up for more than two weeks after they had left the residences.

It's important to remember that of the 280 youngsters I spent time with, 110 were black and 120 were Hispanic; only 50 were white. The shelters and other facilities that minority kids used were not located in their communities; of the nearly 300 shelters established by the federal Department of Health and Human Services, no more than a dozen are operated by minority neighborhood organizations.

The white kids who had spent time in shelters tended to regard them as temporary waystops. They simply didn't raise the issue of whether the shelters had helped them to resolve their differences with their parents. That was something they felt they ought to do on their own, when they were ready. But from the responses of the minority kids, I assumed that the shelter system operated on the same double standard that characterized the juvenile justice system: It tried to reunite those kids and families it deemed treatable—middle-class white kids with basically stable families; it placed troubled minority youths who came from distressed families in foster care, in institutions, or in other out-of-family living arrangements.

As I learned shortly, that conclusion was too hasty. What I ultimately discovered was that the system treated all kids alike— they treated them as delinquents. Simply being on the street was evidence of delinquency. It didn't matter whether you were a poor Hispanic girl who'd been thrown out of your home because you were pregnant or a white kid with a drinking problem. You got the same rough treatment.

I came to this realization by accident. I had a conversation with an old friend. When I finished talking to him, my perspective had changed. What I learned was that except perhaps for youth from the most affluent and influential families, all kids, once they have left their homes and schools, become part of a new caste of pariahs.

It would be hard to imagine anyone better qualified to deal with the problems of a distraught adolescent than Mike Coleman.* I had met Mike ten years before, when we both worked in a national program directed toward poor youth, as well as other disadvantaged groups. Mike had come into that program after helping organize and supervise an innovative employment effort for poor, mostly black and Hispanic youngsters in New York. He had begun his career as a lawyer in the Midwest but, seized by the social concerns of his time, had left the practice of law to practice social betterment. In 1984, when I interviewed him for this book, he was widely regarded as a knowledgeable public policy analyst.

Mike thought deeply about social problems. He approached them from his own distinctive perspective, which blended compassion, humor, and intelligence. He despised bureaucratic jargon and mistrusted policy based on purely statistical calculations. He saw kids not as a class or a social category but as individuals, with distinct problems and needs. When we had worked together I hadn't been surprised to learn that he was writing a novel. As I expected, the manuscript was witty, ironic, and filled with revealing, evocative detail—not the work of your average policy analyst.

I had sought out Mike for an interview because I considered him an "expert" on the employment problems confronting minority youth. Stricken by the common journalistic affliction of tunnel vision, I had not thought of asking him about a subject on which he was clearly the leading expert: His own life. We were sitting in a crowded Japanese restaurant in Manhattan. As Mike listened to my first question, he scratched his beard and then waved his chopsticks to cut me off. "I'll be glad to answer any of your questions about employment," he said. "But first maybe I should tell you what happened to us and our daughter."

Mike and his wife, Susan, were both in their second marriage. She had been married to a man who was now serving time for armed robbery and drug dealing. Mike's story began in the mid-1970s. At that time, Susan had a ten-year-old daughter, Linda,

* Not his real name.

by her first husband. Mike's own daughter was seven. The Colemans also had a new baby boy, then about eight months old. They were living in a small suburban town outside of New York City. Now let Mike tell the rest:

Linda began to show strange behavior. Suddenly, she'd be in the corner of her room yelling I was molesting her. We thought she was just going through a tough period and she'd come out of it. There was some pressure on her. We had a one-year-old son who was easy for everybody to love. I had come on the scene, displacing her father, who had been a violent man and who had beaten her. Her mother hated her ex-husband, and the girl was always hearing that, and she was imagining that her natural father loved her more than anybody. She forgot all about the beatings. She'd say, "All I want to do is go back to my father," which was difficult, since he was in the penitentiary.

I was trying to deal with her very gently, trying to gain her trust. We offered to have her see a therapist or a counselor with us or by herself, but she wouldn't go. It went on and on. If she couldn't get her way with everything, she'd have these tremendous tantrums. She'd break everything she could get hold of. In school, the teachers were saying, This kid fucks up everything—we can't deal with her, get her out of here. I set up an appointment for Linda with a woman who was an authority on child development at a university. Linda wouldn't go. Whatever problems she had, it seemed to me, weren't going to be resolved by being nice and sympathetic.

When she was twelve, we came home and found a note on her bed. She'd failed all her classes and decided to run away. In one sense it was almost a relief. We'd had all this day-to-day tension; everything you know how to do doesn't seem to work. What're you going to do—lock her up someplace? Now things had come to a head, we could take some action. We checked around, found out she was staying with a girlfriend. I called her and said, "I want to pick you up." She said, "No, I don't want to come home." I thought we'd cool it for a day or two, let her think things over, make her own decision to come back. But we started to get phone calls from people who were saying, Your daughter is moving around from family to family. One neighbor said, "If you don't get her back real quick we'll call the police." We got a call from the undertaker, who was the town sheriff. He said—I'll never forget it—"The police are gonna be on you—get the kid back."

That forced me to drop my stoicism. The last thing I wanted was to get this small rednecked town's police involved in our family's problems. So much for community support.

At her friend's house, it was apparent Linda was okay, but she wouldn't go with me. I had to physically carry her out to the car, kicking and screaming. I took her directly to the hospital, where the doctor gave her a shot to calm her down. So what do I do next? We'd heard about a residential program run by Catholic social services. We felt anything which could give her a little bearing, where she could half settle down, we could live with. It troubled me that they didn't focus on analyzing the past of the situation, only the here and now. But we thought we'd give it a try. We visited her every weekend. After six months, the program people said, She's making no progress. She's throwing tantrums, upsetting the other kids, messing up the program. They recommended we put her in a state program.

Literally, I didn't know what to do. She wouldn't come home, they wouldn't keep her there. We tried a private residential school. She lasted a month: same result. We could have tried other private places, but they were all 15–20 grand a year. There was no help whatsoever for a middle-class kid. There was no alternative: She was impossible to live with, the rest of the family was breaking down having her around. I hated to do it but I went to court and took out a PINS (person in need of supervision) petition which enabled me to put her in a state facility.

I was very leery about this state place. It had *bars* on the windows. But the woman we spoke to there was very nice; strict but nice. She assured us they didn't use any drugs at all on the kids. We were told we couldn't visit Linda for the next eight weeks. That was so they could assert control, *right*. When we saw her after two months, she'd gained like 40 pounds. They'd put her on potent, powerful drugs that made her big and fat. Linda told us what had happened: They'd put her in these group therapy sessions. Now this is a twelve-, thirteen-year-old. She'd show up wearing a red baseball cap, and they'd force her to tell them the significance of wearing a red baseball cap at a therapy session. The significance is that she's a teenager who wears a red baseball cap. Period. One night after being criticized by everybody, she lashed out and tried to hit one of the teachers. So they put her on these drugs, and they put her in solitary confinement.

I went to the psychiatrist. I was terribly upset. I said, "Aren't you supposed to be able to deal with this? I mean,

Aren't you supposed to help her?" The psychiatrist hands me a letter. It says that Linda is manic, with suicidal tendencies. They were recommending that she be sent to solitary confinement at a state hospital. At the age of thirteen, they were recommending a kid be locked up in a secure facility. I'd be sitting there reading the letter, listening to the psychiatrist, thinking, "Oooooh, no, what kind of a loser are you?" I asked the psychiatrist how Linda was doing in her school classes. The psychiatrist said, "We don't send her to class unless she behaves perfectly." Well, hell, I thought, I don't have to put her into an institution for that; I can do that.

I asked if she could come home for a weekend. They said, "Just for a weekend." I brought her home and never took her back. I told the director of the place that if they gave me any trouble they'd see a lawsuit the like of which they'd never seen. Later, I found out that other parents had instituted a lawsuit against the place. It was closed down a year and a half afterward.

At home nothing much changed. She'd go along perfectly fine for a month, and she'd go into a tantrum that had nothing to do with any particular way she was being treated. I blew up. I said, "The rest of the family is falling to pieces because of you. I can't let the other kids fall apart. I have no place else to send you. I just don't know what to do."

A few days later, she ran away again. She had some friends in Syracuse. A month or so later she called to say she'd caught gonorrhea, and that I'd better get up there right away. That was an important turning point. I said, "If you're old enough to run away, you're old enough to figure out how to get a doctor." You never know if you're analyzing the situation correctly. But I felt there was a certain gaming element to it. She was running us on a short string. She'd do something and see what kind of a reaction she'd get. Well, my reaction was, Linda, you have to take some responsibility for your life.

After a while she came home again. We tried different things. Nothing worked. She'd run away, come home, run away. Finally, I thought of something I'd never otherwise have thought of as a middle-class person, if not for my professional experience. I sent her to a YCC (Youth Conservation Corps) camp.* It was a residential program for nine months. She worked outdoors, clearing trails. It was real work.

She was there for nine months. Her counselor was a black guy from the Bronx. She couldn't play games with him. YCC

---

* YCC is a state-run residential program in which youngsters work to preserve and enhance public land.

was a third way to go. It was an alternative to being at home or being in an institution. The people in the program recognized that she had problems, but the problems weren't glorified or magnified. They weren't putting her through group therapy sessions. They gave her a chance, and this was very critical, to work through her problems, to get them out of her system, on her own. They were really saying to her: If you're gonna run away, you got to work, you got to assume responsibilities.

When she came home, this kid had really changed. She felt she'd made her own success. She got her high school equivalency diploma. She took a job, which she's held for more than two years. Now she's thinking of going to community college. Something happened recently that showed me just how different she is now. She got into a car accident, $1,100 damage. Another time, she would have ranted and raved. She would have blamed everybody but herself. Now, she quietly explained what happened, she didn't make excuses. She said she'd pay back the damages, every month. She never panicked. I was proud of Linda.

Mike and Linda's story is unusual only for its ending. Mike (and I) had met so many other kids who had gone through periods of rebellion and alienation, who'd left home and wandered the streets, who had landed in punishing and abusive institutions, but who had never been able to make peace with themselves or their parents. What was different about Linda's experience? Partly, said Mike, it was the YCC approach that allowed her to achieve some success on her own. But perhaps the most important element was Mike's relationship to Linda.

"She had someone, namely me, all through that period," he said. "Regardless of where she was, she could talk to me and I wouldn't give her an emotional reaction. And she used that connection all through that time. I felt good about that. Even at the worst times, there was some connection. There was a point with her that I had to call her bluff. But you know, Bernie, the only way I knew when to do that was because I had five years' experience with her. YCC was there, I was there, at the right time for my daughter."

That was not true of the adolescents he supervised in his youth employment program. "A lot of the kids there, seventeen-, eighteen-year-old boys, couldn't find a connection with anybody that was enduring for them. They didn't have someone who they knew deep down had a real affection for them, someone they could go back to, to try and try again. I looked at those kids in my program, they'd gone from one institution to another institution, from one scene to another scene. They'd never dealt with anybody long enough to have somebody who could be both affectionate and know enough about them to help. When it got a little hard to deal with these kids, they just moved them on."

In Mike's employment program there was a black youngster named Eddie. He was constantly in trouble. Mike's assistant, a black man, recommended that Eddie be expelled from the program. "I kept saying, Give Eddie a chance. I was the laughing stock of the kids and the staff. They felt he was gaming me. I thought so, too, but I didn't know how else to keep him in there. One time Eddie pleaded for *another* second chance. I said, Okay. He walked out of my office into this room where there was thirty, forty guys. He's giving them a high sign. And he turns around, and there's a bottle of vodka in his back pocket. I had to let him go. I had no choice. So he went back out on the street. If he'd had a connection with somebody, the kind of connection my daughter had with me, would we have lost Eddie? The fact is, he had nobody. He was out there alone."

Linda Coleman's experience with youth institutions—punishment and rejection—is unremarkable. Her bad luck was in her timing. She had problems at the moment an enormous sea change in social thought and policy was taking place in the United States. A decade earlier, and she might have profited from the then dominant idea that with material investment, compassion, and guidance, institutions and individuals could be rehabilitated. At the heart of that belief was a sense of optimism that every individual, especially if young, has an untapped core of goodness and decency. To reach and activate that critical core, it was felt that treatment should couple supportive therapy with an improvement in the individual's economic and social condition. Describing the prevailing philosophy of the 1960s toward crime and punishment, the social policy analyst Ronald Bayer writes: "More resources, greater effort, more serious commitment—these were the ingredients necessary to realize the promise of rehabilitation."[11]

America's attention to social concern is, as history is measured, a blink. In the late 1960s and early 1970s, efforts were made to divert nonviolent offenders from juvenile justice institutions and to return them to their communities, where they could receive counseling from the youth welfare system. In some localities there had been an attempt to substitute restitution for imprisonment when youths were charged with property crimes. However, those efforts were never accompanied by a comprehensive attempt to confront some of the root causes of juvenile lawlessness. There was no extensive program to provide employment for youths charged with relatively minor crimes. There was no comprehensive inquiry into why those youngsters had failed in school and what educational alternatives should be established for them. There was no comprehensive attack on the poverty that eroded family relationships.

Other countries, such as Sweden, Scotland, Yugoslavia, and Canada, have, with considerable success, limited the extent of punishment for minor crimes by young people and diverted those not accused of adult crimes to social welfare agencies. But in the United States, the fear of violent crime by youth—a fear unsubstantiated by actual crime statistics—has replaced attempts at rehabilitation with harsher treatment. In the late 1970s, twelve states passed laws making it easier for juvenile offenders to be tried and sentenced in adult courts. New York State's Juvenile Offender Law, passed in 1978, included a provision to waive juvenile cases to family court. But a study of 754 cases during a six-month period found that only twelve had been actually transferred to family court.

Many of those short-lived reform efforts were developed as a response to the urban rioting of the 1960s. But by the 1980s the once-restive ghettos of the 1960s were becalmed, temporarily mummified. The inescapable clamor of entire neighborhoods, communities, and cities self-destructing was replaced by the task of subduing individual restive youths, one by one, a task more manageable for conservatives and liberals alike. And so, with reasonable justification, Ronald Bayer could write, "As caution and pessimism have replaced optimism, liberalism has not only lost its vigor, but its luster as well." And he could add, with equal justification, "the liberal outlook has increasingly begun to resemble the conservative perspective against which it had set itself in opposition during much of the postwar period. . . . That is a loss of incalculable significance, one that is bound to affect every aspect of American social life and thought."

In fact, when it concerns youth, the loss is calculable. It may be calculated by examining what has replaced the withered rehabilitative ethic. The first alternative to rehabilitation is indifference, reducing or eliminating services to the adolescents and families who need them most. One bread-and-butter service is jobs. By the early 1980s, 250,000 fewer minority youngsters took part in the federal employment and training programs. In New York, alone, the number of kids in the summer youth employment program dropped from 62,000 in 1978 to 41,000 in 1982.[12] Across the country, the professional staffs serving disadvantaged youths— basic education and remedial teachers, skill instructors, job developers, counselors, program planners—were reduced or eliminated. The basic infrastructure developed over twenty years— community-based intake centers and outreach efforts, skill centers, auxiliary and alternative schools—were being stripped to the bone. Even such agencies as the Employment Service, which do not serve youth primarily, were being cut back.

What was left of the employment effort was directed toward the private sector. Consequently, untrained and unskilled youths with myriad personal problems had to compete with out-of-work urban adults in an increasingly white-collar service economy. The few youths who were helped to find jobs would be those most appealing to private employers—presentable, articulate youngsters who were already doing reasonably well in school and whose home lives were relatively peaceful. The others were too much trouble to deal with, so policymakers chose not to deal with them.

Another alternative to rehabilitation is a policy that might be described as: Lock them up until they outgrow their problems. A full elaboration of this approach is offered by John Mueller, a political science professor at the University of Rochester. Professor Mueller argues that the take from street crime is "ridiculously small"; by his calculations it would take fifty crimes a year to rise above the poverty line. As street kids mature, he says, they are bound to recognize the unprofitability and irrationality of petty crime as a vocation. But what to do with them until they gain that insight? "It may well be sensible, then, to heed . . . call[s] for longer terms of incarceration, that keeps criminals off the streets while age and rationality catch up with them."[12] Professor Mueller apparently believes that most prison inmates emerge from confinement with a community of felons as hopeful, ambitious, and repentant citizens.

The last alternative is a form of therapy that mixes punishment and isolation. This involves stripping youngsters bare of all defenses, denying that they have any value in the world, and exposing them to the humiliation of their peers and all-powerful adult authorities. Redemption comes when they confess their worthlessness. Then they can be remade into new persons.

Linda Coleman got a taste of that treatment when she entered the state institution in New York. But she had parents who were knowing and resourceful and who could rescue her before the damage was irreversible. Others are not so fortunate.

Chillin' Out

Some youngsters I met scared me. They were quite capable, I believe, of killing people as well as destroying themselves, and of causing enormous grief for their families and others who cared about them. Yet even the hardest cases I met went through periods of reflection and self-assessment. They paused to ask: What's happening to me? Where am I going? Is what I'm doing worth it? Can I change? What will happen to me if I don't change?

I don't mean that those periods of self-examination hit them with the stunning impact of revealed truth. Just as children in school gradually change, reach certain thresholds, attempt to adapt to more complex and challenging standards, so, too, do youngsters who find themselves divorced from the central institutions of society. The impetus to change comes from different sources. When boys and girls discover each other, they may be momentarily distracted from the street hustle; romance takes the place, at least until it fades, of family affection and commitment. When a kid puts in time in a juvenile justice institution, he comes back to the street knowing that if he's picked up again he's probably going to serve hard time. When a teenager gives birth, she can't escape the awareness that she has responsibility for two lives now. The most maladapted kid gets tired; he gets worn down when his best friend is killed, when he's spent years pumping junk into his veins, when he's scrambled all his youth for the tough change to buy food and shelter. He begins to wonder what tough changes he's going to have to go through as an adult. It's time, as the kids say, to chill out.

When the chill hits, there are a few kids, a tiny minority of all those I met, who are able to straighten out on their own.

Irene Rogers was one. Irene was the super-bright young woman in Detroit who was forced to leave school by her mother, who wanted her to stay at home to take care of the younger children while she pursued her own religious vocation. As one of Irene's friends in school predicted, Irene became pregnant less than a year after she left.

Another young woman, seventeen, living alone, pregnant, frustrated at every turn, might have crumbled under the pressure. Not Irene.

> Before I left my mother I wasn't sexually active. I didn't even see boys. I couldn't get phone calls at home, my mother was so strict. When I found out I was pregnant, I was kinda dazed. I was afraid to tell my mother, but the way I told her was over a telephone. I said, "Mother, I have something to tell you." And she said, "Well, tell." I said, "I'll tell you later." She said, "Tell me now." And I told her. And she said, "Well, I had a feeling that was going to happen." She didn't have a fire in her or anything like that. All she said was, "Well, it's not as bad as it could be."

Irene was somewhat encouraged. She thought there was a chance her mother would take her back and help her through her pregnancy. One thing she was adamant about: She wasn't going to live with the father of her baby. "I wasn't going to get married just because I'd made a mistake. My life was complicated enough. I didn't want to complicate it any more." But Irene would be more alone than she expected. "I don't know why—she never told me—but my mother stopped talking to me. She just did. From November to June. She was so cold. It was like I was just somebody she had just met. You know, 'How do you like the weather?' And that hurt. She made me feel like she wanted so much from me, and I'd just messed up."

For a while Irene thought about giving up her baby for adoption "so I wouldn't have to tell my mother, but I decided it's senseless to carry your baby for nine months and then give it up. If you have the responsibility to have it in the first place, you can feed it, you can take care of it."

Irene entered a group home for unwed mothers. After her son was born, she returned to school, as much for her child as for herself. "I have big dreams for David. When I get out of here and when I finish college, I want to get a nice, peaceful job so I can put him in private schools." Why private schools? "I'd think if I'm paying for the school, I have a right to know, What is my child learning? I could actually control what happens to him." When David grows up, she says, "he can have friends, and he can get interested in all types of things. But I just don't want him to be a person that wants to scrape by. I want him to have a good background, so he can say, 'My mother raised me right.' Even if he doesn't act like it, he won't be sorry later for the way I raised him."

As might be expected, welfare doesn't figure in her plans. "I'm getting help from the group home I'm in, and I'm thankful, but I'd rather be taking care of myself. To me, if you're on welfare long enough, you just become lazy and don't try to do anything to help yourself. You just sit back."

Irene knows that it isn't going to be easy to remain independent; she knows because she's seen the troubles her sister is having. Carol, a year older, left home at almost the same time Irene did. "I stay out of communication with her," says Irene. "We're very different types of people. She's been arrested for stealing. She has a baby, but she's a gypsy because she loves the street.

"When we were very young Carol would tell the teacher that mother wouldn't feed her and then she would eat all the food she could get and throw it up. She's always been a charmer. She'd act very nice to somebody to do wrong to them. And she was stubborn, a very stubborn girl. If she doesn't change, she will definitely end up in jail or dead before she's even twenty-five. She's a wanderer. She just moves all the time, and I'm afraid she's wandering into trouble."

That's not the direction Irene is traveling. Some months after I talked to her, she called to give me an update. She had gone back to school and was going to graduate shortly. Her baby was fine, and she was planning to move out of the group house and into her own apartment. She had a job lined up, and she had been accepted into a community college in Detroit. The specific reason she was calling was that she wanted to invite me to a conference on adolescent sexuality and pregnancy. Irene was chairing the conference. I apologized for not being able to attend. Later she sent me a copy of her remarks, which began, "A while ago, I was in bad trouble and I didn't know anyone in the world I could ask for help. So I decided the only way I was going to get out of my problems was by doing it myself."

Irene had certain advantages, chief among them that she came from a self-sustaining family. But the fact is that Irene is a rare young woman. She has always been determined to succeed. She didn't want to leave school; she was forced out of it. She didn't want to leave home; she was driven away. When she was alone and pregnant and had no choice but to enter an institution, she used that chill-out period to assess her condition coolly, to marshal her inner resources, and to devise a strategy to improve her life.

Many of the youngsters I met did not possess her clarity of vision or her determination. They needed help to untrack themselves. By untrack, I mean that they needed to reinterpret and redirect the themes that had driven them up to then: searching for independence; securing a place in a community that accepts them; resolving their uncertain relationships with their parents; replacing their home boy alliances with more productive and supportive collaborations, and converting the fuel of adolescent excitement, risk-taking, and volatility into adult striving and achievement.

The first step on this road is a moral and intellectual calculation of how living in the wild affects them and others, now and later. In Dade County, Florida, a study was conducted in 1980 of 100 juvenile offenders and their families. The delinquents were presented with a Moral Development Scale devised by the researchers. The scale was derived from the theories of the Swiss psychologist Jean Piaget, who maintained that as children grow older their ideas about morality change, from assuming that an act that results in their punishment is inherently wrong to distinguishing right from wrong on the basis of what is good or bad for society as a whole.

Conventional, well-adjusted children shift in their thinking between the ages of seven and nine from a preoccupation with their self-interest to a concern with the impact of their behavior on others. The study found that a majority of the juvenile offenders hadn't made that transition. Confronted with different sets of moral dilemmas, they responded more as young children would rather than as adolescents. They were presented with a scenario in which a boy accidentally knocks a pile of fifteen dishes off a table. Another boy defies his mother and takes a single cookie from a jar, breaking the lid. The delinquents thought the first boy had acted in a "worse" way, and was deserving of harsher punishment, because his clumsiness had resulted in fifteen dishes being broken, while the other boy had broken only one lid. As the researchers noted, the delinquents did not include "intentionality" in their moral calculations. The individual's responsibility for his act, a conscious act as opposed to an accident, did not enter into their assessment of guilt—only the amount of damage. Neither did they consider motivation; calculated wrongdoing was no worse—and perhaps better, if the wrongdoer escaped punishment—than an accident.

At the same IQ level, the researchers concluded, "all delinquents, regardless of ethnic background, scored significantly lower than non-delinquents on the Moral Development Scale."[14] Florida Circuit Judge William Gladstone puts a finer point on it: "The delinquent teenagers . . . do not really distinguish between buying a watch, stealing a watch from a table or obtaining a watch by committing a violent robbery."[15]

Chilling out can be an opportunity to grow up. In these periods of voluntary or enforced repose, street kids can take stock of what they're doing. They can calculate the dangers posed to them and to their innocent victims by their continued lawlessness, and they may conclude that the moral cost to them and others is too great. During such intermissions they may decide they are tired of scrambling on the street. The excitement of the danger of the street may begin to wear off. They may be exposed to an adult who has tried to persuade them to change. But change poses difficult questions: Change to what? What's the alternative to the street? What are the rewards for changing?

When your life is on the line, the reward for changing is unambiguous. After a shootout on the street, Ralph Ortiz, the Chicago "gang leader," was arrested when he was spotted carrying a sawed-off shotgun. He spent a year and a half locked up in state institutions in Joliet and St. Charles. When he was released he was sixteen. He returned to his neighborhood and rejoined his gang. He recalls:

> There were people I hurted before I got sent away. They were still trying to kill me. For my own protection I said I was going to join back.
>   And I did. I became president of the gang. And it just made *everything* worse. The streets were running with blood; I could see the blood on my boots. I was askin', "When's

my time gonna come? When am I gonna get it?" I thought the averages were just workin' against me. So I decided to quit. But you can't just quit without gettin' a violation. That's the justice of the gang. That's the way the system works on the street. Three different sections of the gang kicked my ass. One after the other. I was in the hospital for a week. These guys were once my family, but if you're not in the family any more you got to take the rap.

To this very day there are certain areas in this community, I don't even go to, because *they* live there. And if I just walk in front of the house, I get blown away. They don't want to give up. They don't want to let me go.

His leaving was made easier when he found an alternative to the structure and the system of the gang. He met someone who introduced him to a community organization that was putting together an acting troupe. The troupe put on performances at Chicago schools about dropping out, about drugs, about gangs, subjects he knew something about.

I still had a lot of hate in me. Nobody in the group liked me because I was *muy macho.* If anybody said something stupid, I'd slap them. I didn't care who you were. But the people thought I was artistic. I watched them and I really enjoyed their acting and they explain to me how they do it. I understand 'cause I been acting all my life, playing a part in school, with my mom, with gangbanging in the street, with watching my ass in jail. I knew all about acting.

Ralph has traveled to different states with his acting troupe. He is also attending classes at an alternative high school. "I always wanted to be a star," he says. "In the gang I was a star, and doing this I could be a star also. But the real reason for doin' it is, I'm tired of war. I've been through enough war just in this community. I'm really tired of seeing people die—for what? I wanna live."

Bill Craig was also tired of seeing people die. After his closest friend, Johnny Bayley, high on drugs and alcohol, died in a car crash, Bill felt abandoned. Abandoned in the drug trade. Abandoned in the empty houses and railroad sidings of his vagrant youth in Newport. Then love walked in.

Her name was Marie, and he met her in the parking lot of a grocery store. Bill remembers:

> I really looked shitty. I was wearing the same pair of jeans for two weeks. I had long hair and I hadn't washed it for a week. And I was loaded. I went up to her and I said, "I wanna kiss you." She said, "*Really.* I ain't gonna kiss *you.*" I said, "Wanna bet?" and I leaned over and kissed her. I said, "I wanna take you out." She said, "I don't know. I'm not gonna let you take me out and throw me on the bed. I want more than that."

Marie, like Bill, had been a street kid in Newport for years. She had dropped out of school and run away from home when she was fourteen after her father beat her with a 2-by-4. "I was beaten all my life," she says. There were not that many places to hang out in Newport. Marie and Bill kept running into each other. "I was attracted by his personality," Marie says. "It was really good. Most boys want one thing, but not Billy. He wanted somebody to take care of him. To love him."

That's not exactly how Bill remembers it. "I kept saying, 'I don't want love. I don't want it.' After Johnny died, I didn't wanna be close to anybody. But she wouldn't let me go. She was always followin' me."

Marie laughs. "I told him I'm yours, like it or not. I kept buggin' him: Go get a haircut, buy some clothes. When I had some money I went out and bought him a clean outfit. He said, 'I'll score some dope and pay you back.' I told him, 'Just take it. Don't worry about payin' me.'"

Six months after they met, Marie became pregnant. They wanted to move in together, but her mother tried to prevent it. Marie was referred by a city agency to Millie Little, a Newport social worker. After a protracted court battle, Little succeeded in winning "independent living" status for Bill and Marie. She found them a three-room apartment in a fourth-floor walkup. She helped Bill to find a job in a dry cleaning store. "Not all street kids can live independently," she said. "They're too scattered, too unfocused to make it by themselves. Most of the time I try to keep the kid in the family. But Bill and Marie were different. They cared for each other and they wanted the baby. Kids may have a high survival ability on the streets but a very low maturity.

By sacrificing for the baby, Bill and Marie were showing me that they were mature enough to make it together."

Marie says, "We fought for so long and I was about to give up. But Billy says, 'We've been alone; now there's this woman, Millie, who's dependin' on us. We have a *responsibility* to her. We just can't walk away.'"

It would be satisfying to say that by accepting their responsibilities, by committing themselves to an alternative to the brutalizing system of the streets, Bill Craig and Ralph Ortiz and other kids who have chilled out for the long haul have written themselves a happy ending to their unhappy adolescence. But there is more to responsible adulthood than fidelity to wife and child or touring the schools preaching the evils of drugs and gangs. To fulfill good intentions, to bring order from chaos, you have to pay your way. That, in America, is the principal measure of maturity. You have to work.

The winter of 1984–85 was a cheering one for many Americans. More people were working. Some sectors of the economy, high technology in particular, were prospering. Many Americans were expressing their confidence in the future by investing in IRAs and Keogh Plans. But conditions weren't so good for young Americans who were coming off the streets and trying to build a future for themselves.

The unemployment rate for all Americans was around 8 percent; for teenagers it was more than 20 percent. More than 40 percent of Hispanic kids were out of work, and almost half of the black teenagers were looking for a job. The black teenage unemployment rate was more than two and a half times that of white teenagers.

I made a second visit to Chicago and Newport that winter. I wanted to find out how Ralph Ortiz and Bill Craig were doing. The news was mixed. Ralph was still performing at the schools— nonpaying work. In the seven months since I had last seen him he had held five different salaried jobs. He had worked in a ball bearing plant, in a glass company, in a chocolate plant, and in a machine shop, and had hauled garbage. In all but the glass company, he had been hired when business was on the upswing and fired when it slacked off. At the glass company he was told layoffs were imminent. "I left before they laid me off," he said. "The acting at the schools was making me feel good, raising my spirits.

Then I'd spend forty, fifty hours a week sweeping up glass for $3.50 an hour. I guess I'm getting tired of shit work. I can't see myself as a sweeper no more."

In Newport, the smell of beans simmering filled the Craigs' apartment. Bill sat on the floor, his knees pressed up against his chest. Marie occupied the only seat in the living room, an armchair whose springs had finally broken through the tired fabric. There was no heat in the apartment, and she had wrapped herself in an Army blanket. The baby in her lap was bawling. Cartons were piled around the room. Today was moving day. The landlord was raising the rent by $50 a month—some young professionals from Cincinnati were moving into the neighborhood—and the Craigs had to find a cheaper place. Until they did, they were planning to stay in a shelter run by the city. Bill wasn't sure he could afford any rent at all, because he was being laid off by the dry cleaning shop. "I wasn't going to stay there forever," Bill said. "The chemicals really stink, but I was gonna stay until something better came along. I didn't expect to lose it. The guy just said, 'You have to the end of the week.' With losing the apartment and all, I don't know what I'm gonna do."

When the baby's crying drowned out our conversation, Bill picked him up. Rocking back and forth, singing softly to him, Bill carried the baby to the cradle in the bedroom. While he was gone, Marie whispered to me, "I worry about him all the time. He thinks he's failing us. If he don't find work, I'm afraida what he might do. He might end up on the street again."

Bill and Ralph had held a variety of jobs, some legit, some not so legit, while they were still with their parents and later. So did almost all of the youngsters I met. They had held jobs in the public youth employment system; they had worked for small local businesses. Most of those jobs were of short duration and paid the minimum wage or less. They did serve the purpose of providing some pocket change and diverting kids from less wholesome activities.

I am not a missionary composing panegyrics to the work ethic. There are some true believers who place great faith in the magic curative powers of working, but I don't think a job alone can instantly heal the complex of injuries, psychic and social, suffered by the most shell-shocked street kids. For them, work is only one component in a larger strategy of recovery. They need much more. Bobbie A. Jones, who directed public employment programs in Albuquerque during the early 1980s, says, "If we really wanted to serve hard-core unemployed youth, we'd have to do a lot more than we've been willing to do. That hard-core group would need every damn resource we've got.

"I'd need a large class of ESL [English as a second language] or a large class of academic preparation. In the first year almost 90 percent of my resources would be there. In the second year I phase down on that, move on to skills, and when you get to the tail end you have all your resources on job placement. And that's the beginning. After they get the job you give them support and every damn thing they need out there. So you wouldn't be looking for a payoff in less than three years, possibly four years. A reasonably stable nineteen-, twenty-year-old with some work experience, we can brush them up and send them out to a job. But the others? We don't want to make the investment, so we forget about them."[16]

Jones's analysis, I believe, is correct for the hardest of the hard cases; work, by itself, will not transform them. Problems arise when his analysis is used to justify denying stable employment to poor and minority youngsters emerging from adolescence. If you believe that *all* youngsters who have spent time on the street are so personally deficient that they cannot perform in the mainstream of the economy for a long time, then it's not necessary to engage the issue of whether these jobs are accessible to them at all. Deciding in advance that in their present state they cannot meet minimum standards for employment buries the bedrock issue: their exclusion from the primary job market.

If they did have access to a job, I don't think all of these youngsters would become nuclear physicists or CEOs at Fortune 500 corporations. They would have the opportunity, I think, to become what most of us become: reasonably self-satisfied mediocrities. That is not half bad. As many Americans have learned, there are rewards outside of work—in loving families and supportive friends. However, these relationships are hard to cultivate and sustain when you can't pay the rent, afford decent health care, or buy enough food to feed your family.

A decent job can unlock the prison of race and caste in America. For kids who have been branded failures in everything they've tried before, here's a chance to achieve, at last, some relative success. To ask youngsters who are reassessing their lives to reform themselves before the fact—to become model, law-abiding citizens and thoughtful and responsible parents—without first offering them the opportunity to succeed in the marketplace is to blackball them from membership in the American enterprise. To say, as we have, that this class of young Americans cannot take the first step when they are just learning to walk is to cripple them permanently. And not only them.

SIX

Openings and Closings

Eddie Cumberbatch

For many years my closest male friend was a black man named Eddie Cumberbatch.

We met when we worked together on a newspaper in New York. I was drawn to him by his charm, his grace, and his humor. In the 1970s, when I went to a party largely attended by blacks, the host would often try to justify my presence by listing my liberal credentials. Eddie would have none of that. He'd go up to the first attractive black woman he saw and say, "This is Bernie Lefkowitz. He's just as mixed up as we all are. Now why don't you go and teach him to dance."

The highs and lows in our lives seemed to come at the same time. We got divorced. We had disappointments in our work. We recovered from our disappointments and found new pleasures and satisfactions. We believed in our resilience.

Eddie would sometimes talk of his father, who had operated an elevator at Macy's for forty years. He said his dad was never ashamed of his job. "He said in all those years he never shut the elevator door on anybody's face." But the steady work and the steady pay didn't blind Eddie's dad to the limits society placed on a black man in the first half of this century. One night, not long before his father died, Eddie recalled, he looked up over his newspaper and said, "The way it has worked out hasn't been bad. But you'll do a lot better."

We both knew, Eddie perhaps more than I, that doing better did not rest on an individual's talent, pluck, and perseverence alone. In the early 1970s, we worked on a story together in Dallas. We went to a part of town called Mexicana Road, where black families had been suckered into buying houses in a new development for $500 down and a 25 percent interest rate on the mortgage. The developer hadn't gotten clearances from the city before the families moved in. So there was no electricity and water. The streets weren't paved. A few weeks after the houses were occupied, the foundations began to crumble and the roofs started to leak. The city said broken promises weren't its problem. The developer apparently felt the same way.

In the first house we visited, all the members of the family were doing this crazy dance. They darted across the room with buckets, trying to catch the snow falling through the holes in the roof. One of the children, a boy of about seven or eight, was standing at the top of a ladder, holding a bucket over the Christmas tree. "Mary," the husband said to his wife, "will you get our guests a drink? We have to celebrate the New Year."

In long nights of listening to jazz and drinking Scotch, we would recall that New Year's Eve in Dallas. As journalists we believed, devoutly, in cause and effect. Every conflict, every crisis, every injustice we wrote about had to have a cause. That was the way we had been trained to think. How else could you impose reason and order on events that seemed, all too often, to be random and irrational? How else could you explain *why* things happened?

So, in our reporting, we were always looking for the *why* in the hearts of people or in the policies of government. Sometimes the *why* was not that hard to find. We could determine how those families on Mexicana Road, who had worked hard and saved their money to buy their dream houses, ended up on New Year's Eve trying to catch snowflakes in their living rooms.

But other times the *why* was elusive. Why did people try to hurt people whom they didn't know, people who had never done them wrong? Why was it so hard to redress obvious abuses and injustices? When we discussed such matters the word that recurred was *irrationality*. It was my nature to fume about irrationality, to flush with indignation at the unfairness of it all. But Eddie would laugh a quick, knowing laugh and say, "We're professionals. It's our job to answer two questions. Why did it happen? We just can't say it's irrational and leave it at that. We also have to ask: Can we change things, so, maybe, it won't happen again?"

Eddie moved to Los Angeles. One night I got a call from his wife. At about nine in the evening he had been standing at a bus stop across the street from a supermarket and a liquor store. It had been a warm, pleasant evening, and lots of people were on the street. Bystanders told the police that a car filled with teenagers had driven by. One of the youths stuck a shotgun out of the window, pulled the trigger and blasted Eddie. The police called it a "drive-by" killing. "It's been happening a lot," the cop said. "They drive along, pick out a target, and fire away." No one was ever arrested.

For a long time I've tried to find a kernel of reason in this act of irrationality. What was that kid thinking when he saw a stranger on the street corner? What was he feeling when he squeezed the trigger? Did he wonder at all about the life he had just destroyed? I have finally despaired of ever finding the answers to these questions. And I don't have the answers to the questions Eddie would have wanted to ask: Why did it happen? Was there anything anybody could have done to divert that kid from his murderous nihilism? Is there anything anybody can do to prevent other kids from being consumed by pathological rage?

These questions were never far from my mind when I walked down desolation row with the youngsters I have written about. Usually I could brush them aside for the moment, because the kids I was talking to weren't especially threatening or violent; I saw them more as real victims than potential killers. But there were times, a few times . . . A kid says, "Nobody gives a damn about me, why should I give a damn about them?" A kid describes spitting in the face of a stranger, and I wonder, What if she had a knife or gun? A kid tells me about picking out a target on the street, stealing up behind his prey, putting an armlock around the victim's throat. What if the victim resists? What if the kid panics? Then I'd think about Eddie and that night in Los Angeles, and I'd wonder: Where's the line? When does the casual, detached violence of the streets spill over to homicide?

Fortunately, my experience with street kids was similar to what Judge William Gladstone found in Florida when he reviewed his caseload of juvenile offenders—90 percent of the delinquents who came before his court had not committed violent crimes.

I worried about that not-yet-violent 90 percent. These kids weren't killers. There was still a little time before they were swept up in the conscienceless destructiveness of the streets. It was too late to do anything to alter that terrible design that struck down Eddie. But it wasn't too late for most of the youngsters I met. And it wasn't too late for their younger brothers and sisters, still at home and still in school, who would join them all too soon on the street. For all of them I could still ask Eddie's questions: How can the script be rewritten? How can the ending be changed from tragedy to hope?

I found some of the answers in the story of one kid's spectacular rise from the depths of Newark.

Victory over Newark

When I talked to Robert Long, he was about to graduate at the top of his high school class. He had received offers of academic and athletic scholarships to several Ivy League colleges. But at fourteen his future had not looked that promising. His father had left home. His mother, who was working as a seamstress, was drinking heavily, so heavily that she was taken to a hospital in a coma. "I didn't understand why she was drinking," Robert says. "I thought I was doing something wrong. I was asking myself, Was it me?"

Robert didn't find much support outside of his home. "In this neighborhood there's a negative attitude about black kids who come out of the public projects," Robert says. "I was a smart kid, but parents told me, 'I don't want you to play with my child.' Straight out, they said: 'Sorry, you can't come into our house.' "

Almost every kid who came out of the projects in Newark's North Ward could be termed "at risk." Sixty percent of the kids in high school were dropping out; it was estimated that one out of every two kids in that area was born out of wedlock; 60 percent of the mothers were under nineteen, and 75 percent of the crime on Newark streets was being committed by juveniles.

Robert had been going after school to a neighborhood Boys

Club since he was nine years old. When he was fourteen and his family's problems were at their worst, he and a couple of other boys from his shattered neighborhood broke into the club's gym and tried to steal some basketballs. Suddenly the lights went on, and Robert's counselor at the club was standing there. "He talked to me for three hours that night. And he kept pounding at me all that week and the next one. Mainly, he said, 'Your mother's problems are not because of you. It's something she's going through. Now, Robert, you have a chance, a good chance. I'm going to be here for you all through school. I don't want you to let me down, but I also don't want you to let yourself down. You have a gift. You better start using it.' "

The counselor did more than talk. He brought Robert's mother into an Alcoholics Anonymous program. He got Robert's older sister and brother involved in Robert's welfare. But his influence was most important in overcoming Robert's resistance to adults. "After I started talking to him, I began to talk to my teachers, who were mostly white," Robert says. "I could see a lot of them were interested in me. They could see I didn't hang with the crowd. When I was in the cafeteria sitting alone, they'd come over and talk to me. I think they thought I was a kid who could make it and it was worth putting effort into me."

It must be said that Robert made it easy for the teachers. He was handsome. He was a star basketball player. He was the best student in his class. All in all, a solid investment. Robert understands this, and in a way it makes him sad. "So many kids keep it all inside, they just don't trust anybody. And the counselors don't have the patience to get through to them. You have a lot of hard-headed children and just by living in the projects makes them harder. I think they could be turned around, but teachers and counselors don't want to take the time because it takes a lot of work to relate to someone who's afraid of relating to you."

I didn't spend a lot of time with Robert, but I couldn't escape the feeling that this was a young man who someday—and it wouldn't be that far off—would have a medal pinned on him at the White House with the President and other assorted pols basking in the glow of self-congratulation at recognizing an outstanding black American who had made it out of the slums of Newark. It doesn't diminish Robert's substantial accomplishments to point out that however rough his adolescence got, it wasn't as rough as it's been for some other kids I've met. But it was rough enough, and not being omniscient I can't say—and I don't think even Robert knows—what would have happened to him if not for that counselor's intervention.

Three things occurred as he was growing up that made a big difference. Someone was there for him, someone he could believe in and who could believe in him. "The counselor trusted me, and I always felt I had to live up to his trust," Robert said. He also had the opportunity to establish his competency, to achieve success. "People thought I could make it. If they thought so, I did too," he says. The other element in his success was that concerned, engaged adults helped him to strike the right balance between his own responsibility for his welfare and the responsibility of society to give him a shoulder to lean on as he made his way.

The summer I met Robert, which was between his junior and senior year of high school, he was working from eleven at night until seven in the morning at a gas station. From 8:30 in the morning until 1 P.M. he was taking precollege courses at a local community college. From one until five he practiced with the other members of his high school basketball team. And from five to ten at night he slept. "I don't mind working this hard," he says, "because I've been offered scholarships, because the kids at school look up to me, and because the teachers want me to make it. You know, though, when I was fourteen I had a lot of people tell me they didn't think I was going to do so well. They thought I was just another 'project' kid and they wanted to shut me out."

Up to this point, I've been mostly concerned with what I believe would have been Eddie Cumberbatch's first question: Why? I've tried to account for the reasons why some youngsters find themselves alone in America in the prime of their youth. Now I want to respond to the second question I think Eddie would have asked: What can be done to prevent them from following in the path of all those who have lost their way?

The kids I want to discuss in this concluding section are not as advanced as Robert Long; they don't possess all of his natural gifts. Neither are they deranged, as were the people who killed Eddie. They are part of that broad spectrum of kids who have knocked around, who are a little frightened of what the future holds for them and who may be approaching the stage where they are trying to find some access to a safer, more productive life.

I don't mean to overlook youngsters who have debilitating social and psychological problems. They may require long-term intensive therapy. I am not competent to suggest what form their therapy should take, except that it should not be punitive and isolating.

The majority of the kids I met hadn't been crippled yet by their problems. They were functional. They hadn't committed serious crimes, or if they had been in trouble with the law, they were chilling out and trying to redeem themselves. These adolescents had an alternative to residential and institutional care—they could return home, or they were old enough to live independently.

As Robert Long did at fourteen, they were searching for someone they could believe in. They wanted to prove to themselves they could be competent at something. They were trying to strike a balance between assuming responsibility for their futures and finding the people and institutions to help them surmount the obstacles presented by their troubled past. And they needed help to overcome the barriers of race and class.

For these kids, the critical issue was jobs. *The job.* When kids breathed these two words it was as if they were saying: "Open sesame." Get a job, they thought, and I won't be poor anymore. Get a job, they thought, and I'll get respect. Get a job and I won't have to jive any more: I'll be able to play it straight and cool.

So what are their chances of finding stable employment? What are the prospects for a kid coming off the street? Not very good.

To assess their prospects, all you have to do is think about three sets of statistics. The first compares the unemployment of young blacks and of whites. Forget, for a second, the street kid. Consider the prospects of the young black who completes high school. He is two and a half times as likely to be unemployed as the white high school graduate. The black kid who has spent some time in higher education has three times the chance of being unemployed as that of a white youngster at the same level of education. White high school *dropouts* had a 23 percent unemployment rate in November 1985, while black *graduates* had a 37.5 percent rate.[1]

Robert B. Hill, a consultant to a federal task force on youth unemployment, has observed that "employment opportunities are more available to white youth with markedly less educational attainment . . . It should be quite clear that the high rates of unemployment among black youth today cannot be attributed primarily to their lack of education or job skills. [The data] strongly suggest that the unavailability of jobs to black youth is a more important factor than their unavailability for those jobs."[2]

In the past the manufacturing sector of the economy has provided the greatest access to decent-paying entry-level jobs offering opportunity for advancement. That is not true for the high school dropout in the 1980s. In 1985, the Labor Department reported that 2.3 million manufacturing jobs had disappeared since 1980—jobs in steel, construction, and clothing manufacture.[3] The Chicago metropolitan area alone lost 123,000 manufacturing jobs between 1980 and 1983—a decline of almost 20 percent. Employment in steel plants, the hardest hit industry, dropped from 20,000 workers in Chicago to 5,000. Some sectors of the economy have grown—employment in services and retail trade, for example, increased by 4 million jobs since 1983. But as many analysts have found, the wages offered for these jobs are significantly lower than in manufacturing. For example, the average weekly wages in retail are only 46.5 percent of those in manufacturing.[4] There are still some relatively well-paying jobs in manufacturing, but they are in industries like communications, electronics, and computing. Those relatively skilled positions are virtually closed to the dropout or even the high school graduate.

Lost in this switchover in the economy are millions of unemployed and underemployed youths. I'm not referring here only to untrained youngsters. Officials in the government-funded youth training system report that only a small minority of participants actually get white-collar jobs in the private sector, and only a few of that group find employment in major corporations. Since the training system is now directed almost entirely toward employment in the private sector, only the most promising youngsters are trained. "We take only the cream of the crop, the top third of the applicants," says Theodore Small, former director of the Private Industry Council, which does much of the screening of applicants to the training system. "We know that even the best of these young people are going to have a very hard time finding jobs in the private sector."

If youngsters were trained—if they were exposed to a combination of remedial education, skills development, and social counseling—could they compete for the more desirable beginning jobs in the new economy? Conservative analysts say no. They argue that seventeen- to twenty-year-old youngsters are too weighed down by their past failures and their present social problems to work productively; they're just too mercurial, too unreliable, too shortsighted to keep a responsible job. But the actual answer is that we don't know. We don't know because it hasn't been a national priority to prepare them for employment in the private sector. Far less government funding for job training goes to dropouts than to other young people. During the Carter administration, a national task force on youth unemployment led by Vice President Mondale found that low-income youths attending college receive an average of $1,900 from the federal government for job training. High school dropouts, on the average, receive $267; the investment in dropouts is 14 percent of what is spent on college kids.[5] Youngsters who are neglected in school don't get any more attention after they drop out.

How then does the dropout make the tough change from adolescent to adult, from unemployment to wage earning, from marginal worker to independent middle-income taxpayer? Statistics offer only a partial answer; they don't capture the personal nuances of ambition and rejection. It is more enlightening to examine two lives-in-the-round, two dropouts, one black, one white, both poised for the leap across the great divide.

Richard Wilson and Gus Pappas: On the Rise

Richard Wilson's big break came when the cops caught him. Richard is the seventeen-year-old black youngster I met in Tompkins Square Park on Manhattan's Lower East Side. He had talked about the boring, grim sameness of the days he spent on the street. "I'm just another hangout artist," he had said then. "There's only one way I can go—down." That was the general direction he was heading when he was collared by the police as he stood lookout while some of his friends were breaking into a grocery store. Richard's friends scattered, and he was left to explain what he was doing at midnight in front of a splintered glass door as a burglar alarm shrieked behind him. A lightning decision: Take the fall or give up his friends and save himself. He talked; charges were not pressed; some of his friends were arrested; he became a pariah among his home boys. "Some of the guys wanted to end it for me," he says. "But I hid out with my cousin in the Bronx for two months. Then I don't know where to go."

He went straight: He worked. He delivered flowers; he bagged groceries; he cleaned up a church in his cousin's neighborhood; he helped an unlicensed nonunion mover load furniture into a truck (between the hours of midnight and 3 A.M., because there was a moving strike in New York and the boss didn't want to fight with the union). Those were temporary, dead-end jobs. They usually lasted no longer than a few weeks (the supermarket hired him during the Christmas season, the flower store a few weeks before Easter) and weren't the kind of jobs you could put on a resumé. He wanted steady work.

I didn't think it was an unreasonable ambition. I found him a perceptive, responsible, and functional teenager—at least as responsible and functional as any eighteen-year-old could be who had gone through what he had gone through. He was not an emotional cripple. On a moral scale, he could distinguish between selfishness and behavior that would be considered destructive by society. He had reached a kind of ethical maturity. In fact, I thought he was considerably more advanced than some other kids I had met. And one other thing: He was trying.

One evening, after coming out of a movie theater near Times Square, he passed a fast-food restaurant I will call Hungry Jack's. On an inspiration, he walked in and asked the manager, a man named Sam Melvin, whether there was any work. Melvin didn't ask Richard if he had graduated from high school. He didn't ask if he had been in trouble with the police. He asked only, "Do you wash dishes?"

From the grapevine of poor black and Hispanic kids Richard knew all about fast-food operations. He knew that kids who worked for them were very vulnerable. You could receive an increase on Saturday and have it taken away on Tuesday. You could be promoted to working the cash register, but without warning or explanation find yourself mopping the floors. You might be asked to work overtime without pay. You could be coerced into kicking back part of your salary. You could be coerced into doing things that had nothing to do with your job. (I met five young women in three cities who had been sexually harassed by managers of fast-food chain restaurants. It is a measure of their vulnerability that none of them ever thought of going to the police. Faced with sexual demands on the job, they felt they had only two options: quit or give in.) But Richard didn't have a choice. You have to work to live. It was Hungry Jack's or nothing.

Melvin was a straight-shooter. On Richard's first day, the manager promised him, "You do good by me, I'll do good by you." In Richard's first two months he washed and stacked dishes. During slack periods, he cleaned tables, dumping the cardboard trays and plates and plastic utensils into plastic sacks that he carried down a narrow flight of steps to the basement. Then one of the countermen quit, and Melvin offered him the job.

It wasn't a high-prestige or high-paying position, but he learned some things from it that he could apply to any work situation. One was teamwork. Richard saw how the cook kept the burgers moving on and off the grill, how he kept track of the orders and the sequence in which they were placed, not so much because the customers were going to be angry if he screwed up or because he wanted to please the boss, but because the cook was trying to protect Richard and the other countermen who would catch hell if the order was wrong or late. Richard, in turn, protected the cook against the customer's impatience—"The patties were too frozen today, it's taking him a little longer." I was there one day when he was covering for another counterman who hadn't showed up. I heard him telling Melvin, "Gus's mother's been real sick. He doesn't like to talk about it, but that's why he's not here."

The people Richard worked with resembled the people on his block and the people he went to school with, but with one big difference: Here cooperation and teamwork were necessary to survive, in contrast with the voracious competition of the streets.

Richard also learned something about what it takes to make a profit in business. In the fast-food business, particularly, time was the key. Richard had to maintain a certain pace: not so fast as to make the other workers look bad; not so fast that they'd be given extra work; not so slowly that they'd hold up the process. One study of the fast-food industry reported: "One chain is restructuring its total system . . . so that the average transaction will take no more than 17 seconds. Another chain is reported to have it down to 12 seconds. . . . The focus is on the system. Each worker repetitively performs a few tightly organized functions as part of a team."[6]

Richard had mastered some of the subtleties of the system.

I watched him perform an elegant body twist to hide a fallen burger, dust it off, and place it on the tray—all in less than four seconds. Actually, the process at Hungry Jack's was more leisurely than most. I timed Richard, from the moment he placed the order until he delivered it—twenty-three seconds.

An unexpected dividend of the job was the friendship he formed with the other counterman. Gus Pappas was also eighteen, also a dropout. His family had come from Greece when he was five and had settled in an almost totally Greek neighborhood in Astoria, Queens. His father was a house painter; his two uncles were partners in a luncheonette. "I grew up believing that if things got pretty bad and money was scarce, somehow your own kind'd take care of you," Gus told me.

One of his high school English teachers said after Gus had dropped out, "He wasn't stupid; when something caught his interest he'd do rather well. I just don't think he saw the point of school. In his culture, accomplishment is measured by work, particularly when you get paid for it. He couldn't see the payoff in finishing school, going on to college. Maybe it was because he was white, but I thought he'd be happier and make out well in the work world, even without a high school diploma."

Gus's family was not pleased when he dropped out; they were less pleased when he moved in with a friend after he started working at Hungry Jack's. But his uncles said that someday they would consider making him a junior partner in their luncheonette. First he had to prove himself. He had to show them he was capable of holding down a job. He did that at Hungry Jack's. He had been there almost fourteen months; his salary had been increased from $120 to $180 a week; some days when Melvin was sick, Gus substituted for him as manager.

Melvin says that it never bothered him that Gus and Richard didn't have high school diplomas. "If I judged two kids to be equally capable of handling the job, I'd probably hire the high school dropout," Melvin says. "He'll stay longer. He doesn't get as restless as the kids with diplomas. I wanted a hard worker, someone who doesn't bitch all the time. This is menial labor, a factory. You don't need any skills to work here." I asked him whether he thought Gus would stay for a long time. "He'd be stupid to," he said. "There's no future here for anybody. He's been here for more than a year, but he's not going to be president of the company or anything. He'll always be turning over burgers."

That isn't the way Gus saw his future. After he put in his

time at Hungry Jack's, he'd cash in on his uncles' promise of a partnership. He'd save some money, and in five years he'd open his own place. "I can see it in my mind," he told Richard. "Red and white velvet chairs with gold in the wood. Chandeliers. Steaks that flame up right on the table. And a band, too. I want somethin' that rocks."

Gus wasn't all business, though. With his earnings he'd bought and sold two used cars and a motorcycle; he'd break in each new vehicle by offering Richard a ride. A couple of times he double dated with Richard. "If my folks could see me now, with a black guy and his chick, smokin' a joint . . ." he would laugh. Gus had a booming laugh, a nutcracker handshake, and red cheeks. Gus was an easy guy to be with. He'd make you laugh when he told you how he won big at the track by betting on a horse who looked like his maiden aunt. He'd make you laugh describing how the cops almost picked him up when, on a dare, he stole a car and went for a joyride.

Gus reminded me of an earlier model, the kids I knew in junior high. He was the youngster who leaves school to make a living. He didn't want to invest in the future; he wanted the car and clothes *now*. He's not comfortable with academic theorizing; what he wants to learn has to do with business and making money. Doing is what Gus believed in.

Almost a year and a half after he started in the restaurant, Gus left for a three-month vacation with his family in Greece. When he told his boss that he wanted some time off, Melvin said, "Take the time. Business is lousy anyway. Dick can cover for you." Alone now, Richard would spend his free time in the restaurant staring out the window at the packs of black and Hispanic kids roaming through Times Square, wearing their "dew rags"—cloth headdresses resembling the Arabian *kaffiyeh*—under black leather caps. Watching them would make him think, Shit, this job ain't much, but it's better than that.

Three weeks after Gus left, Richard wrote a letter to him in Greece. "Hungry Jack's is no more. . . . A week ago Melvin closed down. He says he might open a bar soon. Meanwhile, I got no job. . . . I keep looking around . . . things are tough, but maybe something will open up soon. It better because my wallet's empty. The thing that bugs me is working here for more than a year and then there's nothing. When they took the grill out, I said there goes 2,000 burgers."

Gus wrote back, "Can't say I'm sorry. The place wasn't nothing anyway. My uncles keep asking me if I want to go into business with them. The money's good and they're not going to fire me. I'll make up my mind when I get back. All I'm thinking about now is the sun and the chicks."

Richard read Gus's letter while he was waiting on line in the unemployment insurance office. He remembers thinking, I wish my uncle owned a restaurant.

The demise of Hungry Jack's did not come as a big surprise to Richard. Business had been declining for months. He knew that, like Gus, he needed a backup. So he took a six-week night course in word-processing. It cost $300, exhausting his savings and necessitating a $120 loan from his mother. Still, he thought it was worth it; he had a trade. Now, the problem was, Where could he practice it?

On the way home from the unemployment insurance office, he passed a bank. It was one of the largest in New York. Officials at the bank say there are approximately 450 entry-level positions filled each year. These include receptionists, mail room workers, maintenance people, clerical workers, and messengers. At that time, entry-level jobs paid between $140 and $180 a week. More skilled positions, such as word processing and operating a key punch, paid better, up to $275 a week. When Hungry Jack's closed, he had been making between $160 and $200 a week, depending on whether he worked overtime.

Well, what the hell, Richard thought, it was worth a shot. That's how he got the restaurant job, just walking in off the street. It could happen again. The bank's headquarters complex is located in midtown Manhattan. In the huge lobby of the main building, there is an elevated semicircular desk manned by three receptionists in bank blazers. At each of the six elevator banks, there are three uniformed guards, stationed beneath closed-circuit television screens. There was a line of people inquiring at the reception desk. Richard walked over to one of the guards.

"Can you tell me . . ." Richard asked.

"What's your business here?" the guard said.

"I'd like to apply for a job," Richard said.

"Who do you have an appointment with?"

"An appointment? Do you need an appointment?"

"Of course. Do you think anybody can come in here?"

"Well, I was just lookin'."

"Look outside," the guard said, pointing to the revolving door. "Outside."

Later I asked a bank official in the "corporate responsibility" department about Richard's reception in the lobby. "It's a huge building," she said, "with thousands of people. There are guards everywhere. To go to the cafeteria you have to wear an ID. I think about how frightening it was for me when I came here last year. It took me a long time to become acclimated, and here I am with thirteen years of work experience. I know my way around the city. I know how to dress. Any kid who comes in here for a job has to be a thousand times more intimidated than I was."

Richard walked down the street thinking, "Screw it, I'll find some other job." Then, not far from the lobby entrance, he saw a sign with an arrow pointing down: "Central Employment Office, One Flight Down." The sign said that the next hiring date would be a week from then.

Richard was very excited when he called me. "I've got a job lined up," he said, breathlessly. I tried to calm him down when I heard that he had no specific appointment, that he was one of perhaps 100 other applicants for what might be four or five open positions. But I couldn't dampen his enthusiasm. "I'm movin' up," he said. "I can feel it. I took the computer course; I'm *qual-i-fied.* I tell you, I'm tired of sweat work. I want me one nice clean job. Just call me white-collar Joe." He said his mother wanted to talk to me. Mrs. Wilson was a devout fifty-eight-year-old woman. She often said that she would die happy if Richard "made a good man of himself." Perhaps because I was white and a stranger who for some reason she didn't quite understand had befriended her son, she had the idea that I had the power to get him a job. "I'm going to church Sunday," she said, "and I'm going to pray for Richard. And I'm going to pray for you, too."

I called the bank and persuaded officials there to let me sit in during the job interview on the condition that I did not identify the bank or the interviewer. On the morning of the interview Richard looked spiffy: He had dressed in a pair of chino pants, a white shirt, a solid green tie and a plaid sports jacket. Mrs. Wilson was a half-hour late for her job because she wanted to make sure her son had a good breakfast and had dressed properly.

The bank's employment office was a large room with yellow walls. Rows of orange armless chairs were grouped in different sections of the room. The chairs reminded Richard of those in Hungry Jack's; they had not been designed for leisurely dining.

Approximately fifty applicants were in the room. The one visible bank representative looked to be in her early fifties. She was seated behind a small white desk. Richard approached her and said he wanted to apply for a job. She swiveled in her chair and glanced behind her at the honeycomb of partitioned offices where job interviews were being conducted. "I don't know if we can get to you today, young man," she said. It was 9:30 A.M. "But you fill this out." She handed him an application form and a small cardboard square with a number printed on it. "Come up when the number is called. Meanwhile, take a seat."

"Where?" he asked in a whisper.

"Where it says 'nonofficer'," she said, quickly looking down at her paperback book.

He sat next to two other black job applicants. One was a young woman who I guessed to be about seventeen. The other was a man dressed in a black shirt and tan pants. He seemed to be in his early twenties.

"What's happenin'?" Richard asked the man.

"Not much, bro," the man said. "I don't think they're hirin' nobody."

"How long you been lookin'?" Richard asked.

The man said he had been searching for a job for about eight months. He told Richard he could type sixty words a minute.

"Do you have a high school diploma?" Richard asked.

"Sure, man, and I went to this school for typing, too, but ain't no difference."

Richard was silent. You could almost hear him saying to himself: Here's this guy who has a diploma and he can't get a job. What chance do I have?

He began to fill out the application form. The questions on the first three lines were printed on a second sheet, separated from the form by a strip of carbon paper. He was using a felt tip pen. When he finished three lines, he realized his printing wasn't coming through the carbon. He picked up the carbon and started printing on the form itself. "Screwed up," he whispered to himself.

The form was relatively brief, twelve lines in all, but three questions were aimed at finding out whether the applicant had some connection to the bank: Had the applicant ever worked for the bank? Did he or she have relatives who worked for the bank? Had the job-seeker been recommended by anyone employed by the bank?

"Why do they keep askin' that?" Richard asked the young woman seated next to him.

"I guess they want to check you out. They don't want Mr. Nobody comin' in lookin' for a job with all the money around here," she said. She had given as a reference an aunt who worked as a typist in the accounting department.

"You think I can use your aunt, too?" Richard asked.

"You crazy, boy?" she said. "Supposin' there's but one job, an' you get it. You think I'm gonna give you my aunt?"

He came to the line that read: "Have you ever been arrested and convicted for any criminal offense involving dishonesty or breach of trust? If yes, please explain." The charges stemming from the grocery break-in had been dropped, but Richard told the man in the black shirt that he had once been picked up for throwing light bulbs at people who were passing by the projects where he lived.

"Should I write it in?" he asked.

"Lie," the man said.

"Lie?"

"Lie."

Richard wrote no after the question.

On the line that asked about his last job, he wrote: "Restaurant Worker."

The next line asked why he was leaving his present job. "Place closed," he wrote.

He also said that he typed 55 words a minute; that he could use an "IBM computer" and that he expected a salary of $5 an hour.

In the box headed "Position Applied For" (which was next to the box headed, "Relatives in Our Employ"), he wrote: "Word processing." Then he wrote: "Clerk typist."

After waiting for almost two hours, his number was called. He was interviewed by Miss Marjorie Keneally.* Miss Keneally is forty-eight years old. She has worked in the bank's personnel

* A pseudonym.

department for nineteen years. She grew up in Far Rockaway, where she still lives. She has two brothers, both cops. Her uncle is an inspector in the Fire Department.

Marjorie Keneally looked across the desk at Richard Wilson. "Now, you worked in a restaurant, Mr. Wilson," she said. "Yes, ma'am," he said.

"And, now you want to be a typist?"

"Word processing. Key punch." He added quickly: "I took typin' in school and I been practicing."

"You know at the bank you have to type at least ninety words a minute."

"Oh, I see."

"We do have some jobs as runners." Richard looked puzzled. "That's like a messenger," said Miss Keneally. "But you have to be bonded. You haven't had any legal problems, have you, Richard?"

He shook his head. He thought about the time he was picked up throwing lightbulbs. "How much does it pay?" Richard asked. "Three-eighty an hour," he was told.

"I guess I want to think on it," he said.

Three-eighty an hour was 75 cents less than he had made at the end of his stay at Hungry Jack's. Besides, a messenger's job didn't sound like a step up. Later, he would say that he thought about asking her whether any other job was open, but decided against it. He thought she would have mentioned it if there were, and he didn't want to sound stupid.

She scanned his employment application. "I see you finished tenth grade," she said. "Are you going to school now?"

"No, I been working."

"Oh, yes, in a restaurant. Do you have a certificate for your typing?"

Richard didn't know what she meant. The night course hadn't awarded certificates.

Miss Keneally took a long, hard look at her watch. It was a little after noon; he was cutting into her lunch hour. "Do you have any other questions?" she asked. He said he couldn't think of any. "Well, if you change your mind about the messenger job, you can come back in. You know how to get out, don't you?" He said he did. He reached across the desk as if to shake her hand, then stopped. Miss Keneally hadn't moved.

Out on the street, Richard asked, "What did I do wrong?"

The next morning, I asked Miss Keneally: What did Richard do wrong?

"If we hire someone like him for an entry-level job we want to know whether he can do more, can he go up one or two grades. But I didn't see any evidence of that. He didn't ask whether he would be promoted. He didn't even ask what he would be doing as a runner. How can I take a chance with someone like him?

"That's the point. I'd be taking a chance if I hired him. No one else but me. I have to guess what the line supervisor wants. If I guess wrong, I'm in trouble. The supervisor will say, 'Oh, Keneally has sent me another honey.' The bank wants kids who have basic skills. If you could train every kid who walked in here to be a typist or a stenographer, we could hire them all."

Like a number of other banks in New York, this one conducts special programs for youngsters referred by social agencies and the schools. Why couldn't Richard Wilson be placed in one of these programs? "That's not Personnel's responsibility," she said. "That's another department."

If a kid like Richard showed some promise, he would still be rejected because he hadn't come through a program. "Look, I take enough risks," she said. "Every time I hire one of these kids I take a risk. You think I want to take a double risk and get involved with the business of another department? The trouble with a kid like that is he wouldn't think of being a messenger."

What happened to Richard was not typical of what happens to the average black or Hispanic teenage walk-in. He was, in fact, treated better than average.* The interviewer asked him a question or two about his previous job. She indicated that a job might be open as a messenger, and she left the door ajar if he changed his mind about it. Many other kids might not have been interviewed at all.

A few weeks later I tried to reach Richard. His cousin in the Bronx said he had left and he didn't know where he was staying. "He said something about joinin' up the military." I called his mother. She didn't know where he was either. He had called her to say that he was still looking for a job. "For a while I thought everything was working out for him," she said. "Now I don't

---

* This was certainly due, to some extent, to the fact that I had arranged to sit in on the interview.

know." This time Mrs. Wilson didn't say anything about praying for him. Or for me.

In New York several thousand entry-level positions have to be filled in banks and insurance companies; other white-collar businesses have similar needs.* The people who are hired bring to their job searches credentials of various kinds: They are preferred over high school dropouts in the competition for entry-level, low-paying jobs because they are Vietnam veterans; they are women returning to the job market; they are adults with substantial employment histories; they are retired people seeking part-time employment; and they are recent high school graduates, some with years of college. Most of this last group are white and clean-shaven. Perhaps a hundred or so of these positions are filled by participants in special programs. And then there's a kid like Richard Wilson.

If Richard had known some people in the corporate world, they might have tried to persuade him to take the job as bank messenger. They might have pointed out that it was a way of getting inside the door; after a while maybe he'd be promoted to the mail room or to the position of office boy. But he didn't know anybody on the inside who could advise him. I supposed I could have told him that, but, to be honest, I didn't want to. I had gotten to know him and I knew he didn't see himself any more as a guy with his cap turned backwards, dodging traffic on his messenger's bike. He had another image of himself, and I didn't want to be the one to tell him that image was wrong, that he had to come down a notch to be accepted.

Richard could read and compute on an eighth-grade level. He had demonstrated stability and reliability—and a desire to reform himself—by holding a job for more than a year and a half and by contributing fifty dollars a week to his family. Until he was rejected at the bank, he thought he had passed his initiation, served his apprenticeship as a worker. He had interpreted his stint at Hungry Jack's as proof that you can get a job, and do rather well at it, without that gateway credential, without the diploma. All he had ever known were "sweat" jobs. In another

---

* Although there is a commonly held view to the contrary, the number of entry-level positions has not been sharply reduced by the increasing automation of the workplace. Studies of the banking and insurance industries show a substantial need for unskilled workers; reductions have occurred principally among semiskilled and skilled workers.

time, he might have chosen the security and union protection offered in an auto or steel plant over the "glamour" of white-collar work; but by the 1980s those industrial jobs were even rarer than white-collar employment.

Richard simply didn't have the credentials that would have made him a relatively safe bet. A study by the Vocational Foundation in New York speaks directly to that point: "In place of the bigotry of race has arisen a new bigotry of schooling," the foundation concluded. This policy is characterized by a "worship of credentials . . . that blocks every route to the ladder up." Each year, the foundation said, "the ante is raised: first a high school diploma, then a special test, then a further degree . . . ."

This system protects "any schooled but shiftless members of the middle class from the competition of unschooled but aggressively hardworking poor people. [It] depreciates the assets of diligence, determination and drive to get ahead that have launched other groups into the middle class, and that every close study has shown to be most important to productivity. And it exalts the assets of the advantaged classes—schooling, testing, computing—that are often irrelevant to productivity in most jobs."[7]

Richard's exclusion should not be seen as solely a problem for black youths. Puerto Ricans and Mexican-Americans are disproportionately clustered in blue-collar jobs remote from the growth sectors of the labor force. As a study by the Public Agenda Foundation pointed out, "They work as machine operators or laborers, in service occupations such as fast-food operations, or in dead-end jobs such as hospital orderlies or security guards. . . . The fact is that a large group of Hispanics is trapped in the lower occupational tiers of the American economy."[8]

While the employment prospects for white dropouts are not exactly bright, their outlook is significantly more promising than for blacks and hispanics. In January 1986, according to the U.S. Bureau of Labor Statistics, the unemployment rate of black teenagers was 41.9 percent, as against the white teen unemployment rate of 14.9 percent. The unemployment rate for sixteen- to twenty-four-year-old black high school *graduates* was 27.3 percent; the rate for white high school *dropouts* was 23.9 percent.

For all young people, exclusion from a job that could offer opportunity for growth is a double blow. It keeps them in poverty and it threatens their future. When researchers analyzed the data compiled in a ten-year national study of adolescents in the labor market, they found that the quality of a youth's first job—particularly status level and productiveness—can affect his or her occupational status as much as nine years later.[9] The stable, productive job, according to the economist Lester Thurow, is "important in developing good lifestyle working habits. Without these habits, an individual may not be able to succeed economically in later life."[10]

Yet when help is offered, it is almost always part of a *preventive* strategy directed toward the kid who's still in school. If you are young and unattached to any institution and trying to make your way, you might as well, in the youth policy analyst Peter Edelman's resonant phrase, "fall into a hole and die." The almost universal judgment in America is that adolescents who have grown up on the street are beyond help.

Training—and Then What?

In intangible ways that can't be measured by credentials, Richard Wilson was an attractive candidate for an entry-level job. At eighteen, he was more together than many other kids who'd spent a good part of their adolescence on the street. And he couldn't get a job. What of kids who aren't on Richard's level? What of kids who don't have the know-how, the confidence, and the work experience to make the leap from the street to a reasonably promising job?

In the past a variety of programs have been proposed to prepare youngsters less advantaged than Richard to enter the job world; a few have been seriously tried. Those programs try to give the kid a taste of what it's like to hold a job; they also try to teach some basic skills and develop the individual's sense of confidence.

In the late 1970s a substantial number of poor and minority youngsters took part in training programs, although the number of applicants was always larger than the number of openings. In the 1980s most of those programs were eliminated. The ones that remained served only a relatively small number of eligible youth, most of them still in school. Nevertheless, it may be productive to review some of the more promising approaches that have been tried in the last twenty years in the hope that someday American policymakers may decide to renew their commitment to disadvantaged adolescents.

One approach recognizes that if a youngster remains in his present environment—in his old neighborhood, surrounded by his home boys—he's going to continue to get into trouble. Programs like the Youth Conservation Corps and the Job Corps relocate the youngsters to a new setting that blends education and work.

Another kind of effort is directed toward more deeply disturbed and disoriented youths. It begins with the assumption that no one program element—whether education or job training—will resolve the diverse and complex problems of these youngsters. So the programs, which are usually sponsored by community organizations, offer a variety of services from psychological counseling to filling cavities to finding jobs. Occasionally, those multiservice projects also provide a place for the youngster to stay while taking part in the program. It should be emphasized that multiservice programs, which are always expensive to operate, are few in number.

A different approach is rooted in the concept of community service. Here the money kids earn and the skills they acquire are less important than the sense that they are contributing to the improvement of community life. When kids rehabilitate abandoned buildings in East Harlem, refurbish a senior citizens' residence in San Francisco's Chinatown, or clean up a refuse-strewn lot to construct a playground in Chicago, they develop a belief in the value of their labor. By doing valuable work, they become valuable people. I should inject one caveat here: The work must be perceived as a real service to the community. Youngsters don't develop a belief in themselves when they spend their days mopping up a bathroom in a community center.

Then there are programs that offer kids who have never been outside their neighborhoods exposure to an environment that simulates an actual work setting. While they are being trained, they feel as though they're working in a big business.

One example of this approach is a Chicago program called Training, Inc. In this secretarial skills program, the training sites are housed in office buildings. Participants dress and behave as they would in an actual job. They eat lunch in cafeterias frequented by employees of firms in the building. Program instructors have worked recently in the private sector and consult frequently with supervisors in companies that may hire graduates of the program. Representatives of personnel departments conduct mock job interviews with trainees; a graduation luncheon for participants is heavily attended by representatives of Chicago firms. The purpose behind the program is to soften the kind of shock Richard Wilson felt when he walked into the lobby of that bank building in New York. Despite its obvious advantages, there aren't many Training, Inc.s around for one reason: It costs about $2,000 to train a youth for fourteen weeks.

Other approaches put all their emphasis on getting a job, however menial. In a program such as Jobs for Youth in Boston, the kids didn't get much time to prepare for working. When I reviewed the program, youngsters on the average received seventeen hours of basic education or counseling. Then they were sent out to jobs in small retail stores, gas stations, and fast-food operations. The proponents of this strategy argue that it has some basic advantages: It puts money into the youths' pockets and provides an introduction to the rules and responsibilities of the workplace for youngsters who haven't worked before. I don't think many of the kids I met would gain a great deal from it; it would put them into the same secondary labor market jobs they've held before. Eunice Elton, a San Francisco labor specialist with three decades of experience in youth programs, says, "I've never put kids in these jobs. The pay is lousy. The work conditions are just this side of slavery. They learn all they're going to learn in three weeks. Then they have no place to go."

Finally, there are programs that stress the importance of remedial education. They operate from the conviction that preparation and training for work are futile if a young person can't read or write. To hold a job, proponents of this approach argue, you have to read on at least an eighth-grade level. For those who can't, it's essential to combine remedial education with stopgap jobs. In some larger cities, street kids can enroll in alternative and auxiliary schools or in federally funded learning skills centers. This is a hard proposition to sell to many teenagers, for whom school is anathema. They have already been told they can't learn. The paradox of the combined school–work strategy is that for so many of these youngsters, success at work is the prime motivator for resuming their aborted education; they have to succeed on the job *before* they gain the confidence to take on an educational system in which they have failed.

Clearly, no single strategy works for all disaffiliated and rejected adolescents. For those with severe social and psychological damage, protracted and intensive counseling and therapy may be necessary before they can benefit from training and job prepa- ration. Some kids may need to get away from the disturbances of their homes and neighborhoods. There are others for whom the first step is simply earning enough money to move themselves and their families out of destitution. Community service would offer some youngsters an opportunity to enhance their self-esteem and self-worth. It's this opportunity that has moved some policy- makers to propose a year of national service for youth, a year in which they would try to rebuild the decaying infrastructure— the buildings, streets, parks, and highways—of their communities and improve the delivery of social services such as day care, recre- ation, and senior citizens' programs. Such an effort would have to be financed by public funds or a mixture of public and private support. During the Depression, when many middle-income peo- ple became poor, funds were provided for such an effort; in the prosperous 1980s, a national service proposal founders because it's considered too expensive.

All of these approaches are of some benefit to different groups of poor adolescents. But they are all compromised by one central defect. They stop short of providing access to stable employment in the mainstream economy. They teach, they train, they simulate a job—and then they tell the eighteen- or nineteen-year-old black or Hispanic kid: You're on your own.

In the last fifteen years one popular approach to training is based on a system called "supported work." In these programs, youngsters are organized into work crews. Kids are encouraged to support each other's productive efforts and to criticize deviation and irresponsibility. In some supported work programs I've ob- served, individual crew members do gain a sense of responsibility for the welfare and progress of the entire crew. But I think this otherwise effective strategy for building cohesiveness and mutual concern is undermined by the program's isolation.

The supported work crews are not integrated into existing private business. They are organized into self-contained units that act as a kind of subcontractor for established businesses—they deliver parcels, they run messages, they finish furniture. But all those activities take place outside the real private sector workplace. In effect, the participants in such programs are quarantined; while they may make a sincere effort to learn a skill and develop good work habits, they don't have a chance to demonstrate their proficiency to an employer. Everything they do is make-believe. They aren't prepared for the actual demands, requirements, and standards that determine success or failure in a real job.

Conventional training projects resemble poor families in that they leave it to the youngster to take care of his social problems. I've described earlier how in many poor families the hearing and visual problems of children are never treated, because it's too much of a hassle to spend days in a public clinic waiting to see an impatient, overworked physician. When participants in training programs run into trouble with drugs, with their families, with their babies, with their housing, with welfare, they are referred to public agencies. Often they never get there, and if they do get there they often become discouraged and leave when the agencies are unresponsive. Their private problems remain private, except when they are manifested in disruptive antisocial behavior. And then it's usually too late to do much about them.

In the training programs, youngsters get the same message they get at home: It's all up to you. You can remake yourself if you choose. But don't blame anybody else if you fail—the fault's all yours. Of course, the middle-class college students I teach get a very different message when they unexpectedly become pregnant or when drug use starts to affect their academic performance. I tell them, the college and their parents tell them, "We'll do everything we can to help you because your life has value—it's worth saving." Of course, when middle-class youths run into trouble they are sometimes treated callously and indifferently, but they are told often enough that their lives have value. It is these repeated affirmations, internalized throughout their adolescence and early adulthood, that help to sustain them during periods of difficulty.

The tension between the responsibilities of the individual and the responsibilities of society have been a constant theme in all of our efforts to intervene on behalf of poor adolescents during the last quarter-century. But in that time there's been a distinct shift in the balance of responsibility. In the 1960s a group of street kids in a training program would have been told: You have some responsibility for resolving your problems and improving your life, but so does America. You have to change, but America has to change too. That's a little different from the current attitude: Nobody's responsible for you but yourself.

When they send out that message, today's policymakers and training program directors aren't only reflecting the current popular wisdom. They're also letting themselves off the hook. By shifting all the responsibility to the individual kid, they don't have to do anything about moving youngsters from the margins to the American center. After spending twelve or sixteen weeks in an airtight chamber, doing "real" work in an unreal world, poor adolescents are left on their own. What happens, of course, is that most of them are left dangling, as Richard Wilson was, in midflight.

It has become fashionable today to say that black and Hispanic youngsters cannot advance from their "underclass" origins because of inherent flaws in character and personality: They are undersocialized; they are uneducable; they want to have babies to qualify for welfare dependency; they prefer criminality to honest labor.

These perceived flaws provide policymakers with a rationalization for treating them as a special—incurable—case in America. They are special only in the sense that poor, minority adolescents constitute the sole group in the country that cannot count on a network of advocates to give them a head start as they approach adulthood. At the end of the nineteenth century and in the first half of the twentieth, young miners of Welsh ancestry in Montana and Pennsylvania were called "uncle Jacks"—they always had an "uncle Jack" who could help them find work in the mines. Asian-Americans go forward in the 1980s with the support of a tight-knit network of family and friends. Gus Pappas, Richard's buddy at Hungry Jack's, was the son of an immigrant Greek family. He knew that when he was ready to assume adult responsibilities, his uncles would be waiting for him.

I can think of only one approach designed to balance the individual's responsibilities against society's responsibilities. It's a kind of updated Uncle Jack strategy for today's generation of young outsiders who are looking to establish themselves on the inside track. It's called on-the-job training. And it's virtually extinct.

Breaking Through

No one has yet devised a precise mathematical system to measure the payoffs to participants and to society from remediation and training programs. There are, however, some approximate benchmarks. The federal office of Youth Programs found that young-sters who received on-the-job training (OJT) in the private sector registered an 18 percent gain in income after a year of working, compared to a 10 percent increase for those who had been trained in classrooms.[11]

In the 1970s federal officials tried to estimate what *society* saved by providing stable employment for poor adolescents. The government considered how much money was spent in wage subsidies and tax allowances to employers who trained these kids. Then it computed how many taxpayers' dollars would have to be spent on unemployed young men and women who received welfare or who were placed in training facilities and penal institutions. By these estimates, on-the-job training returned $2.18 for every dollar invested; by contrast a dollar invested in classroom training returned $1.14 and in the Job Corps $1.30.[12]

One reason OJT is so successful is that it gives a novice worker some breathing space during the critical break-in phase on the job. When I interviewed twenty-five line supervisors and foremen at manufacturing plants and white-collar businesses, they agreed that the make-or-break period for minority youth was the first sixty to ninety days on the job. "The kid's access to the job is in the first few weeks," says Michael Marker, a personnel specialist with Procter & Gamble in Modesto, California. "The white kid, he comes into a company, maybe it's enough he's graduated from high school and he has some self-esteem. It'll carry him through the period when he's still a stranger, feeling his way. A poor black or Hispanic kid doesn't have that going for him. If he screws up, if he shows unfamiliarity with the work, the stereotype of failure is reinforced, for the kid and the supervisor and the other workers. Everybody draws back from him—'What are we gonna do to get rid of this burden?' He's being shut out."[13]

During on-the-job training, the kid learns the rules of the workplace; he learns whom to trust and who's out to get him, and he learns how much time to take for lunch and when he can talk on the job. By successfully completing the training, he can also overcome his own limitations—all the anger, fear, defensiveness, and suspicion that are the emotional staples of street life. The fact that he's been trained and is assured of long-term stable employment is tangible evidence of his worth—to him and his employer. Kenneth DeBey, Denver area representative of the AFL-CIO's Human Resources Development Institute, says,

"When the kid's done with training, he knows he has a marketable skill. He knows he's marketable because he has a job."[14]

The greatest advantage of OJT is that it equalizes responsibility between the youngster and society. It's up to the kid to prove his worth; but he also knows that somebody has decided he's worth investing in. Somebody is teaching him. Somebody is guaranteeing him a job if he learns. Somebody is bothering to tell him, over beers after work, "Watch out for Smith—she's a real pain to everybody, but she's mostly a pain to smart-mouth black kids."

Despite its obvious advantages, OJT has never been a realistic option for most of the youngsters who are the subject of this book. When the federal government was making a sizable investment in training disadvantaged youth, OJT was available to less than one in ten eligible youngsters.[15] Today the odds are more like one in fifty, despite the Reagan administration's emphasis on private sector employment. When major corporations get involved in training youths, the ones they select are almost always still in school and doing reasonably well. What they offer these youths is not very much: part-time short-term employment, with no assurance of a permanent position.

But even that is available to only a few youngsters. After months of negotiations with a coalition of private employers, New York City Employment Commissioner Ronald Gault discovered that "employers were unwilling to bend their employment standards to meet the youth population. They insisted on hiring older workers who had experience. Any others, they weren't interested in."[16]

When training organizations have tried to crack the OJT barrier, they have run up against a stone wall of objections from large corporations and small businesses. Unions at big manufacturing plants have been more interested in preserving the precarious positions of experienced adult workers than in hiring young minority newcomers. Large corporations have resisted the inducements of tax breaks and wage subsidies, arguing that hiring youth—especially dropouts—would destabilize the workplace.[17] When they say they want experienced people to train, they don't mean people who have advanced skills. They mean people who don't represent a risk—people who are older, who have families, who have worked for five, ten, fifteen years. Usually that means white adults.

Small businesses, with high employee turnover, are the most

likely to take a chance on young people. For them the subsidies offered by the government are attractive—and they need warm bodies. But when the training period ends and the subsidies expire, the kids may find themselves out on the street. "It's a risk for the employer," says the manager of a Spanish-language radio station in Albuquerque. "Some of these kids can goof up on drugs. I had a nineteen-year-old girl who couldn't figure what to do with her baby when she was working." He didn't say whether any of his older workers ever used drugs or had babies.

Despite the station manager's experience, a large body of research shows that younger, disadvantaged workers are no more inclined to quit their jobs than older workers when the work is challenging and the salary is fair. As one analyst reported, "There is no evidence . . . that minority and poor youngsters are any less willing to work than their white or middle-class peers."[18] Yet I do think the station manager had a legitimate gripe: Even the most highly motivated youths bring an overflowing bag of social problems to the job. They have a hard time doing the work and solving their accumulated problems at the same time. They need help.

This is the bind. Here you have a group of young people in their late adolescence and early adulthood. They are functionally literate—they read at eighth-grade level or above. They have already held a number of jobs in the secondary economy—low-paying, short-term menial work. Although they don't have the credential of a high school diploma, they are literate, experienced, and ready to make the leap into the mainstream work world. But they also bring with them the remnants of their old street code— defensiveness, suspicion, and close-to-the-surface hostility. The residue of a chaotic adolescence still clings to them: drug abuse, illegitimate children, criminal records, associations with other kids who are still hustling on the street. The weight of their past threatens to sink their chances on the job.

At another time they might have sought work in the public sector, where there was less pressure to prove their competency and reliability instantly. But with the loss of almost 1 million public service jobs since 1981, that is no longer a realistic alternative. In the New York City area alone, it is estimated that 250,000 young people between sixteen and twenty-four are "out of school, out of work, and looking for work."[19]

In the past fifteen years a new employment approach that blends social support and counseling with on-the-job training has begun to emerge in the United States and other "postindustrial" societies, but it has yet to be implemented widely. In the United States this approach was embodied in a now defunct program known as the Youth Incentive Entitlement Projects. The program, conducted in the late 1970s, provided part-time and summer jobs to disadvantaged high school students or to dropouts who returned to school. Employers who hired these youngsters received a six-month wage subsidy.

In 1982 I interviewed employers in three cities where the program was still operating. Eight of ten employers said they kept their young workers on after the subsidy period ended because of one program element: the presence of a counselor at the job site.[20] In Denver, Greg Garcia, the owner of a shop that manufactures security doors, retained three youngsters on a part-time basis during the school year and full time during the summer. "Look, I'm no baby," Garcia said. "I live in the real world. I started working in the beet fields. I had a drinking problem for a lotta years. When I heard about this program, I figured it was time for me to pay something back to the world.

"There was this kid I had. He'd get up at four in the morning, to go to work in a tavern, go to school, then work for me, and then go work for his dad. Some days I know he came in a little high. Shit, I'd get high, too, if I hadda work so hard. Another kid, a black kid, he'd fight at the drop of a hat. I found out the kid's been in six different foster homes. Hey, this kid didn't even have an address. You think, if I was his age, I wouldn't be pissed, too?

"You know, I wanted the job to work out for these kids. But I couldn't have done it all by myself. The counselor from the program, he'd be here two, three times a week. He made all the difference. The kid who got high, he talked to his father, got him to ease off on the work load, and he got the kid to spend time on Saturdays in a drug center. I loved what he did with the kid who was looking for a fight. He enrolled him in the Golden Gloves. *That* gave him something to do with his hands.

"The counselor wasn't only involved with the personal stuff. He helped the kids to work. Look, we get a call for a job out in Aurora, 40, 50 miles away. The kid's got to think: What do I need for this job? Do I have the lead for the welder? The gasoline tanks? The screwdrivers? Even the paint for touching up? At first, it's hard for a kid—for any new worker—to get a handle on all this. So the counselor would sit with them, go over every item, the whole sequence of laying out the job, get them to write out a whole list. After a couple of months, the kid'd have it down himself. Well, the counselor was like an extra crew boss, which I couldn't have afforded, but which made life a lot easier. These kids were motivated from the start. The black kids especially, they wanted to get their feet in the door. You should see them when they actually built a door by themselves and installed it— 'Hey, I've done something.' If they came in all alone it would taken longer to get the hang. But it was like they had an uncle on the job; the counselor was their uncle showin' them the ropes."

When business declined, Garcia had to lay off two of the five youths who were working for him. But he wrote letters of recommendation and made phone calls that resulted in their being hired elsewhere. This doesn't happen often in employment programs. "The program made me feel I had a stake in their future," he says. "I have a long memory. I remember towns around where they said, 'No Mexicans or dogs allowed.' I thought it was time to cut out that crap."[21]

Proving you're competent. Finding someone who believes in you. Assuming responsibility for yourself when someone shows an interest in you. That is what it takes for a kid to cross over from never-never land to the land of golden opportunity. On a very limited scale, that is what the Entitlement project offered its adolescent seekers. Like so many promising social experiments, it lapsed when its funding period ended. There aren't many legitimate business organizations that now provide the kind of nurturance and mentorship that was offered by Entitlement. Yet there are other types of organizations that welcome the outsider. They operate businesses, but not ones regularly featured in *Business Week* magazine. One such enterprise is known as the Five Percent Nation.

A Muslim splinter group, the Five Percenters preach a distorted version of Malcolm X's message of black unity, self-development, and economic independence. Originally they did most of their recruiting in prisons, lockups, detention centers, and reform schools. Now they also recruit on the streets of the most impoverished black neighborhoods in the country. Their appeal is potent: They offer the kids in jail the protection of a militant and lethal organization—and they offer access to power. Join up, they say, and we'll protect you against rape and assault by other inmates. Join up, they say, and we'll deal you into the drug action. After you get out, they promise, we'll bring you into the business— the business of drugs, extortion, loan-sharking, and fencing stolen property.

The Five Percenters are not just another criminal organization. They are an organization with a philosophy, and it's their message that accounts for their appeal among dispirited young black men. The Five Percenters teach that they "possess the power to build or destroy, build that divine nation of God, and destroy all the stumbling blocks that try to stop us."[22] Happiness, they tell the novitiate, is "total and complete satisfaction with one's own self." In other words, the Five Percenters offer something you can't get from a conventional employment program or a pickup job: a system of faith that promises true believers material and spiritual fulfillment.

In New York I met James, a true believer. He had returned recently from a reformatory, and the conditions of his release required that he attend the alternative school where I was an observer. He was the shortest kid in the group, perhaps five-one or five-two, and his round head seemed oversized for his body. When he was preparing to deliver a judgment, which he did regularly three or four times in an hour, he would cock his head to the side and roll his eyes in mock disbelief at a person who could be so ignorant as to utter such total drivel. James was not tolerant of nonbelievers. When Deezie, a young black woman in the class, said she had had sex with white men, James thundered: *"You filth."* When the teacher discussed the dangers of cocaine and heroin addiction, James shook his head despairingly. "Allah teaches us that cocaine is healthy because it's natural, it comes from the soil of the earth," he declared. Once, after class, I found him lecturing to a group of kids that it was a sin to hold up another black man but that it was a "holy act" to steal from whites, because they were "enemies of black people."

You could feel that James's views were screwy and evil and cruel, but you couldn't deny the force of his conviction. He stood out among all the other bewildered and forlorn adolescents as an unshakable monument to faith. He knew who he was and where he was going; the others didn't know what was going to happen to them the next day, the next hour.

James knew he was for real. The Five Percenters had told

him so. They had told him that his misspent and shrunken child-hood had value now that he had discovered the truth. James didn't have to hope for the "big break" that almost never comes. James had found mentors—the Five Percenters and Allah—who would guide him across the chasm that separates childhood and adult-hood, as later they would lead him into the bliss of the afterworld. "I am a righteous brother," James said, "and my future is as bright as the stars."

Can American ingenuity invent an alternative to the Five Per-centers for someone like James? In Massachusetts I found an en-terprise that might have attracted a kid like him. It was not primarily directed toward adolescents, but in its philosophy, in its approach to work, and in its reliance on a network of mentors it had the potential to invent a new future for kids who want to change their lives.

Independence: Living It Up at Fenway Park

The Massachusetts program was called TEE, which stood for Transitional Employment Enterprises.[23] TEE had a philosophy that, as enunciated by its founder and president, Peter Cove, went like this:

> We do not believe in trying to change the individual. We believe in improving the prospects of getting a job. We have learned that there's an army of people out there who want to work, and would work if they had access to jobs. Our task is to provide that access. Once they get the job, they will master the skills necessary to keep it. We have faith in the competency of the individual.

Indeed, faith in the capacity of the individual—the belief that people will be productive from day one on the job and will get better as time passes—had been elevated to scripture. I spent almost four months observing the TEE effort in Massachusetts and New Hampshire. One morning stands out in my memory. Cove was preaching to a breakfast meeting of wary businessmen at a motel on Massachusetts's Route 128 high-tech belt. Wearing a hand-tied blue and pink bow tie and twirling the waxed ends of his mustache, Cove promised his audience:

"Our people will work as hard, if not harder, will turn out to be as dependable, if not more dependable, are as trainable, if not more trainable, than the average worker hired off the streets."

By "our people" Cove was not referring to teenagers, although there are some people in the program in their late teens and early twenties. The job-seekers served by TEE were for the most part somewhat older, mothers on welfare and retarded people. In 1983 and 1984, when I was studying the organization, the average TEE worker was a woman in her late twenties or early thirties who received Aid to Families with Dependant Children (AFDC). She had dropped out of school and had little or no work experience. A majority of the participants were black or Hispanic.

What they had in common with TEE's other clientele—retarded people—was that both groups had lived sheltered or circumscribed lives. If the welfare mothers had worked at all, they had worked in public programs in jobs specifically designated for welfare recipients. They were a "special" class doing "special" work. While their most committed advocates tried to improve their services and benefits, they did not usually encourage them to expose themselves to the standards and competition of the private sector. David MacKenzie, counsel to the Massachusetts State Senate's Ways and Means Committee, had found that when he worked as a legal services attorney representing welfare recipients, the overriding philosophy was "Play it safe." He said, "Welfare workers were just not going to open their clients to risks, and their attitude was contagious—it spread to the recipients themselves. It was just *safer* to stay on welfare."

Retarded citizens had also been treated as *special* cases. Some 800,000 in the United States had attended special classes or special schools. Approximately 200,000 had lived in large public or private institutions. More than half had worked in "sheltered" workshops. In those workshops, their work was usually repetitive and unvarying. They were paid mean wages, averaging thirty-five cents an hour. They had little if any opportunity to upgrade their jobs, get a promotion, or face a new challenge. If they did get impatient, they were reminded, as welfare mothers were reminded, that the "sheltered" job is *safe,* risk-free.

At a certain stage, they began to get restless. They wondered, as Richard Wilson wondered: Can I do more? Can I get out of this bind? Can I become independent? And that was the point when they discovered TEE.

Some job-seekers were referred to TEE by the welfare system or by other public and private agencies. Others were attracted by the organization's advertisements. When they entered TEE's offices in Boston, they found themselves in what was essentially a nonprofit employment agency—with a twist. The organization found real jobs for them in the private sector. They were *not* temporary or make-work positions.

If they met their employer's standards, they would be hired permanently after a three- to six-month tryout period. If they didn't pass the tryout, TEE promised to find them another job. The TEE job candidates would have to compete with other TEE participants and regular job-seekers from within and outside the firm. If anything, these jobs were harder to hold than other positions in the business world. It was not unusual for a TEE worker to be employed in company departments that had a history of 50 to 60 percent turnover.

Despite those obstacles, TEE placed 65 percent of its job-seekers. A study by Brandeis University found that 90 percent of former TEE participants continued to be employed a year after the program, 80 percent after two years, and 72 percent after three years. Since 1975 it has found employment in the private sector for more than 2,500 people.

TEE was successful because it offered an attractive deal to both the potential employer and the employee. TEE promised a prospective employer: We will find a suitable worker for you. If the employee doesn't work out, we'll get you a substitute. "If I want three entry-level workers, like dial-a-prayer, I dial TEE," said James Howell, a senior vice president of the First National Bank of Boston, where a number of TEE workers are employed. "TEE takes care of the nuisance during the swing period. If I don't like any of them, we start all over. If I like them—I hire them."

For the service, TEE charged companies between $3.25 and $6 an hour. With those funds, TEE paid in 1983 a minimum wage of $3.35 an hour, plus fringe benefits, salary increases, and bonuses during the tryout period. It also picked up the tab for recruitment, pre-employment screening, interviewing, and job-matching. It also paid the salary of the TEE supervisor who was present at the job site. Cove estimated that it would cost the average company between $10 and $15 an hour to recruit and train entry-level employees. That was the deal TEE offered the private sector.

This is what it offered prospective employees: an opportunity to prove themselves at work; on-the-job supervision by a TEE employee who helped them develop their skills and counseled them in their private lives; the minimum wage plus bonuses and increases depending on their performance, and a reduction but not elimination of their welfare benefits as their salary increased. The training, TEE emphasized, occurred on the job. The participants didn't have to wait before they started working.

A lot of promises have been made to participants in employment programs. When Carol Slawson* walked into the lobby of the Shawmut Bank of Boston, she didn't know whether the promises TEE made would come true. More than that, she didn't know whether she was capable of doing the job. She was thirty years old. The last time she'd held a job was ten years before. During that time she'd raised four children at home. Throughout her adult life she had been on welfare.

During her first week, her face would often be creased with doubt. As she looked across the room at Glenn Wilts, the TEE supervisor at the bank, her eyes seemed to plead: Help me, I'm lost. "The bank showed me how to log the checks in and compare them with the statements, and there was a dozen different forms to fill in. I said, 'I'll never know all these things.'" She couldn't even pronounce the name of the department she worked in. "I'd say to people I worked in recon . . . something. Reconstruction, maybe. Finally I wrote the word out and stared at it for an hour. It took maybe four days before I got it right—reconciliation."

Throughout this difficult break-in period, Mrs. Wilts was there to support her. She suggested, for instance, that Carol make out work cards that detailed each of her responsibilities on the job. Mrs. Wilts also reassured Carol when some of her co-workers at the bank were cold and indifferent to her because she was still receiving welfare funds, and because she got the job with the help of an outside organization.

Where Mrs. Wilts's intervention made the most difference was outside the job. During the orientation sessions at TEE, speakers from various banks had counseled the participants to keep their private lives and work lives separate, not to let their problems at home undermine their performance on the job. Good advice in principle, but hard sometimes to practice.

* Her name has been changed.

Mrs. Slawson was having problems with her landlord when she moved to a new apartment after a few weeks at work. The conflict made it difficult to concentrate on checking accounts and bank statements. But after talking to Glenn Wilts for several hours, Mrs. Slawson was able to resolve the problem.

> I would have felt uncomfortable talking to the bank supervisor about it, but I had to talk to somebody because it was driving me crazy. But Glenn, she was somebody who was sensitive to a woman on welfare. She told me how to get the information I needed and how to approach the landlord. Between her advice and my feelings we worked out a plan. The bank supervisor's interested in me, *the employee.* Glenn's interested in me, *the person.*

The landlord, however, was a piece of cake compared to the welfare department. In her first month at the bank, Carol was taking home $140 a week. Welfare regulations provided that she would receive some payments as well as medicaid and a certain amount of food stamps until she earned more than 110 percent of her grant. But two weeks after she started, she got a letter from the welfare department that said all payments to her would be stopped—food stamps, medicaid, the housing allowance, all of it. This threw Carol Slawson into a panic.

One principal purpose of having a job was to become self-sufficient. With four children, how do you become self-sufficient on $140 a week?

> They gave me two weeks' notice. Two weeks and I would be completely cut off. I was between mad and infuriated. I said to myself, I didn't have these problems until I got a job. I'd been dealing with welfare a long time. Even if I managed to finally straighten this out, I knew it was going to take me a week of sitting in the welfare office. What would the bank say? Sure, I'd get my welfare. But I'd lose my job.

It took Glenn Wilts three phone conversations, lasting an hour and a half, to establish that Mrs. Slawson was eligible to receive a partial grant until she was hired by the bank and her salary was increased.

When I finished my study of TEE, Mrs. Slawson had worked at the Shawmut Bank for almost four months. In that time, she had consistently received superior work evaluations from the TEE representative. Bank officials said she was likely to be hired soon. But the best indicator of her progress may be her own attitude toward the work.

When she first appeared at the job, her dominant emotion was fear. Now it was boredom. "When you first come in, it's all so scary and exciting. But after a while, the work is repetitious and it's so boring. But that hasn't stopped me," she said. "I've tried to help all the other TEE workers on the floor, and when the bank hires me, the job will be different." She was also thinking of taking night classes in computer sciences, if she could raise the $90 for the fourteen-week course.

Carol Slawson wanted not just any job, but a job that challenged her. It's normal to be ambitious; she had entered the mainstream of the work world.

That passage from fear to ambition had left its imprint on her family life as well. "This has given my children something to follow. If somebody asks them, 'What does your mother do?', they can't say, 'She sits at home.' They have to ask within themselves, 'If my mother did it, why can't I?' Now at dinner, my daughters say, 'I'm gonna be a secretary or a nurse or go to college,' and they know they can do it because I did it." In a sense, she has become a model to her children, which is not something that most of the youngsters I met experienced in their own childhood.

Compared to some other TEE workers, Mrs. Slawson had a relatively easy time adjusting to her job. In Bedford, Massachusetts, Judith Sadowski, a TEE counselor-mentor with a master's degree in social work, spent a lot of her time washing dishes in a hotel kitchen where young retarded men and women worked.

"David, who was seventeen, was hired as a pot washer," she recalled. "The first week he was at the job, I was doing 50 percent of his work. The next week it was 35 percent. Finally, I let him do it all. At the same time, I was telling him, 'You're doing a fine job, you just need to work a little faster.' "

She knew that while job performance was important, so too was David's appearance—even in a hotel kitchen. "You focus on whatever the trouble is," she said. "It might even be the way David dressed, whether he shaved, whether his hair is clean, whether he brushed his teeth that morning. You might have to remind him to use deodorant. That sounds pretty basic, but you know some of our kids haven't had anyone tell them that."

For David, as it was for Carol Slawson, the real payoff from

working came with a newfound sense of independence. On the
night he got his first paycheck from TEE, David left the hotel
kitchen and took one bus and two trains to get to Fenway Park
in Boston. There he purchased tickets for six home games that
the Red Sox were scheduled to play during the following two
weeks. The tickets cost $42.70. David was a very big Red Sox
fan. Then he took a bus home to the Boston suburb of Brookline.
The trouble was, he took the wrong bus and wound up in Harvard
Square in Cambridge. He tried calling home a few times, but
the line was busy. So he called the Brookline police and told
them he was lost. A police car was dispatched to pick him up,
and he arrived home an hour later.

"I was very tempted to give him hell," says his mother, Helen.
"I knew he didn't have the strength to work every day and then
go to the ball game every night. Besides, I'm not sure that was
the best use of his money. I was also very upset that he got lost.
But in a way, I was thrilled. Positively thrilled. All through David's
childhood, I had been moving him toward this idea of independent
living. And whether I approved of everything he did or not, he
was acting independently."

The price of achieving independence is not cheap. TEE estimates that it costs $3,000 to train and employ a former welfare
recipient. It may cost up to $10,000 a year to secure employment
for a retarded citizen. "We're expensive but not costly," Peter
Cove says. Cove meant that it would cost much more if they were
not working. The organization calculated that forty-eight former
welfare recipients who were hired permanently would pay a total
of $78,000 annually in federal and state taxes, while about
$384,000 was saved in reduced welfare grants through the year.
While the state of Massachusetts was helping to subsidize the
TEE program at a cost of $1,000,000, it was realizing a return
on its investment of 152 percent in increased taxes and reduced
welfare grants.

Similarly, while the $10,000 annual expenditure for retarded
people is substantial, TEE projected that taxpayers save $1,800
a year for each individual holding a full-time job. But that's only
the short-term return. A life of social and economic dependency
for a thirty-year-old retarded person who's capable of gainful employment is estimated at more than $385,000.

The value Massachusetts places on TEE's work is suggested
by its support of four other local organizations using the TEE

model, at an annual cost of almost $6,000,000. State Assistant Welfare Commissioner Robert Cornetta said, "Traditionally we've trained people, but after they have all this training, they can't get a job. It's awful. But what TEE has done is take people with almost no training or preparation and put them on a job very quickly, and most of these people meet the standards of the company."

The economist Eli Ginzberg once told me, "I don't see how in a civilized society, you can say to people you're supposed to work and then not offer them the chance to work." I believe that a national apprenticeship system, borrowing from the TEE approach, would give a significant number of unemployed out-of-school youths access to economic self-sufficiency. Not all, but some.

There's never been an extensive national test in this country of a job-first, education-later strategy. Most previous programs have required dropouts to enroll in remedial education programs while they are working. The TEE approach would alter that cycle. In a discussion paper on employing youth, the organization said, "We propose changing access to and availability of the workplace before changing the individual. The result should produce a cycle that creates successful job experience leading to successful education and training which leads to increasingly successful labor market participation." Past experience, TEE said, suggests that "the cycle that now exists is unsuccessful education which leads to unemployment."

With the loss of many industrial jobs, TEE contends, an effort to add new jobs to the economy must accompany any new national program to find private-sector employment for youth. I am not sure that an increase in jobs would significantly improve the prospects for youth. Between 1970 and 1983, about 22 million jobs were created by the economy, but only 0.1 percent, or some 22,000, went to black male youths. More than 9.5 million jobs were created from the trough of the recession in November 1982 to January 1986, but teenagers, minority and white, who represent more than 18 percent of the unemployed, suffered a net job loss during the economic recovery, according to the Bureau of Labor Statistics. Whether you blame racism or a generalized mistrust of poor youngsters or a premium on academic credentials, the private sector has resisted employment of impoverished minority youths, even when offered the assurances and support of an organization like TEE.

The only practical alternative now, I believe, is to direct youth employment efforts toward those sectors of the economy most responsive to public opinion and political leadership. One expanding sector of the private economy comprises industries that rely heavily on defense contracts. Their reliance on federal expenditures obligates them to a sincere effort to meet equal opportunity goals. The defense industry is not an insignificant part of the economy. It could absorb a sizable chunk of unemployed teenagers. It could, that is, if the national administration linked the defense buildup to a buildup in opportunities for excluded young workers.

Another natural target of a national apprenticeship strategy would be businesses that receive tax incentives, low-interest government loans, and other special breaks from the public treasury. There are businesses that sometimes realize a great profit with the investment of development money provided by taxpayers. It would not be ungenerous to ask them to pay a little of it back by investing in youth.

That is what is being asked in St. Paul, Minnesota. There, local government has tied a youth employment effort to the development of the St. Paul Energy Park. The park, whose businesses rely on high technology and energy conservation, will contain both businesses and residential housing on a 300-acre site. The principal developer is the St. Paul Port Authority. The development of the park will create roughly 4,000 jobs, according to officials.

Richard Thorpe, director of the city's employment and training system, will try to employ youths in the different phases of the park's development. In the first stages, he wants to put them in landscaping and construction-related jobs. Later, after businesses open, he wants to place them in retail, service, and maintenance positions. With the support of the mayor and the Port Authority, he has secured a clause in all construction contracts that requires builders to set aside 20 percent of the jobs for trainees in the program.

"It's not a guarantee," Thorpe said, "but it gives us a foot in the door. The companies have to demonstrate a best effort, as they would in affirmative action. They simply can't give us lip service. They have to sit down and say, Okay, these are the jobs. We've got to be able to say, What about this one? How much training does it really take? And the guy says, A year, and we say, No, we'll do it in three months."

St. Paul's effort starts with a relatively brief remedial education course and an orientation to work attitudes. It then moves to skills training. Once the trainees are on the job they will receive intensive counseling and peer support.

Training youngsters for work in a community that is being developed, Thorpe argues, allows youths to change interests and vocational direction as they grow up. "Three years from now the same kid who laid the sewers may want to move into manufacturing or sales or into health services. We'll be there to help him do that. The important thing is that right from the start they've been part of the community's life and growth."

If the energy park plan succeeds, Thorpe hopes to apply the same strategy to other publicly funded development projects. "It's the mayor's feeling and my feeling that if we have a development effort going on here, it shouldn't be creating jobs for people in the suburbs."

Thorpe also points out that many private sector enterprises receive indirect public support through tax incentives, bonds, and other inducements. "There's a strong feeling in St. Paul that anything that occurs here that's fostered by public monies should be part of our effort to provide jobs for people who are shut out," he says.

In December 1979, the National Commission for Employment Policy recommended that the federal government include a provision in grant-in-aid programs and contracts that requires employers to consider hiring job-ready young men and women. That recommendation, which some unions and employers have opposed, has never been fully implemented, although local administrations in Denver, San Francisco, and other cities have tried to link public grants for development to jobs for disadvantaged youth. When the beneficiaries of long-term tax abatements and low-interest government loans build skyscrapers in New York, construct a new sports stadium in New Jersey, or redevelop the harbor area of Baltimore, they should be asked how many youngsters they plan to train and employ in those profitable enterprises. It is estimated that the cost of training one million poor dropouts would be approximately $5 billion annually;[24] the cost should be shared by government and the private sector.

Training without access to a job only heightens frustration. It is the task of political leadership to persuade those public-spirited entrepreneurs that they have a stake in the future of the children of the streets. I am not talking about inspiring the philanthropic spirit. I am talking about their pragmatic stake in preserving the public good. The cost of that grows every year as expenditures increase for social services, welfare, and incarcerating juveniles.

But I am not confident that the present political leadership has the interest or the will to engage the private sector in such an effort. Based on its past record, I don't think the business community is going to be eager to volunteer. In the absence of business involvement, I think it will be necessary to develop a new public sector program that will provide an apprenticeship for unemployed youngsters.

I know that mention of public sector employment conjures up the specter of the old CETA program. CETA was fatally compromised by scandal, favoritism, bureaucratic bungling, and a lack of accountability. In other words, it suffered from the same defects as some defense contractors, Wall Street investment houses, and banks that have engaged, on some occasions, in certain money-laundering operations. Many analysts believe that eventually a new national public employment initiative will emerge, better managed than CETA, providing needed community services and alert to abuses and the possibility of corruption. Unless a wave of public-spirited voluntarism sweeps through the private sector, government intervention will be, as it always has been, the only recourse for an excluded generation.

Without public or private support, it's not hard to guess what will happen to these youngsters. We can foretell their fate by considering the experience of the adolescents who are the subject of this book. Of the core group of 280 youngsters, one year later I heard from or was able to reach fifty-two. It is difficult to keep track of people whose addresses are subway trains, park benches, abandoned basements, and cardboard boxes.

The fact that they communicated with me or that I was able to find them suggested that they might be in a little better shape than the larger group. They were still looking for a lifeline, still trying to make a connection to the outside world.

The few who were making some progress tended to come from working-class and middle-class backgrounds. Although they may have had serious conflicts with their parents, they did have, in their own experience, a model for advancement. They had also developed important attachments in their own lives. In Detroit Irene Rogers had finished her high school work and was going on to college partly because she was an intelligent and ambitious young woman but also because she was determined to make a better life for her son. Myra Robertson, who lived in isolation in an Appalachian hollow, didn't make it all by herself either. She had the support of the David School in Floyd County, a deeply engaged and committed institution. Bill Craig in Newport has kept out of trouble because of his commitment to his wife and child, although his living conditions and employment prospects are tenuous at best. Whatever gains he has achieved he owes, at least in part, to the investment of a concerned adult—Millie Little, the social worker in Newport. He knows she's there for him and his family, not only now but in the years to come.

Some kids are straddling the line. I later heard from Richard Wilson. He'd held and lost three fast food jobs in the five months after being rejected at the bank. Actually, his latest job was a step up. He was cooking hamburgers instead of serving them. But he didn't seem very happy about it. "I can't keep doin' this," he said. "I gotta make some money somehow."

Most of the kids had dropped out of sight. They were either out on the street or they had been swallowed up by some institution. After months and years of looking for steady work, they had lost hope. They wouldn't be counted in the official unemployment rate, because they had given up on finding a job. If they had been counted in 1985, the overall unemployment rate for all teenagers would have increased from 18.4 percent to 27.6 percent.[25] But no one in the Labor Department keeps track of ghosts.

The young people I met in the years between 1982 and 1985 are yesterday's story. Today's story is in the junior highs and high schools—the next generation of kids who will hit the streets. They haven't invented their lives yet. There is still time to help them.

The Next Generation

The streets took a heavy toll of the youth of Chicago in the winter of 1984. On the Near Northwest Side of the city, a youth had been shot on the steps of his high school. Another had died of a drug overdose a few blocks from the school she once attended. A fourteen-year-old boy had been stabbed to death in a neighborhood park because he refused to join a gang. Altogether, the Reverend Charles Kyle had performed funeral services for eighteen adolescents who had dropped out of neighborhood schools.

Father Kyle, associate pastor of St. Francis Xavier Roman Catholic Church, was upset at the loss of young lives.[26] He was also upset because he had just completed a two-year study that showed that many Chicago high schools were concealing the real dropout rate. And he was upset because the schools didn't seem to care very much that students were leaving or that those who were still in school were being victimized by youth gangs.

He decided that the community needed a forum for its grief and anger. So he held a memorial service for those who had died. In the early evening of March 26, 1984, some 500 parents, relatives, and community members gathered at St. Mark's Church. An old, scarred wooden coffin had been placed in front of the pulpit. It symbolized the sudden, violent deaths of some of the thousands of youngsters who drop out of Chicago's schools each year. "After you close that coffin and hear that mother cry, it's a sound you never want to hear again," Father Kyle told the mourners.

After the service, a dozen pallbearers, all parents and relatives of children who had died that winter, carried the coffin to Roberto Clemente High School, where Father Kyle said that 75 percent of the freshmen who entered the school failed to graduate. In the school auditorium, Father Kyle said, "I've buried eighteen kids under eighteen who've been killed on the streets. Every time I ask the mother, 'Where did he go to school?' The answer's always the same—'Oh, he dropped out.' The last kid I buried, I went back to the high school principal and said, 'I want to talk to you about José.' The principal said, 'Wait a second, I'll get him out of class.' I said to him, 'You can't do that. He's dead. I buried him.' I wanted to scream, 'Doesn't anybody care what happens to the kids in this school?'"

The reforms Father Kyle proposed centered on schools. He wanted an end to the underreporting of the actual dropout rate. Accurate reporting, he believed, would lead to a recognition of the seriousness of the problem. He wanted a full explanation of why students were dropping out and what needed to be done to retain them. He wanted parents to have a greater voice in how their children were being educated. He wanted students to be protected in and around their schools. "How can kids learn if they know that not the teachers but the gangs are running the school?" he said. If a youngster is failing courses or missing school, the last person to find out why, says Father Kyle, is the counselor. A first step toward reform, in his view—and mine—is the replacement and redefinition of an ineffective and potentially harmful counseling system.

Kyle also wanted fuller disclosure by the schools of their punitive practices. Specifically, he'd like to know more about the procedure for review and appeal of punishments. He would review the entire range of rules and practices that encourage—"The word is 'invites,' " Kyle says—students to drop out: suspensions, expulsions, public humiliation, beatings, and, in some localities, *jailings*. "All kids want discipline. They want structure, they want order in their lives," he said. "But they also want justice. Now we only have the appearance of justice."

Lastly, Father Kyle thinks schools should have some responsibility for students who leave. After they disappear, do they go to another school? Do they join a gang? Do they leave the community? Are they working? Are they pregnant? Are they living by themselves or with their families? Are they seeking their futures in the streets? He asked these questions of the schools he studied. The answer he got was that they didn't know. "When a kid leaves, is that the end of it?" he asks. "Does *anybody* care what happens the day after? If we bothered to find out, then maybe we could find a way to continue their education."

The movement to hold schools accountable for students who fail and drop out has gained momentum in the last two years. The heat generated by Kyle's study led to an investigation by the state legislature that basically confirmed his findings and promised some reforms in inner-city schools. One reform, achieved before the legislature's report, concerned the seemingly marginal issue of what youngsters do with their summers.

In 1978 and 1979 some 3,000 Atlanta students took the standardized Metropolitan Achievement Test before and after their summer vacations for two years in a row. The results showed that the summer hiatus had a negative effect on year-to-year learning among disadvantaged youngsters, while the more privileged kids did better on tests.[27] Researchers have estimated that 80 percent of the difference in year-to-year learning between advantaged and disadvantaged youngsters originated during the summer. In Chicago before 1984, if a high school student failed a course he would have to pay tuition to repeat it during the summer. Kids whose families could afford tuition started the next school year on an equal basis with their classmates. But not poor kids, who could not afford summer school. When the tuition requirement was abolished, *all* children had an equal shot at the benefits of education. I need not dwell, at this point, on the obvious fact that being in school during the summer offers an alternative to gangs, drugs, and hanging out.

Another significant school reform has to do with absences and academic failure. In some states a set number of absences is grounds for failure, regardless of why a student is absent or how well the student is doing in the course. In Texas, for example, five unexplained absences during the school term means automatic failure. It doesn't make a difference if your mother is in the hospital, your father is an alcoholic, your brother is shooting up, and your sister is pregnant. Those circumstances are not accepted as adequate explanations for absences. If you're out of school you've failed. In New York, the State Education Commissioner ruled in 1986 that high schools may no longer fail students or withhold course credit for excessive absences as long as the students are maintaining a passing grade.[28] The teachers' union objected to the ruling, complaining that it was an example of 1960s-style leniency. The state, I think, proceeded from the unremarkable observation that constant attendance is very difficult for a child whose family is in turmoil. It may have also concluded that time spent is not the only measure of achievement; the effort involved in passing a course while the rest of your life is unraveling deserves reward, not punishment.

Time is important in another sense. *Brrring.* 2:45. A couple of thousand students head for the door. Another school day is over. It's difficult for some teachers to imagine that some kids would really like to stay a little longer, would really use the school as a refuge—if the doors stayed open. There are kids who would rather belong to a school club or intramural organization than a street gang. Some kids pick up loose change during the days; they might want to go to school at night. Some kids might want to shoot a few baskets in a school gym instead of an inner-city playground, where half the guys have their heads bent over a can of spray paint. There might be a few kids who would like

to find an adult to talk to, just an adult. And then there are kids
who are looking for nothing more than a warm place to sit.

All of this should be obvious to anyone who looks out at
the surrounding neighborhood from a school window. It is obvious to Billy Reagan, school superintendent in Houston. "I don't
really think that with the way society is today, we can make much
of an impact unless we change our whole delivery system," Reagan
says. In 1984, when I spoke to him, Reagan had established the
city's first year-round extended-day elementary school; it was open
until 5:30 and it operated on a cycle of sixty days in school and
twenty days out, year-round. "The first thing we found is that
kids come right back after the short intercession," he says. "What's
the second thing? They lose only one-third of what they usually
lose, particularly in language. You can do a beautiful job in sex
education, in counseling, in remedial instruction, because you've
got time to do all kinds of things. You can bring and collapse
the services around the children."[29] The results were so promising
that Reagan decided to shorten the already brief intersession by
running classes in a neighborhood church.

By 1986 the Houston Independent School District was operating eleven year-round elementary schools and was studying the
feasibility of establishing full-time year-round high schools. The
cost of starting a year-round school was 25 percent higher than
that of running a school with a traditional schedule. But the increase in annual costs was less in the year-round school, because
more students were served over a longer period of time. The
year-round schedule seemed to improve learning ability. At conventional schools, 56 percent of the students were at grade level;
in the year-round schools more than 62 percent were performing
at their grade level.[30]

"My dream," says Superintendent Reagan, "is to restructure
education to respond to the realities of today's students. I want
to make school *their* place, another home for them. If we give
them access, I believe they'll grab it." And he adds, "There's
no way you're going to meet the needs of poor kids with the
remote, uninvolved system that operates today."

The Engaged School

The high schools attended by most poor and minority students
are nothing but fragmented. Joseph C. Grannis, an educational

analyst, writing in the early 1970s, observed that most of these schools operated on the "factory" model.[31] Students work on identical materials, producing identical products, as workers do on the assembly line. Teachers assign; students recite. The successful student grasps, memorizes, and feeds back the teacher's lesson plan. The student never sees the teacher do anything but teach; never sees the teacher solving problems or producing something as adults outside the school do.

A limited form of competition is encouraged in the "factory" schools. It is a competition based on how much information is absorbed and the speed with which it is fed back to the teacher. But there is not much reward for individual initiative, originality, and creativity. All but the most outstanding students labor in isolation; they are not considered capable of effective teamwork and collaboration. One summer I tutored in reading a fourteen-year-old Hispanic boy who attended a "factory" school in the South Bronx. I found him one afternoon thumbing through a book on Latin America in the library of the community center that sponsored the tutoring program.

"Are you interested in reading about these countries?" I asked him.

"The kids in my class divided up in groups and did projects on South America," he said. "But I wasn't allowed to because I was failing *geometry*." In this school, the freedom to engage in creative teamwork is offered only to those students who meet the school's uniform standards.

As in an actual factory, authority in the factory school accrues to those adults with the power to punish. Success comes to the student who flatters and emulates the paternalistic boss of the enterprise—usually the principal and his or her surrogates. "Sometimes, however, the students reject the system," Grannis noted. "They sit in sullen silence or they range themselves against the teachers and the school and bring the works to a futile halt." Obviously, the ultimate rejection is dropping out. If enough students drop out, say 70 to 80 percent, they can shut down the plant.

The experience of the last twenty-five years suggests that most students who spend their school days rushing from one assembly line to another, from one crew boss to another, are as confused and disoriented as Charlie Chaplin was in *Modern Times*. They collapse in exhaustion, or they try to sabotage the production system. Within these schools, the most important innovation will not occur by changing the curriculum or introducing computers. It will be the presence of a core teacher, a mentor, an adult to whom the students are responsible, and who is responsible to them. Somebody who can define what the center of the beehive is all about—the reason for going on, for learning, for growing up. Somebody who knows as much about what the students face outside the school as about their performance in the classroom. When a kid disappears, the core teacher/mentor doesn't respond by shredding the kid's card in his rollbook. He finds out what's happened to him and why, and tries to make education, in whatever shape or form, accessible to the lost child.

Again and again, I found that the same pattern was repeated: The kid who managed to climb out of the morass of poverty and social pathology was the kid who found somebody, usually in school, sometimes outside, who helped him invent a promising future. In practical terms, the presence of the understanding, concerned, yet demanding mentor transforms the meaning and quality of education. The school no longer views the student body as 2,000 indistinguishable humming brains. It responds to the individual students as social creatures whose private lives bleed right onto their workbooks and scratch pads.

Here and there across the country a new kind of school has emerged from the wreckage of the obsolescent factory model. It replaces the failed, insulated institution that modeled itself after the isolated frontier fort encircled by savage tribes. This evolving institution goes by different names. Some analysts call them "moonshot" schools—schools that put as much effort and intensity into educating and guiding their students as the country did in putting a man on the moon. I prefer to call it the "engaged" school. By that I mean a school engaged with the other forces and institutions that shape a young person's development.

For years the education and social welfare bureaucracies resisted intermingling, as if each had a disease that could fatally infect the other. Teachers thought welfare workers, if situated near and in schools, would encroach on their professional status. Welfare workers did not want teachers meddling in the personal lives of their clients. So the two systems operated in separate spheres; little information or advice passed between them, and they never integrated their services to troubled youths. Now some school systems are beginning to recognize they must try to coordinate their efforts with the network of social, economic, and health services in the community.

In an intermediate school in the Chelsea section of Manhattan, one teacher has been relieved of his classroom responsibilities and placed in charge of a staff of ten social workers and counselors. Much of the program's $150,000 annual budget is spent on efforts to assist students with personal problems that interfere with school attendance. When a student is frequently absent, the school, instead of sending letters to parents, sends a full-time "family worker" out for a house call. The program staff says the information gathered is kept confidential, and family visits are informal.

Sometimes when a kid's truancy rate rises, the school reduces his course work until the root problem is resolved. Then he is eased back into the regular schedule. The kid is not failed because he played hooky.

A more expansive effort involves almost 2,000 students, who were identified as potential dropouts, from eight New York City high schools. The students were offered a cluster of services, including personal and family counseling; diagnostic vocational evaluations; some 400 educational internships each year; vocational skills training in an outside agency; and part-time jobs. It is significant that the program was designed by an outside organization, thereby avoiding the bureaucratic in-fighting and protection of turf common to many school programs. The program reports that 92 percent of the participating students either stayed in school or graduated.[32]

Student surveys should be treated with some skepticism; students often react to pollsters as they do to teachers—they tell them what they think they want to hear. But I think some credit must be given to the findings reported in a survey of the program's participants: 92 percent said that the schools were preparing them for a career as compared to 41 percent before the program started; 61 percent said they went to school all the time, compared to 27 percent at the outset, and 77 percent said they felt as if they belonged in school against 45 percent at the beginning.

The integration and coordination of services is one element in an interactive strategy. By itself, I don't think it will achieve enduring gains for the most estranged youngsters, and it may create yet another layer of unresponsive bureaucracy. To be effective, I think an interactive approach must involve responsible adults in and out of the community who are not associated with the social service system or the schools. Usually when outside adults are involved in the schools, the involvement takes the form of a one-day stop at the high school. A successful business person or professional or show biz personality preaches a sermon on the redemptive power of hard work, honesty, and perseverence to a group of respectfully disbelieving teenagers. I'm thinking of something a little more lasting than that.

I spoke with Blandina Cardenas Ramirez, a member of the U. S. Commission on Civil Rights, in her home town of San Antonio. Our talk took place a few hours after I met an enormously courageous girl who was trying to stay in school despite the fact that half of her family had been blown away by drugs and street violence. Ms. Cardenas said the community of her own childhood had been much more peaceful. "I grew up in a community where people were poor," she said, "but there was a basic health there; there was strength. A year did not go by in the lives of my parents that they did not receive one of those high school graduation invitations saying "Thank you for helping me get through school," from a youngster who was not a member of the family. *I have never gotten one of those.* The fact is that that community is removed from me, and I am removed from them. My husband and I are socially, economically outside. I really think that those middle-class blacks and in my case, middle-class Hispanics, have to figure out some way to make it back. That may be my own guilt trip, but I think there has to be a link back in a person-to-person way. Not in an abstract way, but person-to-person."[33]

That link doesn't always have to involve conventionally successful people. It may be enough to engage people who have come through hard times and have managed to stabilize their lives. Project Redirection, a program that served adolescent mothers at eleven sites throughout the country, involved older women as counselors. They ranged in age from early twenties to late seventies. The women spent a minimum of five hours a week with each teenager. They served as their friends and confidants. They were the link between the program staff and the adolescents. As mentors they taught by example how to be effective parents. In a way, they did a lot of the same things TEE counselors did for welfare recipients in Massachusetts. An analysis of the program found: "The relationship was often particularly close when teens became estranged from their families; for these participants, the community woman sometimes served as a surrogate mother."

Rather than taking a tour of an insurance company in a part of town that is as remote to poor teenagers as the North Pole, schools might try to persuade corporations to send one of their managers across the tracks. Not for a day or a week, but for months. That may sound far-fetched, but it has happened when public education and private enterprise decide they both have a stake in the success of kids. The United Parcel Service, for example, detached executives from its offices around the country to work for two- to three-month periods in an employment-education program in Oakland, California. The UPS executives helped to develop jobs and counseled kids once they started working. In Hartford, black and Hispanic businessmen left their jobs temporarily to help schools set up nonprofit businesses that employed adolescents.

If some corporations are willing to furlough their executives, then schools might consider furloughing some of their teachers. Send them out of the classrooms to students' homes where they can teach mothers and fathers and other siblings to read and write.* That's what the David School in Floyd County, Kentucky did, with encouraging results. Send the teachers out also to the places where kids work. More is involved in the transition to adulthood than mastering a few work skills. Ray C. Rist, a professor at Cornell University, describes the passage from school to full-time employment as a "complex endeavor for young people, involving not only occupational choices, but choices about living arrangements, education, spending larger sums of money, assuming adult roles and any number of other changes."[35] The teacher who is present at the workplace can help student-workers sort out these choices on the spot, as they develop.

If all this talk of schools and communities interacting, of teachers who trek into the lives of their students and responsible adults who navigate their way back to the lost communities of their youth, sounds as though I'm proposing alternatives to the deeply disturbed families and communities of poor children, then let me go all the way and say it: That's exactly what I mean.

---

* Most studies of academic failure agree on one point: The youngsters who have the hardest time have parents who themselves failed, dropped out, and had children when they were adolescents. One program that offered those parents help at home in childrearing not only improved the parents' lives but also resulted in a 15 percent gain in their children's IQ scores over those who didn't participate and a 38 percent gain over older siblings who grew up before their parents received the training.[34]

"There is an enormous need to visualize and to create a rather general alternative institution in American life for young people," says Richard Boone, president of the Field Foundation in New York. "Alternative to the schools. Alternative to the street. In many cases, alternative to the current family."[36]

Some of the millions of youngsters who are exposed to the turmoil, drama, danger, and bravado of the streets may lack the discipline and concentration required to master academic abstractions, even when education is offered in a relatively unregimented and socially supportive environment. Many may not respond to the most responsive schools; the streets have left too deep an impression on them. But, as we've seen, street kids "chill out"— they experience moments of reflection and introspection; they're afraid they're getting in too deep. How do we capitalize on those periods? What alternatives can we offer them to the unending cycle of intergenerational crime and dependancy?

I think what we can offer them is an opportunity to demonstrate competency. Let's stop for a second and think about their present and future not in the conventional terms of social waste or as a threat to respectable society. Let's think of their adolescent crisis in their own terms, from their own point of view. Based on all the time I've spent with them, I believe they perceive their central crisis as one of competence. The only thing they believe they're good at is consuming. They know how to buy sneakers, drugs, records. But so many of them don't believe they can do anything else.

"I've seen it a million times," says Richard Boone of the Field Foundation. "Kids cover their inadequacy by bravado. They cover it sometimes by violence. Somehow we've got to struggle to open up space which entitles young people to do something other than school learning and make-work. They have to gain the experience of how to work and they have to gain the feeling that they in fact know how to do something. Not that they're going to carry that with them necessarily as their principal career, but the confidence and self-esteem and, ultimately, the productivity, that's related to that feeling is very, very big. We basically deny them that."[37]

In the California education system there is a partial recognition that some students require an alternative to school. In 1981, legislation was passed permitting fifteen-year-olds to leave school

for a semester and those sixteen and over to leave for up to
two semesters.[38] Middle-class kids may use their time away to
travel. But for poor youngsters it's only a partial answer to their
problems, because they don't have a place where they can develop
competency.

Student furloughs make sense only when they offer youngsters an opportunity to move into an alternative network, an esca-
lator that raises them out of poverty and anarchy. Otherwise,
they end up like Richard Wilson—stalled at the starting gate.
Boone and other analysts envision a social and economic ladder
with distinct rewards and opportunities as you climb. This may
involve residential programs such as the Job Corps or the type
of community service experience that allowed Linda Coleman,
the daughter of my friend Mike Coleman, to prove her competence. Such an alternative system would provide a chance to combine work and school or to return to school full time when the
youngster feels ready.

The key is the opportunity to advance once you have established competence. And advance not only in the confined areas
of public sector employment. The most glaring failure of previous
youth employment efforts is that they choke off ambition. They
are based on the assumption that all kids are like Linda Coleman,
that all they need is the first chance and they'll go on from there.
That's not true of kids who have sustained great damage; they
will need multiple challenges and successes, a continuing sense
of incremental development. And that will require a much deeper
and longer involvement by the private sector—involvement and
responsibility for other people's children.

In rare instances that responsibility has been demonstrated
by private industry. During the 1980s the Control Data Corporation in Minneapolis trained and placed more than 300 graduates
of Job Corps and CETA. Some went to work for the company,
but others were placed in other businesses. Helen Jirack, a Control
Data job developer, says, "It made all the difference in the world
that I could call a company and say I was representing Control
Data. If I was working on the CETA staff I don't think I would
have gotten a tenth of the commitments—and Minneapolis is a
pretty advanced, enlightened community. Control Data is what
opened the doors."[39]

The significance of what Control Data did is not that it opened
the doors to a stable job. The significant thing to those kids was

that they were rewarded for their effort. "If I had a magic wand, I'd create a network in which kids could see growth," says Richard Boone. "They've got to look back over their shoulders and say, 'Look what we did.' We wouldn't simply be moving them in and out of a program, but up and down, with notions of what they are going to be and how they are preparing themselves for that. Obviously the point is to allow them to discover their own value."

And what if they failed? What if they floundered and weren't ready to advance? "They wouldn't be rejected, they wouldn't be thrown out on the street," says Boone. "You'd try to move them into another position on the same level. You'd find a place for them. A place that gives them some money for their work, which has some minimal, marginal prerequisites of the work ethic, but a place that affords them a piece of status."

Many of the young men I met, and not a few of the young women, considered the armed services as the great escape clause in their lives. "Gonna get me an Armeeee job." During the Vietnam War, when the military was in desperate need of functional minds and bodies, the Defense Department started an experimental training program called Project 100,000. Between October 1966 and December 1971, the different branches of the military ran an intensive literacy effort, lasting thirteen weeks, for some 100,000 functionally illiterate recruits. In that period, the participants scored a reading gain of 1.5 grade levels, a rate three times higher than the public school norm. In 1974, the military followed up on the Project 100,000 participants. It found that they were more likely than non participants to complete their high school education, and to hold a higher-skilled, better-paying job. One researcher concluded: "This experience . . . suggests that functionally illiterate adults can, in fact, be raised to functionally proficient levels with education and training." The analyst proposed that the peacetime military be encouraged to reserve 20 percent of its entry-level slots for poor youngsters with limited education who would be trained in a program similar to Project 100,000.[40]

Income. Status. Advancement. In the military or in civilian life, those objectives will not be easily attained for the population I have been discussing. One survey estimates that nearly 20 million Americans are not able to read. The National Assessment of Educational Progress estimates that 13 percent of all seventeen-year-olds, 44 percent of black youths, and 56 percent of Hispanic adolescents are functionally illiterate. There are 4.9 million 16–24-year-olds who don't have a high school diploma and aren't in school. Some 243,000 people between the ages of twenty and twenty-four have never held a full-time job.[41]

Offering them access to opportunity will cost a few dollars. Some of the money should go to youngsters *and* their families. As Senator Moynihan of New York suggests, the personal tax exemptions for low-income working families need to be increased. One reason why 40 percent of the poor are children is that welfare payments have remained at a low level for many years, while the cost of living continues to escalate. (In Mississippi, welfare payments for a family of four come to $120 a month.) At the very least, welfare needs to be indexed to the inflation rate.

But it's not purely an issue of spending more money. It's also a question of rethinking our priorities. In education most of the funds for remediation and special education have gone to the elementary schools. We need to redirect some of that money to junior high schools and high schools. The gains kids achieve at an early age need to be sustained in their adolescence. It's foolish to assume that impoverished children will continue to achieve at the same level as more privileged children because we were kind to them when they were four or five years old.

Perhaps one-third of the youngsters I spoke to expressed an interest in returning to school. But they had been out of work and away from their families for so long that they couldn't afford the cost of resuming their education. For those youngsters who can't wait for years to earn a living salary—particularly those with children—it is worth considering enactment of a new version of the GI Bill, which enabled millions of veterans to reenter the American mainstream. This would provide a stipend to cover basic living expenses while youths attended school. The private sector may want to contribute to the stipend because of the anticipated decline in the number of young semiskilled and skilled workers entering the labor market. It would not be unreasonable to ask the young veterans of the street to repay their debt after they achieve some success, as college students repay their loans years after graduation.

Some social planners contend that piecemeal educational, social, and economic programs will make little headway against the corrosive blight in the most deprived communities. With the memory of San Antonio's Edgewood, Houston's Fifth Ward, and

Newark's North Ward fresh in my memory, it's hard to argue with them. Fifteen or twenty years ago, planned communities where family life, education, work, and leisure were intertwined attracted the interest of some middle-class families. Adventuresome civil servants in Washington were competing for mortgages in the planned town of Reston, Virginia. Civil Rights Commissioner Blandina Cardenas Ramirez wonders whether a modern planned community should replace the slums of Edgewood in the underutilized air force bases on the outskirts of San Antonio. She envisions an American-style kibbutz, where people have a stake in their community, where their children have a chance to learn, where parents can raise their young in some peace and security, and where young people coming of age have a chance to prove their worth to themselves and their mentors. Reborn communities. Regenerated families. Reclaimed lives. I'd be curious to find out what happens when people feel they have something to lose. We know how they feel when they've lost everything.

There is no shortage of visions, no dearth of imagination. But in the America of the 1980s there has been precious little encouragement to realize our dreams. A few of the ideas I've described were tried, and they produced promising results for a while. Then they were abandoned. Others were buried in the file cabinets of foundations and government agencies. The perspective that rules this decade generates a policy of avoidance, punishment, and containment. What we didn't see didn't bother us. When we could not ignore the products of poverty—when they cornered us on a dark street—we demanded harsh retribution. We said to this generation of parking lotters: Isn't it time for you to assume responsibility for your own lives? The injustice in this demand is that we never gave them the opportunity to assume responsibility. We never allowed them access, which is the least we offer our own children. I don't think we will ever know whether these young Americans are beyond repair until we offer them an alternative to the parking lot.

Suppose we don't offer them an alternative? Suppose we don't offer them a share in the American enterprise? What will happen to them? Can they survive? Yes, says Willie Sosa. Yes, he tells us, you can grow up alone in America and survive. But he also tells us the price he had to pay—the cost to him and his buddies on the streets of Newark.

Willie Sosa's Story: War and Peace

At sixteen, Willie was chilling out, looking to escape the streets. This is how he got away:

> I wanted a way out. A lot of my friends' brothers were in Vietnam, and I felt patriotic enough to want to go. Some of them had come back bugged out, but then I seen some that didn't go that way. They were doin' good, and I still remembered how bad they were when they were kids. They changed and I wanted to change. Also, I seen a John Wayne movie about Iwo Jima and that threw me. I said, Hey, this is me.

Willie tried to enlist when he was sixteen but was rejected when the Marines found out that he was too young. He was accepted when he was seventeen years, three months old. After boot camp, he was sent to Okinawa and then to a base in Thailand that served as a staging area for bombing raids and ground forays into Cambodia and Laos.

> We were a support unit, so we didn't see the kind of action that a ground troop would see, but there was the bombing and the mortars and the constant threat of the VC comin' in and hittin' us, and the bodies comin' in. That's when the war was basically winding down. We weren't losin' that many men any more. It was just so depressing because we were just so close, and sittin' ducks, and at the same time we can't do anything about it.
>
> I had to get all of that intensive training out of me. I was trained to fight, I wanted to get into the ground-pounding, but we couldn't. They had me carryin' the garbage into town and the people along the road were jumpin' on the truck and you drop a garbage can just so they can stay away from you. I started to ask, "Why am I here? I don't see I'm doing anything positive." And then a lot of my sergeants and a lot of the guys would come back to the rear after fighting and they were tired. They didn't want to go in any more.
>
> We kept high every day just to not think about either going in or never going in. I think it was two weeks out of the six months I spent there that I was straight. I used every drug you could name, from speed to opium to Buddha sticks, which is opium and marijuana, to heroin. We was involved in everything. As soon as we woke up, we woke up with a

drug in our mouth. To forget how far we were, and how close we were.

So here I was in the Marine Corps, thinking it was all going to be so beautiful and so nice and my whole dream fell apart. Because I didn't understand the purpose of the war, I didn't know what was going down. They sent me to Okinawa and I really went on a binge. I took twenty-two pills; it was a bugged-out scene, I got ripped off in town for 200 some dollars. I OD'd four times. Once I walked into the cafeteria and looked down and I wasn't wearing any shoes. Finally, the MPs got ahold of me, but I was gettin' ready to rotate so they didn't press charges. They knew I was stoned and where I came from. They'd seen a lot of that.

Willie was sent back to the Marine camp in California and then was granted thirty-nine days of home leave.

I was back in my environment again. I said, "I'm not gonna get high, I'm gonna chill out here, get into girls, go to dances." I'd saved a few thousand an' I gave my mother some money, like I used to give her when I was out hustlin' the bars in Perth Amboy when I was nine, ten. But after a few weeks, I cracked. I was doin' 6, 7, 8 quarts of beer a day, pills, methadone once a week. I decided fuck it, I went AWOL, and I stayed AWOL a year and nine months.

A couple of things happened during this time that made me stop and think. We mugged this guy in the park. What we did is we cornered him, five of us, and we mugged him. We split his head open. I punched him in the head, there was blood all over my hands. We took off his clothes, and he ran down the street naked. I looked at the blood when I got home and I just said, "Hey, I can't go on hurtin' people, man."

One day, my friend and me was dealin'. We had a discussion about dope with this guy who was lookin' to score. I told the guy, "Look, we shouldn't fight," and I tried to calm him down. The guy punched me in my mouth, knocked me down, just busted my lip. I was bleedin' all over the place. My friend got mad and he left and he came back with guns. He gave me a gun. We cornered the guy on the playground. We just started shootin'. We unloaded the six bullets and we missed him and then he started firing back and we ran. The bad thing, I always remembered, I could have killed somebody that day. I could have murdered. I never wanted that to happen. That influenced me a lot.

But I needed somebody to show me the way. And that was a friend who'd also been in the Marines. He'd become a Muslim. He was preachin' at me every day. He convinced me. He was a guy I'd grown up with and I trusted him. The Muslims was a beautiful family, the way they treated each other. I went into it because I needed somebody. I was destroying everything and I knew it. Any religion that would have come to me I would have took it. I was reaching out for something. I didn't know the ideology behind it, but the scene was so-o-o-o good. For four months I was a devout Muslim. I gave up the drugs, went to school at night to get my high school diploma, started in community college. I knew I wasn't going to stay a Muslim, but for the time I did, it turned my life around.

I decided I had to square myself with the Marines. I couldn't be AWOL the rest of my life. That was the next big thing. When I went back in I met this sergeant, Staff Sergeant Brown, a very heavy dude. He was my mentor. He sat me down, and we'd rap, and he'd tell me, "Look, man, you're Puerto Rican and I'm white and I know I've got a lot of advantages. Let me tell you, you're already considered a shitbird, and you're really going to have to be straight with me."

He said, "Treat me fair and I'll treat you fair. I'll give you all the breaks you need. I'll never try to hurt you." He was so compassionate and understanding—unlikely for a Marine. He understood the peon, the little guy. He'd also been in Vietnam, so he knew what was going down there. So he gave me that shot, and I never let him down. There's no overtime in the military, but I worked overtime for him. It was fantastic, I rearranged the whole place—the files, the tool cabinets, the tools, and everything. He gave me two meritorious promotions. I was determined to do everything I could for the guy because he was fantastic.

Sgt. Brown tried to persuade him to reenlist, but when the sergeant came down with emphysema Willie decided to leave the military.

I didn't want to stay in without my sergeant, 'cause he was the one I trusted. I told him I decided to try to struggle out there, to make it. Then he said, "Goodbye, I'm always going to remember you because you're an example. And I'm always going to use you as an example, I hope you don't mind." And I said, "No, I don't mind—you can do that." Because of him, I stuck with it, and I dealt with it and I handled it.

Willie returned to his neighborhood in Newark and took a job as a youth worker for La Casa, the community organization there.

> I don't say I completely changed, that I don't drink. I do. But I don't smoke marijuana, I don't get in over my head. When I got back I looked around and mostly all my buddies I grew up with are either alcoholics, they're on drugs, they're dead, or they're in prison.
>
> There's only two of us today that are still tryin'. That's me and my buddy who turned Muslim, and that's all. Because when you grow up in an environment like that, it's not an easy thing to say, "Boom, I forgot all about it—I'm a new man."
>
> When I talk to a kid, I say to myself, I can picture myself goin' through what he's goin' through. He reminds me of myself: the stealin', the robbin', not being able to read and write too good. And bein' a sweet kid, but really a rough and rugged kid at the same time. There's two sides to this kid, and I can identify there. I feel it for him. And I say I'm goin' to try and help this kid as much as I can. I guess that's where commitment comes in, bein' able to identify.

So Willie Sosa and his friend were the only survivors in their group. Willie went on to establish his competency working with the kids of the North Ward. He assumed responsibility for his life. He turned it around. Willie deserves much of the credit for his reformation. But credit must also go to that Marine sergeant who could see the sweet kid inside that rough and rugged kid and who, although he came from a different background, could identify with Willie and could offer him the bond of commitment.

When America begins to identify with the children of the streets, when it realizes that its future is bound up with their future, there will be more Willie Sosas who grow up to tell how they turned it around. It's about time.

Notes

CHAPTER 1 ABSORBING TIME (pp. 1–25)

1. Joan Didion, *Slouching Toward Bethlehem* (New York: Dell, 1961, 1968), p. 84.

2. *Runaway and Homeless Youth,* fiscal 1983 report to the U. S. Congress by the Family and Youth Services Bureau of the U. S. Department of Health and Human Services (Washington, D. C.: U. S. Government Printing Office, 1985), p.i. These estimates are highly tentative, because they do not include many poor and minority youngsters who have left home and school and whose absences have not been reported to government agencies. In 1983 witnesses before a U. S. Senate Subcommittee put the number of runaways at 1.2 million, with an average age of fifteen.

3. Douglas Glasgow, *The Black Underclass: Poverty, Unemployment and Entrapment of Ghetto Youth* (San Francisco: Jossey-Bass, 1980), p. 84.

4. Claude Brown, "Manchild in Harlem," *New York Times Magazine,* September 16, 1984.

5. Study by the Congressional Research Service and the Congressional Budget Office, as reported by the *New York Times,* "*Study Finds Poverty Among Children Is Increasing,*" May 23, 1985.

6. Godkin Lectures delivered by Senator Moynihan at Harvard University, April 8–9, 1985.

7. *"Study Finds Poverty Among Children Is Increasing,"* New York Times, May 23, 1985.

8. Data compiled by Federal Bureau of Labor Statistics, spring 1985, and reported by the Roosevelt Centennial Youth Project, a Washington organization that tracks the academic and economic status of poor youths.

9. Gordon Berlin and Joanne Duhl, "Education, Equity and Economic Excellence: The Critical Role of Second Chance Basic Skills and Job Training Programs," issued by the Ford Foundation, August 30, 1984, p. 9.

10. Roosevelt Centennial Youth Project report, February 1985.

11. Survey by the National Bureau of Economic Research, reported in "Joblessness Among Black Youth: Clues to a Wayout," *Business Week*, February 18, 1985, p. 20.

12. Emanuel Tobier, "The Changing Face of Poverty," report for Community Service Society of New York, November 1984, p. 21.

13. Moynihan, the Godkin Lectures.

14. Survey conducted by Professor Lawrence Bailis of Boston University at a conference held at the Ford Foundation in New York on June 5, 1984. Bailis surveyed more than 300 community-based organizations in forty-five states.

15. Warren G. Bennis and Philip E. Slater, *The Temporary Society* (New York: Harper Colophon Books, 1968), p. 52.

16. Charles E. Murray, *Losing Ground: American Social Policy 1950–1980* (New York: Basic Books, 1984), pp. 227–28.

CHAPTER 2 TO THE BRINK (pp. 26–47)

1. Anna Freud, "Adolescence," in *Adolescence: Contemporary Studies,* edited by Alvin E. Winder and David L. Angus (New York: Van Nostrand Reinhold, 1968), p. 17.

2. Sandor Lorand, "Treatment of Adolescents," reprinted in Winder and Angus, eds., *Adolescence,* p. 25.

3. Erik Erikson, "Youth: Fidelity and Diversity," in Winder and Angus, eds., *Adolescence,* p. 41.

4. *Ibid.,* pp. 41–44.

5. Bernard Lefkowitz, "Renegotiating Society's Contract with the Public Schools," *Carnegie Quarterly* (Carnegie Corporation of New York), Fall 1984/Winter 1985. The quote is drawn from Alvarado's testi-

mony before the National Commission on Secondary Education for Hispanics on February 28, 1984.

6. Author's interview with Schrank, March 14, 1984, New York.

7. *Chicago School Watch,* a 1985 publication of Designs for Change, a Chicago social research organization.

8. The "success" story was written in 1984 by a youth participating in a remedial program conducted by the Brighton Center, a service organization in Newport, Kentucky.

9. Unpublished 1984 report by the Brighton Center.

10. Author's interview with Nienaber in Newport, Kentucky, January 10, 1985.

11. Erikson, "Youth: Fidelity and Diversity," p. 35.

12. Bernard Lefkowitz, "Jobs for Youth: What We Have Learned," report for The Edna McConnell Clark Foundation, New York, 1982, p. 10.

13. Daniel J. Levinson et al., *The Seasons of a Man's Life* (New York: Ballantine, 1978) p. 331.

14. *Ibid.,* p. 337.

CHAPTER 3 CHILDHOOD (pp. 48–92)

1. Bernard Rosenberg and Harry Silverstein, *The Varieties of Delinquent Experience* (New York: Schocken Books, 1983; original pub., Waltham, Mass.: Blaisdell Publishing, 1969).

2. *Ibid.,* p. 164.

3. *Houston Chronicle,* November 19, 1979.

4. *Houston Chronicle,* October 6, 1979.

5. Author's interview with Dr. Susan Pokorney, Houston, January 1984.

6. Statistics appear in Bernard Lefkowitz, "The Funding Partners Community Care Program," report to the Robert Wood Johnson Foundation, May 1984, unpublished.

7. Author's interview with Robert J. Blendon, Princeton, N. J., December 1983.

8. "Updated Report on Access to Health Care," a Robert Wood Johnson Foundation special report, Number One, 1983.

9. Author's interview with Dr. Will Risser, Houston, January 1984.

10. Author's interview with Brenda Shapiro, Miami, February 1982.

11. The statistics on physical impairments are from a report on high school dropouts by Carol Heschmeyer and Kathleen McKean Woodcock for Colorado State University Cooperative Extension Service, 1981, p. 11.

12. Author's interview with Dr. Judith Amster, Miami, February 1982.

13. Annual report by the adolescent health center of Paseo High School, Kansas City, Missouri, 1983.

14. The importance of parental verbal skills is discussed by the researchers Gordon Berlin and Joanne Duhl, who write:

> Research shows that a child's home environment is an important determinant of his or her later achievement. . . . Reading theorists agree that there is a strong correlation between oral and written skills, and that beginning readers draw upon their knowledge of oral language in learning to read. That knowledge is initially acquired from one's parents. Children whose parents are poor readers are likely to have poor vocabularies, which puts them at an initial disadvantage in school. In fact, the amount of reading done at home and parent's level of education bears a consistent and significant relation to a child's achievement in school. [Berlin and Duhl, "Education, Equity and Economic Excellence" (note 9, Chapter 1), p. 12]

15. Peter Blos, *The Young Adolescent: Clinical Studies* (New York: Free Press, 1970), pp. 127–128.

16. Andrew Billingsley and Jeanne Giovannoni, *Children of the Storm: Black Children and American Child Welfare* (New York: Harcourt Brace Jovanovich, 1972), p. viii. Emphasis in original.

17. *Ibid.*, p. 250.

18. Robert Schrank's recollections of his childhood are drawn from the author's interview with him, New York, November 1984.

19. The following quotes are from a draft of an article Schrank wrote in 1984, "Coming Attractions: The End of Work."

20. Author's interview with I. Roy Jones in Detroit, December 1984.

21. Eleanor Holmes Norton, "Restoring the Traditional Black Family," *New York Times Magazine,* June 2, 1985.

22. *Ibid.*

CHAPTER 4 SCHOOL DAYS (pp. 93–154)

1. Horace Mann, Twelfth Annual Report, cited in Richard H. deLone, *Small Futures* (New York: Harcourt Brace Jovanovich, 1979) pp. 41–42.

2. Berlin and Duhl, "Education, Equity and Economic Excellence" (note 9, Chapter 1), p. 8.

3. Statistics on early childhood education were compiled by the National Center for Education Statistics; see "Early Schooling Is Pressed," in *New York Times*, November 17, 1984.

4. "Barriers to Excellence: Our Children at Risk," report by the Board of Inquiry of the National Coalition of Advocates for Students, Washington, D. C., February 1985, p. 3.

5. Laurie Olson and Rebekah Edwards, *Push Out, Step Out: A Report on California's Public School Drop-Outs* (Oakland: Citizens Policy Center, 1982), p. 27.

6. Edith Stern, "Jim Crow Goes to School in New York," *The Crisis*, XLIV (1937): 201–2.

7. Author's interview with Earlene Levicy, December 1984, Detroit.

8. James B. Conant, *Slums and Suburbs* (New York: McGraw-Hill, 1961), pp. 1–2, 144–47. Emphasis added.

9. "After 20 Years, Education Programs Are a Solid Legacy of Great Society," *New York Times*, September 30, 1985.

10. "Barriers to Excellence," p. 74.

11. *Ibid.*, pp. 18–19.

12. Berlin and Duhl, "Education, Equity and Economic Excellence," p. 11.

13. Ernest L. Boyer, "The Test of Growing Student Diversity," *New York Times*, November 11, 1984.

14. "After 20 Years," *New York Times*, September 30, 1985 (note 10 above).

15. On Hispanic children, "Make Something Happen," a national study conducted by the Hispanic Policy Development Project, issued in November 1984, p. 1.

16. Father Charles Kyle, "Los Precioses: The Magnitude of and Reasons for the Hispanic Dropout Problem in Chicago—A Case Study of Two Chicago High Schools," doctoral dissertation, Northwestern University, June 1984, pp. 5, 10, 24, 27–29, 31, 34.

17. Author's interview with Hamilton McMaster, Chicago, November 1984.

18. Author's interview with James Vasquez, San Antonio, January 1985.

19. "Barriers to Excellence" (note 4 above), p. 14.

20. Olson and Edwards, *Push Out, Step Out* (note 5 above), p. 10.

21. For one example of a study that shows a high percentage of Hispanic students leaving school to go to work, see William A. Diaz, "Hispanic

Youth Employment: An Overview," issued by the Hispanic Policy Development Project, March 1983, p. 20.

22. The Benito Juarez High School dropout study was conducted on October 11 and 12, 1984, and a draft report was completed on October 19, 1984.

23. Vasquez interview.

24. A. B. Hollingshead, *Elmtown's Youth* (New York: John Wiley & Sons, 1949), pp. 177, 178, 331. Emphasis added.

25. Theodore B. Sizer, *Horace's Compromise: The Dilemma of the American High School* (Boston: Houghton Mifflin, 1984), pp. 36, 37.

26. Author's interview with David Jackson, director of Kentucky's Department of Dropout Prevention, in Bernard Lefkowitz, "Renegotiating Society's Contract with the Public Schools," *Carnegie Quarterly*, Fall 1984/Winter 1985, p. 4.

27. Conant, *Slums and Suburbs* (note 9 above). Emphasis added.

28. Author's interview with Manford Byrd, Chicago, November 1984.

29. A fuller account of Project Apex appears in a report the author wrote for the Ford Foundation. Bernard Lefkowitz, "Dropouts and Work," July 1980, pp. 122–23.

30. Author's interviews with Danny Greene and Joan Ford, in David, Kentucky, January 1985.

31. "Discipline Problems in Kentucky Schools," survey conducted by the Kentucky Department of Education, Division of Alternative Education, 1980, pp. 3, 4, 5, 6, 8.

32. Olson and Edwards, *Push Out, Step Out* (note 5 above), pp. 18–19.

33. "Kentucky's Children at Risk: The Inequities in Public Education," prepared by Kentucky Youth Advocates in Louisville, June 1984, p. 21.

34. *Ibid.*, p. 22.

35. "Our Children at Risk: The Crisis in Public Education," Massachusetts Advocacy Center, 1984, p. 11.

36. "Kentucky's Children at Risk," p. 21.

37. Sizer, *Horace's Compromise* (note 26 above), pp. 168–69.

38. Olson and Edwards, *Push Out, Step Out*, p. 18.

39. Author's interview with Houston School Superintendent Billy Reagan, Houston, February 1984.

40. The 1959 interview with the Los Angeles youth counselor appears in Lucius P. Cervantes, *The Dropout: Causes and Cures* (Ann Arbor,

Ann Arbor Paperbacks, University of Michigan Press, 1969), pp. 69–71.

CHAPTER 5 STREET LIFE (pp. 155–218)

1. Cited in "Brazil's Time Bomb: Poor Children by the Millions," *New York Times,* October 22, 1985.

2. David Shaffer and Caron L. M. Caton, "Runaway and Homeless Youth in New York City," report for the Ittleson Foundation, New York, January 1984, pp. 34–36, 44, 65.

3. Paul J. Lavrakas, Susan Bennett, and Richard A. Maier, Jr., "Newark Community Assessment Report," Center for Urban Affairs and Policy Research, Northwestern University, Evanston, Illinois, June 1984, pp. 5, 18, 36, 37, 40, 47, 69, 71.

4. Andrew B. Hahn and Robert I. Lerman, "Representative Findings from YEDPA Discretionary Projects," Center for Employment and Income Studies, Brandeis University, 1982, p. 3.

5. "Youth and the Juvenile Justice System," a draft of a discussion paper prepared for the National Council on Crime and Delinquency, Hackensack, N. J., 1982, p. 3. (Unpublished.)

6. Bonnie Snedeker, "Youth Prospectives—The Lives Behind the Statistics," This is one of a series of reports on youth employment issued by the Labor Department's Employment and Training Administration. (Washington, D. C.: U. S. Government Printing Office, May 1980), p. 74, 77, 79.

7. William E. Gladstone, written testimony before the Subcommittee on Juvenile Justice of the U. S. Senate Committee on the Judiciary, Washington, D. C., July 9, 1981.

8. Mark A. Thennes, "Juvenile Justice Reform in America," *Youth Policy* (Youth Policy Institute, Washington, D. C.), November 1985, p. 24.

9. James Wooten, "Minority Incarceration: Troubling Facts Show Inequities," *Youth Policy,* November 1985, p. 25.

10. Shaffer and Caron, "Runaway and Homeless Youth," pp. iii, vi.

11. Ronald Bayer, "Crime, Punishment and the Decline of Liberal Optimism," *Crime and Delinquency,* April 1981, pp. 170, 182.

12. Author's interview with Robert Taggart, former administrator of the federal Office of Youth Programs, Washington, D. C., January 1982.

13. John Mueller, "Crime Is Caused by the Young and the Restless," *Wall Street Journal,* March 6, 1985.

14. "The Juvenile Offender Survey Project," prepared by Andrew Kaplan, June Pimm, and Diane Baker under the sponsorship of Judge William E. Gladstone, funded by the William and Tina Rosenberg Foundation, Miami, June 1980, pp. 7, 8.

15. Gladstone, testimony before Subcommittee on Juvenile Justice.

16. Author's interview with Bobbie A. Jones, Albuquerque, February 1982, cited earlier in Lefkowitz, "Jobs for Youth: What We Have Learned" (note 12, chapter 2), pp. 8, 9.

CHAPTER 6 OPENINGS AND CLOSINGS (pp. 219–281)

1. Monthly report of the Roosevelt Centennial Youth Project, November 1985 (see note 10, chapter 1). The organization bases its reports on the most recent statistics provided by the U. S. Bureau of Labor Statistics.

2. Cited in *A Review of Youth Employment Problems, Programs and Policies,"* a report issued by the Vice President's Task Force on Youth Employment (Washington, D.C.: U. S. Government Printing Office, January 1980), vol. 2, p. 9.

3. "U. S. Study Details Employment Shift," *New York Times,* June 8, 1985. The decline in manufacturing jobs in Chicago is described in testimony by Susan Rosenblum of the Midwest Center for Labor Research, before the National Board of Inquiry of the National Coalition of Advocates for Students, April 26, 1984.

4. David Dembo, project coordinator of the Council on International and Public Affairs, letter to *New York Times,* September 6, 1985.

5. David Robison, "Youth Access to Private Sector Jobs: The Sorcerer's Apprentice," in *A Review of Youth Employment Problems,* vol. 3, p. 7.

6. Lefkowitz, "High School Dropouts and Work," a study by the author for the Ford Foundation (note 30, chapter 4), p. 90.

7. Vocational Foundation, "Our Turn to Listen," New York, 1977. p. 32.

8. Keith Melville and Harvey Lauer, "Moving Up to Better Education and Better Jobs," study by the Public Agenda Foundation for the Hispanic Policy Development Project, February 1984, p. 9.

9. Kathryn Shield, "Youth and the Employability Gap," unpublished report to the Taconic Foundation, New York, October 1981, p. 34.

10. Thurow's comments cited in "Youth Unemployment," a working paper for the Rockefeller Foundation, September 1977, p. 11.

11. Robert Taggart, "A Review of CETA Training: Implications for Policy and Practice," W.E. Upjohn Institute for Employment Research, 1981, p. i.

12. *Ibid.*, p. i.

13. Author's interview with Michael Marker, Modesto, California, March 1982.

14. Author's interview with Kenneth DeBey, Denver, February 1982.

15. Robert Taggart, *A Fisherman's Guide* (Kalazamoo, Mich.: W. E. Upjohn Institute for Employment Research, 1981), p. viii.

16. Lefkowitz, "Jobs for Youth" (note 12, chapter 2), p. 19.

17. The scarcity of promising entry-level employment for poor and minority youth is documented in many studies, including the Vice President's Task Force on Youth Employment (note 2 above), Berlin and Duhl (note 9, chapter 1), and Shield (note 9 above).

18. Laurence Steinberg and Ellen Greenburger, "The Part-Time Employment of High School Students: A Research Agenda," *Children and Youth Service Review*, II (1980): 13–14.

19. Herbert Bienstock, "Young People in the New York Labor Market," report for the Center for Labor and Urban Programs, Queens College, New York, December 1981, p ii.

20. The entitlement program is discussed in Lefkowitz, "Jobs for Youth," p. 10.

21. Author's interview with Greg Garcia, Denver, February 1982.

22. The quotes from Five Percenters literature appeared in material shown to the author by James, a young man recruited into the organization while he was in prison.

23. The account of the TEE program is drawn from Bernard Lefkowitz, "Changing the Odds: A Profile of Transitional Employment Enterprises," unpublished, March 1984.

24. Aaron Bernstein *et al.*, "The Forgotten Americans," *Business Week*, September 2, 1985, p. 51. The estimate is based on data provided by the Manpower Demonstration Research Corp. and the Center for Labor Market Studies at Northeastern University.

25. The extrapolated unemployment rate is based on statistics reported by the U. S. Department of Labor's Bureau of Labor Statistics, as cited by the Roosevelt Centennial Youth Project, November 1985.

26. The discussion of dropouts in Chicago is drawn from the author's interview with Father Charles Kyle, Chicago, January 1985.

27. Berlin and Duhl, "Education, Equity and Economic Excellence" (note 9, chapter 1), p. 16, drawing on the work of Barbara Heyns, *Summer Learning and the Effects of Schooling* (New York: Academic Press, 1978).

28. "Teachers May Not Fail Students for Absence Alone, Board Says," *New York Times,* January 25, 1986.

29. Author's interview with Billy Reagan, Houston, February 1984.

30. Statistics on year-round schools in Houston provided to the author by the Houston Independent School District, March 1986.

31. Joseph Grannis's description of the "factory school" appeared in *The Learning of Political Behavior,* edited by Norman Adler and Charles Harrington (New York: Scott, Foresman, 1970), pp. 140–41.

32. August 1985 bulletin of the Roosevelt Centennial Youth Project.

33. Author's interview with Blandina Cardenas Ramirez, San Antonio, January 1985.

34. Berlin and Duhl, "Education, Equity, and Economic Excellence," p. 13.

35. Ray C. Rist, "Confronting Youth Unemployment in the 1980s," *Children and Youth Services Review,* vol. 2, nos. 1 and 2 (1980), p. 13.

36. Author's interview with Richard Boone, New York, February 1982.

37. *Ibid.*

38. Olson and Edwards, *Push Out, Step Out,* (note 5, chapter 4), pp. 46–47.

39. Author's interview with Helen Jirack, Minneapolis, February 1982.

40. Berlin and Duhl, "Education, Equity and Economic Excellence," pp. 36, 37, 38, 56.

41. August 1985 bulletin of the Roosevelt Centennial Youth Project.

INDEX

Index